Working with Children,

Adolescents, and their Families

Also available from Lyceum Books, Inc.

ADVOCACY, ACTIVISM, & THE INTERNET by Steve Hick and John McNutt

GENERALIST PRACTICE IN LARGER SETTINGS: KNOWLEDGE AND SKILL CONCEPTS, by Thomas Meenaghan and W. Eugene Gibbons

INTRODUCTION TO SOCIAL WORK: THE PEOPLE'S PROFESSION, by Ira Colby and Sophia Dziegielewski

CASE MANAGEMENT: AN INTRODUCTION TO CONCEPTS AND SKILLS, by Arthur Frankel and Sheldon Gelman

TEAMWORK IN MULTIPROFESSIONAL CARE, by Malcolm Payne, foreword by Thomas M. Meenaghan,

MODERN SOCIAL WORK THEORY: A CRITICAL INTRODUCTION, 2E, by Malcolm Payne, foreword by Stephen C. Anderson

CROSS-CULTURAL PRACTICE: SOCIAL WORK WITH DIVERSE POPULATIONS, by Karen Harper and Jim Lantz

CLINICAL ASSESSMENT FOR SOCIAL WORKERS: QUANTITATIVE AND QUALITATIVE METHODS, by Catheleen Jordan and Cynthia Franklin

STRENGTHENING REFUGEE FAMILIES, by Daniel Scheinfeld and Lorraine Wallach

MANAGED CARE IN HUMAN SERVICES, edited by Stephen Wernet

SCHOOL SOCIAL WORK: PRACTICE, POLICY, AND RESEARCH PERSPECTIVES, 4E by Robert Constable, Shirley McDonald, and John Flynn

Working with Children, Adolescents, and their Families

Third Edition

Martin Herbert and
Karen V. Harper-Dorton

5758 S. Blackstone
Chicago, IL 60637
lyceum@lyceumbooks.com

Acknowledgements

We are indebted to all the families in our lives—our families, families we have worked with, and families we encounter—who have taught us so much about those things they celebrate and those things about which they grieve.

© 2002 by Martin Herbert and Lyceum Books, Inc.

Published by

LYCEUM BOOKS, INC.
5758 S. Blackstone Ave.
Chicago, Illinois 60637
773+643-1903 (Fax)
773+643-1902 (Phone)
lyceum@lyceumbooks.com
http://www.lyceumbooks.com

Published in North America under license from The British Psychological Society and Blackwell Publishers Ltd, a Blackwell Publishing company

Library of Congress Cataloging-in-Publication Data

Herbert, Martin.
   Working with children, adolescents, and their families / Martin Herbert and Karen V. Harper-Dorton.
      p. cm.
   Rev. ed. of: Working with children and their families / Karen V. Harper-Dorton, Martin Herbert, 1999.
   Includes bibliographical references and index.
   ISBN 0-925065-64-1 (alk. paper)
   1. Social work with children. 2. Social work with teenagers. 3. Family social work. I. Harper-Dorton, Karen V., 1942– II. Harper-Dorton, Karen V., 1942– Working with children and their families. III. Title.

HV713.H17 2002
362.82'53—dc21   2002019508

Contents

Contents

Contents

Contents

Figures and Tables

About the Authors

Martin Herbert is Professor Emeritus at Exeter University. He was previously Director of the School of Social Work and Professor of Psychology at the University of Leicester. He later joined the National Health Service full time and was in charge of the mental health service for children in Plymouth. This post was succeeded by a move to Exeter where he directed the doctoral course in clinical psychology as Professor of Clinical and Community Psychology. He was appointed to the Consultant Clinical Psychologist post in the child and adolescent department at the Royal Devon and Exeter NHS Healthcare Trust. He now specializes in personal injury psycho-legal work and the training of foster parents. He has published books and journal articles on various topics dealing with the psychological problems of children, adolescents and adults. Many of his books have been translated into European and Asian languages. He is a Fellow of the British Psychological Society.

Karen V. Harper-Dorton is Professor of Social Work, the School of Applied Social Sciences at West Virginia University. She holds the appointment of Director, Reverend Beatrice Ruth Burgess Center for West Virginia Families and Communities. She formerly served as Dean of the School of Social Work, West Virginia University. She served as Assistant Dean of the College of Social Work and Director of the Master of Social Work Program, The Ohio State University. She has published books and professional articles and has served as a consultant and trainer for social work agencies and nonprofit organizations. Having had numerous funded grants, Dr. Harper-Dorton continues to serve as Principal Investigator on child welfare and information technology projects.

Preface

We all know that each child (for convenience this term also covers adolescents) and each family is different, yet society and indeed our world depends on our children and families to populate, nurture, and manage the world for all of us. Children and families are at the very base of our existence and are intrinsic to the social construction of our civilization. We all know about children and families from our experiences of growing up and perhaps parenting. It is likely that many of you reading this book will bring your personal experiences of working with children and families to each chapter. Intended for students and practitioners in the broad field of human services, particularly health service practitioners and social workers, this book informs its readers about intervention, empowerment of those we serve, and evaluation of our work as practitioners.

The range of interventions made in the lives of children and families is as broad as the collection of professionals and paraprofessionals who provide services. Social workers, health visitors, counsellors, medical professionals, psychologists, and others engage children and families in treatment intended to reduce or alleviate suffering and problems. Regardless of the intervention, helping has the potential to build upon their strengths, thus empowering them both as individuals and as family systems. As intervention ends and children and families live their lives, it is hoped that their encounters with professionals and with intervention will contribute to greater self-direction, self-sufficiency, quality of life, and positive images of self and others. This book conveys improved quality of living as the outcome most desired by ourselves as helpers and for clients as consumers of our services. As clients take charge of their lives and happiness, they experience a new sense of self and ability to be assertive and powerful enough to take at least some control over their lives. It is this sense of empowerment that has the potential to nurture individuals' coping, confidence, success, and growth in personal, economic, social, and political realms.

Locke, *et al.* (1998) caution that the term "empowerment" is overused to the extent that it is at risk of losing its meaning for most purposes. Nevertheless, "empowerment" as found in the social work and clinical literature conveys images of increased personal strength, growth in self-esteem, health, self-confidence in the pursuit of personal happiness, and potentials for greater assertiveness, leadership, and participation at all levels of our social environment (Hodges, *et al.*, 1998; Kopp, 1989; Parsons, *et al.*, 1998; Saleeby, 1997; Simon, 1998; and Webster-Stratton and Herbert, 1994). Becoming empowered is a process of development and change that occurs sometimes through treatment and often in response to life experiences of success or positive reinforcement. Regardless of the modality of intervention that may be offered along the range of human and social systems, that is, the individual, family, group or community organization, accentuating autonomy, self-direction, success, and competence is empowering, particularly for the clients, the children and families who seek our help.

It is this process of assessment, intervention, change, development, and individual and family empowerment that is at the center of our work with the children and families that we write about. Building upon the strengths of children and families, we begin with assessment, give examples of intervention, and bring attention to underlying theories and assumptions. We complete the journey at the point of community and social networks, the natural and common environment where people live and nurture others.

Leo Tolstoy observed that "all happy families resemble each other, every unhappy family is unhappy in its own way." The first part of this quotation may not be altogether true, but the second half certainly is. This means that as the reader you cannot expect simple answers to questions. Every child, every parent, and all families are unique; so no generalized advice can meet all cases, every circumstance, or a particular individual's special difficulty.

Written for those who work with parents, adolescents, and children in various family contexts, this revised edition strengthens the emphases of earlier editions and includes a new section on work with adolescents. Theoretical approaches to understanding behavior are expanded and aspects of helping that are psychological and social in what they have to offer are brought into focus. Attention is given to assessing and intervening in personal relationships and interactions that take place within families and the problems to which they commonly give rise—not only for their members, but also for the community in which they reside. New chapters address empowering children and families to go beyond their immediate problem solution and to find renewed involvement in social and community networks. The final chapter discusses the importance of evaluating both our practices and programs as we answer demands for accountability and enter new and changing service environments which now include managed care and requirements for briefer treatment and cost containment.

This book is not prescriptive as there are no shortcuts to understanding families or to engaging them in problem resolution. But, we hope that ways of assessing and thinking about family problems and intervening in problem situations are communicated. Further, the breadth of family troubles and various psychological and social assessments and approaches for intervention is extensive, and a comprehensive review would be well beyond the scope of this book. However, readers are encouraged to explore the literature cited throughout the volume for those theories, techniques, and practice and research methodologies of particular interest to them.

Part 1, "Taking Account of Children, Adolescents and Their Families," introduces you to the multiplicity of family problems and approaches for assessment. For the sake of convenience, the word "child" will generally include those who have reached their teens (i.e. adolescents). A variety of theoretical models presented for understanding and assessing human behavior include social learning, medical, psychometric, personal construct, psychodynamic, family process, empirical research, and ecological systems. The case of the Hayes family is introduced and continues throughout the book. This case demonstrates assessment and intervention from a social learning perspective.

Part 2, "Understanding Development and Change in Families and Children," presents stages of normal growth and development and provides comparisons of problem behaviors both in the family and in the social environment. Child and parenting behaviors and responsiveness are discussed and include problems such as emotional and physical abuse and neglect, family breakup, loss and change, patterns of parenting, and issues in single-parent and reconstituted families.

Part 3, "You as Helper," addresses the process of intervention, from initial assessment through goal setting, intervention, and termination. Methods and techniques for contracting and working with children and families are discussed. Professional concerns for competent practice are raised in this part.

Part 4, "Empowerment of Families and Evaluation of Practice," highlights the importance of carrying growth and new skills for self-sufficiency beyond the agency and into daily living in homes and communities. The merit of extending client empowerment into social and community networks is presented. Mentoring is presented as an important extension of agency-based intervention and can link family and social networks. The common concern of evaluating effectiveness and efficiency of practice and programs is explored in relation to professional accountability and to the changing human service arena of managed care and cost containment. Considerations for ethical practice of evaluation and service delivery are also presented in this section.

Illustrative case material throughout the book highlights the ASPIRE step-by-step assessment process linking theory and practice with evaluation. Flow charts and checklists are included to assist you in assessing client situations and monitoring your interventions and outcomes. The appendices include examples of actual work with parent and divorce groups.

Recognizing that no single theory is adequate for application to all problems in the practice of working with families and children, we hope that the variety and scope of psychosocial theories and techniques presented will serve in our quest to strengthen and empower families in their daily lives. Based on the premise that children and families have capacities for growth and change, building on their strengths is central to this book. Finally, professional accountability and assessment of our work bring us to our own potential for extending and building personal and professional competence.

PART I
Taking Account of Children and their Families

Let us imagine for the moment, and for many it will be close to actual experience, that you are faced with several clients—a family—clamouring for help, with what seems like a very large and very daunting number of what to them seem insoluble problems. Everyone is thoroughly miserable, except the teenager who claims to be "above it all." The mother feels hemmed in between the demands of Grandmother, who lives with them, and the commands of a fretful, strong-willed toddler. Father is feeling truly middle-aged and rather anxious. He faces the possibility of being laid off, and he feels he gets little sympathy, or for that matter attention from his wife who seems wrapped up in the children. Grandmother is worried about her health and finds the children noisy and impolite, although she does enjoy making a fuss of the youngest. The middle child, aged 10, feels rejected and is having trouble at school; she is beginning to refuse to go—to the concern of her parents. The house is tense; and the atmosphere, particularly in the mornings, fraught with bickering and tears.

Given this sort of situation, where on earth do you start? It must be said that this is but one of an immense variety of scenarios which might unfold before the social worker or some other professional who works with parents and children. The problem, indeed, may be a lot worse and more menacing.

Families are all different and come with a variety of problems. Some are stressed and define their lives as being problematic for them. Others are multiproblem with serious issues such as deep resentment, violence, abuse, impoverishment, mental illness, terminal health problems, children in custody of others, children for whom they seek custody, and many other crises. It is misleading to think that troubled families will be troubled in the same ways just as it is misleading to assume that all children live in two-parent families. Families have many forms including biological families, stepfamilies, families with only one parent, adoptive families, gay or lesbian families, biracial families, and reconstituted families. Families and children are our most valuable social unit and must be treated with dignity and respect for the importance they bear in our world.

Of course, the threshold of vulnerability or annoyance varies from person to person; one individual's "devastating" life-event has "nuisance value" only for another hardy being. But, while the magnitude of their problems and the possible need for intervention are assessed, everyone deserves at least the dignity of being heard, and attended to with due concern. And therein lies the difficulty: What is a problem, and when can a problem be considered to be serious, especially in the realm of psychosocial events involving human relationships and interactions, with which this book is mainly concerned?

There has been a move away from putting children with problems into categories with names such as physically handicapped, mentally subnormal, delicate, maladjusted, subject to specific learning disability, and so on. Current practice is to access the needs of individual children relative to their circumstances. Special needs are specified in terms of what the child requires above and beyond those requirements normally supplied for all children. Thus they might include psychological or speech therapy, special diets, medication, aids to mobility, physiotherapy, and special educational provision or accommodation for learning disabilities. Along with the moves goes a trend toward wider integration of children into the community. This concept of community care requires a close alliance between professionals and parents (see Sutton, 1994).

This is not a book about intervention into details of different disabilities and special needs in their accommodation. Instead, it is about problem solving and helping strategies which can be applied to a variety of situations and problems that might involve children and their families. Basic knowledge and skills are presented for use with families in search of solutions to problems. Assessment and short-term intervention are presented to empower and support permanency of families in their community context. In the process of learning to work with families, many fine resources are available to deepen information. For example, resources include: major theoretical approaches to family therapy (Becvar and Becvar, 1996; Dadds, 1995), clinical interviewing with children (Greenspan and Greenspan, 1991; Jones and McQuiston, 1988), strengths and problems in contemporary families (Mason, *et al.*, 1998), and children with disabilities (Seligman and Darling, 1997). Troubled families often experience and sometimes seek help with problems such as:

Children
- children with behavioral (management) problems;
- children with emotional problems (for example, fears, phobias and obsessions);
- children with special needs (disabilities);
- children who have been fostered or adopted; and
- children who have been abused.

Adults
- parents who cannot cope (for example, who are unskilled or simply demoralized);
- parents who are unresponsive, unattached to their children;
- parents who are abusive, who lack self-control;
- parents who are coercive, argue incessantly, or fail to communicate meaningfully; and
- parents in reconstituted, divorced, and stepfamilies.

In the chapters that follow we shall be considering the following questions:

Question 1. **What**, precisely, is the nature of the problem(s) the client(s) want help with?

Question 2. **Why** have these problems arisen, and why (with time) have they not gone away?

Question 3. **How** can I help my clients, or better still, help them to help themselves?

All members of the helping professions are faced constantly with choices for themselves and their clients. In this, their role is similar to that of parents and their children. The choices parents make, and the decisions they take, have a potent influence not only on the way their offspring will "turn out", but also how enjoyable and relatively problem-free their journey from childhood, through adolescence, and on to adulthood proves to be.

This book is intended to help you to assess problems and to initiate actions that stimulate change in families who are "stuck" in self-defeating, unproductive, and growth-inhibiting patterns of living. Information about child development, child-rearing, and family relationships will be provided. Information provided is intended to help the reader gain basic knowledge and understanding leading to practical strategies for helping parents, and helping children learn to help themselves.

CHAPTER 1

Assessing Children and their Families: Where to Begin

The "What" Question

One of your earliest choices is where to concentrate your attention in what may present itself as a welter of conflicting claims, complaints, and accusations. Some of the problems will reside mainly within an individual, such as fear, but even then they will have repercussions. The individual's parents (or partner) worry about his or her suffering. Or the problems put constraints on the activities of the family: as when vacations are not possible because a mother is agoraphobic, feeling anxious about leaving the house; when a father's erratic outbursts inhibit the children from bringing friends home; or when a hyperactive child's disruptive/destructive behavior makes shopping a nightmare. In some families, problems arise from relationships and interactions such as the give-and-take transactions between people. For example:

- Mother–Father   Disagreements about the children, quarrels over decisions, other marital difficulties.

- Parent(s)–Child   Management difficulties, disappointments over the child's achievements or lack of them; feelings of rejection at the child's apparent lack of affection toward them.

- Child–Parent(s)   Resentments about being "babied"; complaints about unfairness and favoritism or in the case of an adolescent it is likely to be frustration at not being allowed to do "grown-up" things.

- Child–Child   Sibling rivalry, jealousy.

5

Your client(s) may be one of these persons—a child refusing to go to school, one or both parents angry or disengaged, or all of the family members feeling unhappy. You might even have to work more widely in the neighborhood, at the school, or with other agencies in the community. Who the client is, is in fact an unclear question, and one to which we shall have to return.

Some workers like to have all the family members at their interviews, some prefer to see the parent(s) first of all, with or without the children present, and then gradually work their way around to talking to other key members of the household. Whichever way you tackle the initial interviews, you are trying to assess what is going on, what the problems are, under what circumstances they occur, and what changes (i.e. outcomes) would be desirable for a viable and happier situation to be created or restored for the family (see Sutton, 1999).

Exploration: Observing, Asking, Listening

To explore the "what" question, you will bring into play your observation, questioning, and listening skills when you meet with the family. This meeting, an interaction, is the process of the family seeking intervention or asking for help and the professional assessing and exploring in order to clarify the problem as presented. This coming together to collect information is the interview. It is the process of defining the problem, offering help, and agreeing to work together toward an initial plan for finding a solution to the problem, that begins the intervention process. Asking a series of questions, engaging in exploration for facts, and practicing open and careful listening occur during an interview. Insoo Kim Berg (1994) offers a careful description of interviewing processes and techniques from the initial stage of intervention through defining the problem, setting goals, contracting for intervention, conducting a session, and terminating the intervention. Interviewing is a skill, shaped by the methodology or theoretical approach that most informs the professional. The interview is the starting place, the springboard to intervening in problem configurations in the lives of families and children. It is the medium for initial assessment and for intervention and determination of outcomes of the intervention. Interviewing is not an end in

6

itself but a tool to aid assessment and treatment and is explored later in Part I.

Before we look at particular approaches to assessment from which the professional can choose in his or her endeavor to help a family, there is an important general consideration: the perspective or model of helping to be adopted. Cliff Cunningham and Hilton Davis (1985), authors of a book on children with special needs, have a useful device for working out where you stand with regard to your role vis-à-vis your client: on the one hand, the expert model and on the other, the consumer model. The collaborative model lies between these two models.

In the expert model the professionals view themselves as very much in charge because of their expertise, responsibility, and therefore decision making. The client is relatively passive as a recipient of advice, "prescriptions" about health or behavior, or possibly therapy of one kind or another. At the other extreme, clients are viewed very much as consumers of the professionals' services, with the right to select what they believe is most appropriate to their needs. Decision making is ultimately in the parents' control; professionals act as consultants and teachers. Negotiation and discussion play a large part in the professional relationships.

In the partnership or collaborative model, practitioners perceive themselves as having expertise but sharing it and imparting it to parents and other non- or paraprofessionals so that they mediate or facilitate much of the training or therapy of the child and parents.

Not all models suit all problems. What is important is that a worker should know what his or her assumptions are. The authors referred to previously (Cunningham and Davis, 1985) help you to uncover your orientation to problems of children and their families with the following questions:

- Have I met the family?
- Do I consider the child in the context of his/her family?
- Do I have regular, two-way communication with the family?
- Do I respect and value the child as a person?
- Do I respect and value the family?
- Do I feel the family has strengths to help the child?

- Have I identified the parents' abilities and resources?
- Do I always act as honestly as possible?
- Do I give them choices about what to do?
- Do I listen to them?
- Have I identified their aims?
- Do I negotiate with them?
- Do I adjust according to the joint conclusions?
- Do I assume they have some responsibility for what I do for their child?
- Do I assume I have to earn their respect?
- Do I make the assumption that we might disagree about what is important?
- Do I believe they can change?
- Have I tried to identify the parents' perceptions of their child?

A high proportion of "yes" responses suggests the generalized use of a consumer model; many "no" responses indicate an expert model.

The model you adopt will be determined not only by the agency you work in, the clients who seek help at that agency, but also your view of human nature. The way you construe problems and the solutions to them reflects your beliefs about families, their problems, and their strength to make progress and change.

Problem Parenting

We referred earlier to the difficulty for the worker of deciding when a problem can truly be considered to be serious. When should we begin to worry because behavior, whether it is a child's or adult's, goes beyond the bounds and can be said to be abnormal or dysfunctional? In other words, when is a problem really a problem?

There is no simple answer to this question. One would be hard-pressed to find absolute distinctions between the characteristics of parents who come to be diagnosed or assessed as problematic by psychologists, psychiatrists or social workers and those of other unselected parents. The judgment of what is abnormal (that is, a deviation from a norm or standard) is essentially a social one. Certain adults fail to meet particular

8

expectations on the part of society for what constitutes appropriate parental behavior. Unfortunately, terms like "normal" and "abnormal" are commonly applied to parents as if they are mutually exclusive categories. The point is that the attributes and actions which society judges in its evaluation of good and bad, normal and abnormal parenting are ones that in some degree or other are manifested by most adults (see Figure 1a).

Figure 1a demonstrates how a wide range of parental behaviors can be reduced to two major dimensions that can be described as Love–Hostility and Autonomy–Control. Thus we have parental transactions that are warm and loving at one extreme and rejecting and hostile at the other, and then again activities that are restrictive and controlling versus ones that are permissive and promote autonomy. According to this model an antagonistic parent is one who combines hostility and restrictiveness, while a protective parent is one who is both loving and restrictive.

Figure 1a.   The range of parental behavior types within two major dimensions: autonomy–control/hostility–warmth

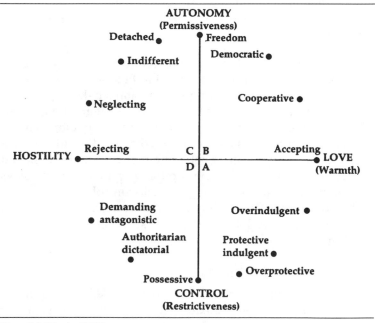

Figure 1b. Details of children's behavior as influenced by the two major parental dimensions: restrictive parenting and permissive parenting

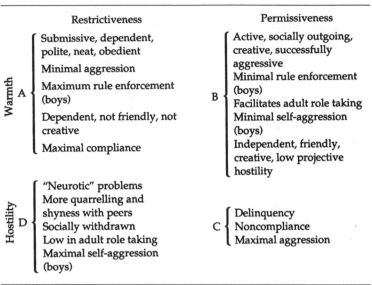

	Restrictiveness	Permissiveness
Warmth A	Submissive, dependent, polite, neat, obedient Minimal aggression Maximum rule enforcement (boys) Dependent, not friendly, not creative Maximal compliance	B { Active, socially outgoing, creative, successfully aggressive Minimal rule enforcement (boys) Facilitates adult role taking Minimal self-aggression (boys) Independent, friendly, creative, low projective hostility
Hostility D	"Neurotic" problems More quarrelling and shyness with peers Socially withdrawn Low in adult role taking Maximal self-aggression (boys)	C { Delinquency Noncompliance Maximal aggression

(Adapted from W.C. Becker, 1964.)

You can also see how the potential long-term consequences of these parental behaviors – illustrated in Figure 1b – guide us to a view of the kind of parenting which entails risks.

Signs of abnormal parenting involve exaggerations, deficiencies, or harmful combinations of behavior common to most, if not all, parents. Thus we would be concerned about overprotective and underprotective behavior by a mother or father, and we would be concerned about a punitive parent who displays a combination of hostility and poor self-control.

The differences are mainly quantitative; differences not in kind but in degree. The same (as we shall see) can be said of children's problems.

Children With Problems

Parents' enjoyment of their children is likely to diminish rapidly and give way to anxious concern, and perhaps anger and resentment, when they show signs of abnormal or deviant behavior and emotion. Parents and teachers begin to worry about children when their actions persist in the following:

- being understandable, that is, when their moods, attitudes, or behaviors defy good sense and lack reason or meaning;
- being unpredictable, such that there is a Jekyll-and-Hyde-like quality of changeability, disconcerting switches in mood, friendliness, and cooperativeness;
- rebellious and uncontrollable in the sense that adults are unable to impose their authority and/or their children seem unwilling or unable to control their own behavior.

Most parents and teachers have observed undesirable forms of behavior in a particular child or adolescent at one time or another and tend to be resigned about such manifestations. "Well, that's what you'd expect, isn't it, of a toddler or teenager." It is when such actions are frequent and intense that real concern is felt; in other words, it is often a matter of degree. There are, however, organic conditions or adverse temperamental (constitutional) conditions in which there is an emotional overlay which, therefore, may be accessible in part to psycho-social interventions.

At what point is it inappropriate to be philosophical about your client's difficulties? When should your mental "alarm bells" begin to ring; when do you cease saying to clients, "Ah well, she'll grow out of it"?

At the most-general level you might ask yourself:

- What are the consequences of the child's actions, benign or unfavorable?
- Does the child's style of life prevent her from leading a contented life in which she is able to enjoy social relationships, and play and learn effectively?
- Does the child's behavior, in terms of his development toward maturity, represent a retrogressive trend? That is, does he resort to thumb sucking and temper tantrums as a way of deflecting mother's attention from the rival baby sister?

11

By the way, you could substitute parents for child in most of these questions to assess the seriousness of their problems. Every stage of development is marked by certain life tasks— physical, psychological, and social skills and challenges that have to be mastered by the child, the adolescent, and eventually the adult. Some of the more important of these tasks can be indicated in chart form (see Table 1).

Table 1.   Developmental Tasks

Age period	Characteristic to be achieved	Major hazard to achievement
Birth to 1 year	Sense of trust or security	Neglect, abuse, or deprivation of consistent and appropriate love in infancy; harsh or early weaning.
1 to 4 years	Sense of autonomy— child viewing self as an individual in his/her own right, apart from parents although dependent on them.	Conditions which interfere with the child's achieving a feeling of adequacy or the learning of skills such as talking.
4 to 5 years	Sense of initiative— period of vigorous reality testing, imagination, and imitation of adult behavior.	Overly strict discipline, internalization of rigid ethical attitudes that interfere with the child's spontaneity and reality testing.
6 to 11 years	Sense of duty and accomplishment— laying aside of fantasy and play, undertaking real tasks, developing academic and social competencies.	Excessive competition, personal limitations, or other conditions which lead to experiences of failure, resulting in feeling of inferiority and poor work habits.

12 to 15 years	Sense of identity—clarification in adolescence of who one is, and what one's role is.	Failure of society to provide clearly defined roles and standards; formation of cliques which provide clear but not always desirable roles and standards.
15 to adulthood	Sense of intimacy—ability to establish close personal relationships with members of both sexes.	Cultural and personal factors that lead to psychological isolation or to formal rather than warm personal relations.

(Adapted from E. Erikson, 1965.)

Look at Table 1 and make some notes about the life tasks which most concern your clients at the moment. Ask them about their present priorities and preoccupations. The topic of family life maps (Chapter 3) will examine how one individual's life tasks and those of other members of the family are interconnected.

The newborn infant needs to develop a sense of trust and, later, a growing autonomy. A lasting sense of trust, security, confidence, or optimism (as opposed to distrust, insecurity, inadequacy, or pessimism) is thought to be based upon affection, a degree of continuity of care giving, and the reasonably prompt satisfaction of the infant's needs (Erikson, 1985). Some parents may be too immature or preoccupied by personal problems to do this. The major hazards to the development of a perception of a benign, trustworthy, and predictable world in which children initiate independence seeking and perceive their own actions as having meaningful consequences are neglect, abuse, and indifference. Extreme inconsistency and other social and physical conditions interfere with the child's sense of personal adequacy or hinder the acquisition of skills. Such influences are likely to produce a child who behaves in a troublesome manner. Incidentally, physically handicapped children are massively over-represented in the population of youngsters with behavior problems. If such children can be helped to become more competent, then they may have less recourse to problem behavior.

Two-Way Traffic: Parent-to-Child; Child-to-Parent

In many ways children's behavior can have as much effect on their parents' actions as their behavior has on them. So when parents meet certain extremely difficult or temperamental factors from a very tender age, they can be overwhelmed for a time and change the direction and manner in which they intended to bring up their child. These individual characteristics may show themselves in moodiness, overactivity, defiance, oversensitivity, unpredictability, biological irregularity, and unadaptability to changes in routine. The impact may be greater on adoptive parents because they may ascribe the difficult behavior to deprivation experiences, rejection of themselves by the adopted child, or even "bad blood".

What is important is that you assess the way clients construe situations and attribute meaning to what is happening to them.

The Case of Avril Hayes

This is what one mother, who referred to the first author, said about her child:

> *From the first day that I saw my daughter Avril I realized that she was more lively than her sister Stella and wouldn't be content to be in a room by herself. She would scream and I went through endless months wondering if I was feeding her incorrectly, whether she had a pain or was unhappy. But I finally came to the conclusion that she just wanted company ... but on her own terms. I wasn't allowed to make a fuss of her but she didn't want to be alone. Meanwhile, other problems were emerging. She would never sleep during the day like other babies and eventually wouldn't sleep much at night either. She would scream, bite, or kick when I went to cuddle her and this showed itself particularly at bathtime and changing time. Guilt was my first emotional feeling towards my baby – pure unadulterated guilt. Guilt because no one really wanted her; guilt because I had foisted a child upon my family (I was the only one who welcomed the pregnancy) who was proving to be*

every parent's nightmare. For me protectiveness came very quickly after guilt. I would protect her against the world if necessary. But love was hardly noticeable except in my fierce protective instinct. How can you love a baby who alternately screams and cries for 18 hours out of every 24, who won't feed without an all-out battle, who shows no response when you pick her up, cuddle her, talk to her, play with her, or just try to love her? Avril caused violent quarrels between my husband and myself (things unknown previously) and arguments between relatives on how to deal with her. I did so try to show my love for her, but she just didn't appear to want it.

By the time Mrs Hayes came to us at the Child and Family Consultation Centre she had lost all confidence in herself (a loss of what psychologists call self-efficacy). She was thoroughly depressed and demoralized and doubted whether anyone could help her. The case of Avril and her family is continued in the following chapters as an example of working with a family having difficulty.

Perceived Self-Efficacy

An eminent theorist, Albert Bandura (1976) is of the opinion that human behavior is subject to two major categories of influence: efficacy expectations and outcome expectations; these are the constituent parts of perceived self-efficacy. They are distinguished because a parent may believe that a particular strategy reward or discipline will produce certain outcomes such as improvement in a child's behavior. However, the parent may have serious misgivings as to whether there is sufficient patience and consistency to bring about such a desirable outcome. All psychological procedures designed to bring about change, whatever their type, are thought by some professionals to depend on beliefs about the level of skill required to bring about an outcome and the likely end result of a course of action. Efficacy expectations are thought to be the most important component. The main effect on outcome expectations is through the strengthening of efficacy expectations, for example, the self-expectation that "I am able to do it!" In their approach, successful helping depends on the degree to which the interventions create or strengthen the client's expectations of personal efficacy. It appears that verbal persuasion has only relatively weak and short-lived effects on such expectations. Performance accomplishments, on the other hand, are very potent; hence the success of techniques like behavior rehearsal and modeling. In rehearsal or modeling, clients practice skills that have been demonstrated to them.

Fortunately most parents, with little or no training, rear their children, with the help of other socializing agents, into socially acceptable and broadly rule-abiding adults who respect societal norms around them. Despite variations in family pattern and style of parenting, all societies seem to be successful in transforming helpless, self-centered infants into more or less self-supporting, responsible members of their particular community. In other words, they become socialized. Indeed, there is a basic preparedness on the part of most infants to be trained, an in-built bias toward all things social.

Summary and Comment

This chapter has been concerned with the individual and his or her relationships; also with what goes wrong with them. We have seen that abnormalities of parenting and childhood behavior vary greatly. Problems represent, most often, exaggerations, deficiencies, or handicapping combinations of behaviors, emotions, or attitudes common to all people. You are very likely to have to deal with, or refer elsewhere, the following categories of problems:

1. Excessive behaviors that require reduction or elimination (e.g. dangerous actions, self-injurious behavior, aggression, phobic avoidance, etc.).
2. Appropriate behaviors that occur in the wrong context, for example: cooperation with delinquent enterprises; honesty that hurts—Q: "How do I look?" A: "Awful." These problems require training in determining when to do what.
3. Deficits that need to be made good, for example, incontinence, selective or elective mutism, poor self-control, etc.

Applying similar criteria to pinpoint deviant parental behavior, we have physical abuse or overprotectiveness as an example of excessive behavior, the continual provision of help when help is no longer required by the child as an exemplar of inappropriate behavior, and unresponsive parenting as typical of the deficit type of parenting response.

We judge the seriousness of problems in terms of their disabling and/or distressing consequences for the individual and for others. Parents will often come to you with their self-confidence, morale, and self-esteem in tatters. Give them back their dignity by the manner in which you talk to them, treat them as "experts" with regard to aspects of their own children, and appropriately involve them as partners in the helping endeavor. In boosting perceived self-efficacy, deeds speak louder than words. In the chapters that follow, you will find interventions and techniques for helping families along with solutions and coping skills for problems they seek to resolve.

CHAPTER 2

Approaching Assessment:
Step-by-Step

Children are usually a source of great pleasure and endless wonder to their parents. These joys are sometimes tempered by the concern and heavy sense of responsibility that also accompany parenthood. Such pleasure may be transformed into anxiety and the wonder into puzzlement when the child begins to behave in a peculiar or erratic manner. Children who have not, at some stage of their development, been the cause of quite serious worry to their mothers and fathers are unique.

Families, like individuals, also have their ups and downs and go through stages—some more difficult than others. Family life can be the source of tensions and problems for its individual members in their various roles: as parents, grandparents, stepparents, substitute parents, children, and teenagers.

This book concerns itself with problems that arise within families, particularly between parents and children or caretakers and children. The research literature on parent/child relationships is pervaded by the belief that optimal care and training of children during the impressionable years of life will prepare them for present and future problems and even prevent many problems in their lives (Crain, 1985; Kagan, 1984). When one considers the intimate, protracted, and highly influential nature of parents' relationships with their children, it seems self-evident that the quality of such relationships must have a vital bearing on the development of the child's personality and general adaptation. This weighty responsibility for which many parents are poorly prepared creates stress and feelings of inadequacy among some parents and even guilt among others.

It is worth noting that although society delegates its most crucial functions to the family, there is little formal education or training offered to prospective parents. The informal learning and experience once offered to older children caring for younger siblings in large families, or the help from the experienced members of the extended family and from relatives living nearby may not be available to the relatively small and often isolated family whether it be biological, step, adoptive, or single parent.

The Family as a System

Systems theory helps explain interactions within the family system as it adjusts and changes and defines its boundaries (Janzen and Harris, 1997). The family is a basic social system, a social organization; or as defined in the literature, two or more individuals who share space, have emotional ties, establish relationships, share commitment, and have established roles and tasks to accomplish functions of the family. The family system negotiates intimacy and is the basic institution for socialization where children learn family rituals and social and cultural values in the context of family life. Systems theory is not a theory about behavior or intervention but an approach to understanding various organizations of people and institutions Systems theory offers a way of organizing information from multidisciplinary approaches to behavior (Longres, 1995).

Consistent with systems theory, families are comprised of subsystems such as parents and sibling subsystems which make up the whole system. Families establish boundaries that define the family and its subsystems. Permeable boundaries allow exchanges of energy and information to occur internally among the family's subsystems and between the family and its external environment (Anderson and Carter, 1990; Germain, 1991; Zastrow and Kirst-Ashmann, 1997). The social environment which the family interacts with includes a variety of other systems such as communities, organizations like schools, jails, hospitals, and the variety of organizations that employ family members and support physical and social needs of individual members. The family changes and evolves as differentiation occurs for the members and for the family as a whole in response to adaptation to pressures from internal and external

19

environments. Families change over time and seek balance within and around family boundaries (Becvar and Becvar, 1996; Nichols and Schwartz, 1991).

An ecological systems perspective provides a framework for approaching systems and their ecological environment and is useful in understanding interactions within the family system as it adjusts and changes and defines its boundaries (Janzen and Harris, 1997). It is a subset of general systems and focuses on adaptations and accommodations that occur as systems change and evolve in relation to their environment (Kilpatrick and Holland, 1995). According to Kilpatrick and Holland (1995), six major concepts from Germain and Gitterman (1987) are essential to working with families. First, families have reciprocal exchanges with the environment as transactions flow into and out of the family system. Second, demands for exchanges and changes are defined as life stresses that produce negotiation of relationships within and between systems. Third, coping occurs as systems adjust, or as families make accommodations and adjustments in response to internal and external stresses. Fourth, habitats or settings of physical and social contexts define realities of systems such as families. For example, communities, cultures, and basic resources support functioning for family members and for the family as a whole. Fifth, a niche includes the statuses, rights, resources, opportunities, and deficits that define physical and social realities for families. Sixth, relatedness or connectedness evolves as social systems such as families establish their particular place in community and environmental networks. These six concepts help define the family as a system and provide points for intervention in the system.

Intervening in the family system and in its interaction with the environment is informed from an ecological systems approach. This perspective informs understanding families' adaptations and provides for intervention in various life transitions including interactions within and outside the family in its exchange with the environment.

Family systems include more than simple exchanges with the environment. From a systems perspective, the individual family members are seen as the elements or sub-units.

Whatever happens to one or more of its elements such as mental illness in the mother or father, the death of a sibling, or serious marital disharmony can affect the entire system. The heightened emotional intimacy and interdependence of the members of our small, intimate contemporary families are thought to place a great burden on parent(s) and children. Parent(s) are the crucial and therefore potentially weak link in the chain of rearing children where socialization occurs.

In an ecological systems perspective, children are influenced by the rules, culture, and activities of their family system. Families, parents, schools, and neighborhoods are immediate systems in the individual experiences of childhood (Fraser, 1997). Taking care of young children is likely to be more stressful for some parents than others, especially in situations of poverty, poor housing, abuse, neglect, death of a family member, and other crises. An old and popular aphorism is that "there are no problem children, only problem parents." In the context of the practices and case example that follow, we shall see that this is an oversimplification.

Reviews of the literature repeatedly point to the conclusion that there is little evidence of a connection between specific parenting practices and later characteristics of the child (Crain, 1985; Garbarino and Binn, 1992; Kagan, 1984). Available evidence suggests that what is important in child rearing is the general social climate in the home, particularly the attitudes and feelings of the parents, which form a background to the application of specific methods and interactions of child rearing. For example, the mother does best who does, with a sense of confidence, what she and the community to which she belongs believe is right for the child. Feeding and potty training and the like are important elements of the child's daily activities; but it is the social interactions they mediate, the manner in which parents undertake these tasks, that give them significance. It is how the young child is looked after that is crucial, and it is the social and psychological context of the care that matters rather than its chronology and mechanics.

The implication of all this is that a good deal of the worker's attention is focused on the present rather than the past. This is not to say that you should neglect the client family's history.

The important thing is to get the balance right, a matter we shall return to. Another implication concerns the manner and form in which you get to talk to the members of the family. There may be disagreements about the formal arrangements and theories about how best to achieve change, but there is likely to be a consensus that all members should be interviewed.

The Interview

The interview is an essential method for gaining access to parents' and children's problems. It sounds deceptively simple and straightforward to say, "I am going to interview the Smith family to find out what lies behind the referral." But you need to be clear about the answers to several questions before you intrude on the privacy of a home and its family.

- Do I have the right and the family's permission to conduct this and subsequent interviews? This can be a significant problem for social workers who frequently have to wear two hats called "care" and "control," and whose intervention may be unwelcome, especially for involuntary clients such as those in child abuse and/or custody referrals.
- What do I wish to find out (what are my objectives) in the interview?
- Whom do I need to speak to in order to fulfill my objectives? (All the family members, parents only, the child alone, his/her brothers and sisters?)
- Do I invite them to meet me as a full family group? Do I speak to the mother first? Both parents together? Should the child be present initially?
- How do I begin the interview?
- How do I best express some quite complex and potentially threatening ideas?
- How do I reassure them about confidentiality?
- What is the best way of eliciting reliable and relevant information? How do I deal with their tendency to digress or to set an agenda which avoids key issues?
- Indeed, what is relevant information?
- How do I terminate the interview without leaving clients feeling "up in the air" or threatened?

These questions raise ethical concerns of clients' rights and have a bearing on intervention concerns such as the development of rapport with clients; using communication; summarizing and memory skills; obtaining accurate, relevant, and meaningful information; maintaining a good working relationship; conducting one's business in a professional and ethical manner; and so on.

Communication. Working with all members of the family in conjoint family sessions requires broad communication skills. Interviewing children demands skill, patience, and respect for children. Young children tend to be talkative but are limited in their ability to reflect their experiences insightfully. Adolescents are often introspective and have a way of becoming monosyllabic when asked personal questions.

Children are not always very good at expressing their fears, frustrations, or uncertainties. They cannot always tell their parents, let alone a comparative stranger, how they feel, but they have a language that adults can learn to translate—the language of behavior and fantasy. What they do in everyday life and what they say indirectly through play or story telling can be most revealing.

Projective techniques. There are advantages to using projective techniques for assessment including: play, puppets, dramatic creations, completing stories or sentences. These techniques permit an almost unlimited variety of responses. The client has to fall back on his or her own resources rather than stereotypical, socially desirable answers. These techniques have their critics but are invaluable if used cautiously as aids to communicating with children. The caution refers to interpreting the protocols—the made-up stories about pictured events, or the posted "letters" containing statements about feelings and attitudes to various members of the family. It is recognized that children identify with the central characters in their stories; project their own feelings, especially unacceptable or difficult-to-acknowledge impulses or attitudes, onto the fantasy figures; and attribute various motives and ideas that are essentially their own into the play or other creative situations and plots.

Gil (1991) and Moon (1990) provide examples of working with children and youth in play and art therapies, respectively.

When the child is too loyal, too frightened or ashamed, or too inarticulate to speak about feelings or painful events in the family, it may be possible to express these things in the evolving story. Stories can be constructed, leaving spaces for the child to fill in about a boy or girl of similar age. Thus you begin, "Once upon a time there was a boy/girl. What did he/she most like doing?" .... "What did he/she not like doing?" .... You gradually introduce, among neutral themes, topics such as secrets, fears, worries, preoccupations, family tensions, parental behaviors, and so on.

Sentence completions are useful:

"I like to . . . ."
"What I most dislike . . . ."
"My best friend . . . ."
"I wish . . . ."
"My dad . . . ."
"My mom . . . ."
"If only . . . ."
"In my home the nicest thing is . . . ."
"The worst thing is . . . ."

With stories told as a response to pictures, you need to be cautious about your interpretation. There is a tendency for us to project our own "psyches" into our interpretations or to superimpose our "theories" onto the projective protocols.

Nevertheless, play, drama with puppets or miniatures, or stories are undoubtedly an invaluable adjunct to work with children. You would do well to have a store of miniatures, anatomically correct dolls, drawing materials, and pictures available for use with families and children who come to you.

The Formulation

The formulation about the client's problem is the bridge between the assessment, the intervention plan, and its implementation. It is arrived at by several stages summarized by the mnemonic ASPIRE (Sutton and Herbert, 1992).

Stage 1, Assessment (AS):

(I)   *focus on the 'What?' question—i.e. what is/are the problem(s)?*

(II)   *focus on the 'Which?' question—i.e. which of the problems are to be addressed and in what order?*

(III)   *focus on the 'Why?' question—i.e. why have the problems arisen?*

Stage 2, Planning (P):
     focus on the 'How?' question—i.e. how are we (practitioner and clients) going to address the problems?

Stage 3, Implementation of the intervention (I)

Stage 4, Rigorous evaluation (RE)

Stage 1: Assessment (AS)

The *what*, *which* and *why* questions are directed towards the precise identification of the antecedent, consequent and symbolic conditions which control the identified/targeted behavior problem(s).

This linear ABC analysis is elaborated into a recursive sequence such that Cs become As, which generate new Cs, and thus ramify to affect the actions of others in the vicinity of the main protagonists (say, mother and child). The main assessment tasks are twofold:

Identifying Target Problems

Point 1 in Figure 2 underlines the importance of a developmental context such as a child's fearfulness or aggressiveness. The question arises from the essential normality of these emotions—universal responses to a wide range of life events and normal adaptations to particular environmental circumstances, thus functional in the sense of having positive survival and reward value. The parameters that separate behaviors defined as problematic from the anxieties, avoidance, fears, indecisiveness, and the sheer number of problems with which they are associated are also important diagnostic criteria. Their implications for the individual's well-being and "effective"

Figure 2.   A conceptual framework for an assessment of behavior problems

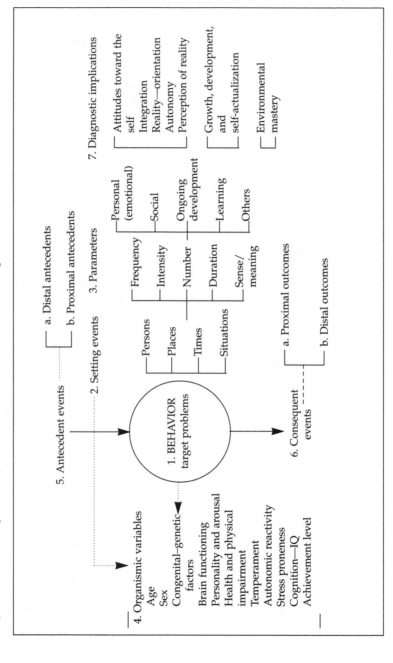

functioning provide a further diagnostic guideline for the practitioner (see point 7 in Figure 2). The meaning of the problems for the child—the sense made of them, the payoff they provide—and indeed for his or her family, constitutes a vital element of the overall assessment.

Identifying Controlling Influences

Two categories of influence are generally considered: current environmental variables (antecedent and consequent events (see points 5 and 6 in Figure 1), and organismic variables (see point 4). The contemporary causes of problem behavior may exist in the client's environment or in his or her own thoughts, feelings, or bodily processes (organismic variables), and they may exert their influence in several ways, as antecedent stimuli either, or as outcomes (consequences) of a reinforcing kind. Proximal (current) influences (point 5b) are direct in their effects and close in time to the actions they influence. They are functionally related to behavior and can thus be tested in therapy—as hypotheses about causation—using single case experimental designs.

The identification of the current problem and its contemporary antecedents and consequences may be assisted by information about the patient's past (e.g. attachments, health, reinforcement history, attitudes, life events) (see point 5a in Figure 2). But the information is gathered primarily as a source of clues to contemporary conditions that influence the elicitation and maintenance of symptoms rather than as primary treatment objectives in themselves. This places most emphasis on providing the child and/or parents with *new* learning experiences.

Beginning Your Assessment

We have looked at various conceptual issues and methods which set the stage for the actual assessment. In Flow Chart 1, we describe in summary form the ten steps you might take in seeking answers to the *what* and *why* questions from Stage 1 of the ASPIRE procedure.

Flow Chart 1. The Assessment Process

INITIAL SCREENING		PHASE I
	Step 1.	Explain how you intend to work. Foster a good working relationship.
	Step 2.	Obtain a general statement of the problem(s).
	Step 3.	Specify the problem(s) more precisely.
	Step 4.	Elicit the desired outcome(s).
	Step 5.	Construct a problem profile.
	Step 6.	Introduce the idea of behavior sequences by looking at your client(s) typical day(s).
	Step 7.	Establish problem priorities.

ASSESSMENT		PHASE II
	Step 8.	Work out a family life map.
	Step 9.	Make an estimate of your client's assets.
	Step 10.	Ask your adult clients about their goals, e.g. for their children. Ask the child about his or her wishes and requirements.

FURTHER ASSESSMENT	PHASE III
	Collect more detailed "baseline" data. Give clients homework tasks, e.g. keeping diaries, frequency charts, etc. of daily life, behaviors, or whatever data are relevant.

INTERVENTION	PHASE IV
	(One or possibly two interviews)

Step 1.	**Foster a good working (therapeutic) relationship.** (a) Explain who you are and how you expect to work.

	(b) Establish a warm, friendly, and professional relationship, i.e. work systematically.
Step 2.	**Provide the client(s) with an opportunity to state the problem as they see it.** (These questions can be adapted and directed toward the child.) (a) Begin with an open-ended question: "Tell me in your own words what is causing you concern ... Take your time." (b) Summarize at intervals that are not intrusive to clients. "May we pause for a moment to see if I have understood correctly what you have said? I want to be sure that I get things right. As I understand it you are concerned about ..." Allow sufficient time for the clients to express themselves. Supplementary questions (probes) can be useful at this stage. "What is going well in the situation you are concerned about at present with regard to ___ (say the child)?"; "How does ___ contribute to family life?"; "Has anyone else expressed concern about ___?"; "Is there anyone— a teacher, friend, or whoever—who does not see this worrying side to ___, because he/she is different when in their presence?"
Step 3.	**Begin to specify the problem(s) more precisely.** (a) Ask for examples—preferably recent ones—which will illustrate the problem situation(s): "Tell me, in detail, what happens so that I can see it in my mind's eye." "What leads up to the confrontation or problem? Who says what ... to whom, who does what ... to whom, with what consequences?" "How does an episode usually end up?" The use of role-play may be helpful.

29

(b) Find out when, how often, with what intensity, and in what particular circumstances (what people, places, situations) the problems occur.

(c) Discover the details surrounding the onset of the problem(s). "How long has this been happening?"; "Are there any particular circumstances—life events— that may have been of significance because they occurred at the time that the problems made their appearance?"

(d) "How have you tried to deal with the problems up to now? ... With what result?"

(e) "Who helps you cope with the problems?" "Does anyone hinder you, as you see it?"

(f) "You probably have some ideas, perhaps a theory, as to why this is happening. Would you like to try it out on me?"

Step 4.	**Find out about desired outcomes.** "I am going to ask some questions to help us clarify what you and I should work toward. If, as is likely, other members of the family are involved, we will need to consult them." Note that families in conjoint sessions can respond to the question of what they want help with.
Step 5.	**Draw up a problem profile.** Take account of the complaints and desired outcomes of all the members of the family.

Let us take time off for the moment to look again at Avril and her family. They were referred to our center for Avril's problem. But it wasn't that simple.

Avril, aged four, demanded an inordinate amount of individual attention, monopolizing her mother's time wherever she was and whatever she was doing. She clung to her and followed her everywhere, even to the toilet, refusing to let her out of her sight, even for a few moments. Avril would not play with other children, including her sister who had no real problems. By the time she was referred to us, her behavior problems, including aggression, self-centeredness of an extreme kind, and other antisocial actions, were rampant and having serious implications for herself and her family. The problems were real enough, but there were other issues which required attention (see Table 2).

A glance at this problem profile tells us why those who call themselves systems theorists are agreed in focusing not on the individual but on the system of relationships in which they interact. We are not describing family therapy in minute detail in this book, but there is some overlap between home-based behavioral psychotherapy work and family therapy. After all, the latter is not so much a school of therapy as a basic redefinition of the therapeutic task itself. A systems approach places the emphasis on the individual as a member of various social systems of which the most important is usually (especially for children), but not always, the family. Therapists attempt to conceptualize the problem in a more horizontal (rather than vertical-historical) manner, viewing the client as part of a family group in which the relationship of the members, each with the other, has a bearing on his or her present predicament. The older treatment model tended to point to the identified patient as the focus of attention, for example, the child referred to the child guidance clinic. Diagnostic thinking has since been considerably influenced by what are called interactional frames of references consistent with systems thinking. The family as a system should always be considered in terms of its interaction with other community systems such as the neighborhood, school, and social and health service agencies.

The value of this open-ended approach is (a) it does not assume that the family is "the problem"; nor (b) does it jump to the conclusion that the child has "the problem." Rather it helps you to tease out, by careful and systematic assessment, the many possible problem areas for intervention. Salvador Minuchin (1974), the eminent family therapist, gives the example of the treatment of anorexic patients and their families: taking the child into the hospital; encouraging her to eat

31

Table 2.   Family Problem Profile

Examples of problem	*Settings*	*Desired outcome*
Mother asks Avril to go up to bed. Avril ignores; if mother insists she says "No."	Bedtime, supermarket visiting	Avril should comply more readily
Avril demands attention or some task of mother, nags at her until she complies; tantrums if mother refuses her command or does not "obey" immediately.	Home, supermarket (especially when mother is busy)	Ask nicely, wait patiently, be more reasonable
Avril pinches, pulls hair, hits. Is also rude. When mother is driving car/attending to others (when sister teases).	In the car/home/ almost anywhere when thwarted	Develop self-control, tolerance of frustration
Makes contemptuous remarks about/to father (e.g., "You're fat"; "You're stupid").	Home	Learn to be polite and respectful
Father opts out of confronting Avril; rushes off to work in the morning apologizing to mother for leaving her to manage Avril's tempers. Obviously pleased to be "escaping."	Home. Tells mother she is best at dealing with Avril	Father to play his proper parental role
His wife is always weepy, miserable, and lethargic. She doesn't enjoy life or sex anymore.	Everywhere	Be her old cheery affectionate self
"They treat me like a baby."	Home/playgroup	Treat me like my sister
"They spoil Avril"; "She gets away with things I get punished for."	Everywhere	Treat us the same

(Adapted from M. Herbert, 1987.)

through a behavioral program; initiating family "lunch" sessions; providing individual therapy for the child; and marital work for the parents. These interventions are, nevertheless, only separate moves in the direction of changing patterns of behavior in the family system which he sees as maintaining the problem manifested by the child.

Group Processes

Increased understanding of the effects of group influences on individual behavior has also modified views of what should be taken into account in assessment. It has become necessary to consider whether behavior on the part of an individual is to be seen primarily in individual terms or is more readily explicable in terms of group processes. In a residential context group processes assume particular significance and may themselves, rather than the individual, constitute the unit of attention (Johnson and Johnson, 1987).

It is a small wonder when we look at the history of Avril that we had a complex case on our hands: a depressed mother, an unhappy child, a discontented sister, a frustrated and confused father, and a generally miserable, tense family life.

Avril, from early in life, had been a difficult and hyperactive child. From the day of her birth Avril would cry day and night. The nights were particularly difficult. Mrs Hayes spent most of them nursing her to allow the rest of the family to have some sleep. There were also serious feeding problems. The parents were worried that Avril would starve herself, so forced feeding was necessary for several months. It could take up to three hours to feed the baby. Indeed, she was an unusual child in other ways. She was difficult to amuse, taking only the most fleeting interest in toys. She seldom smiled. Her moods were volatile. When she didn't appear to be depressed and withdrawn she was often screaming for attention. Her mother and father found it impossible to enjoy their youngest child as she was so difficult to rear. She hated any change in routine and was predictable only in her unpredictability. Mrs Hayes felt guilty for having the child when she had been advised not to and would fiercely protect Avril, even though she might secretly agree with the criticism. Finally, because of the marital tension and lack of her husband's support when dealing with Avril's behavior, Mrs Hayes reached a low point of depression, involving physical and nervous exhaustion; all this further minimized consistent and effective mothering of her child.

Thinking in "ABC" Terms

At this point, we shall begin to think in "ABC" terms— Antecedents, Behaviors, Consequences. This basic learning equation brings us to the next step in assessment. We shall return to Avril as we progress throughout this book.

Step 6	**Teach your clients to think in terms of behavioral sequences.** This will provide us with an understanding of some of the significant influences that trigger and maintain unhappy interactions within the family. Provide the client with materials to collect information and set homework tasks.
Antecedent events	What happens? What events precede, lead up to, set the stage for
Behavior/interaction	the problematic behaviors/interactions being complained of; and
Consequence	what happens after the event? What social (or other) outcomes flow from the problematic interaction?

This is the basic learning equation; the ABC analysis or functional analysis. It provides a helpful description of the key elements of an interpersonal situation and their interrelationships.

The records in Figures 3a, b, and c elicit information about the behavior of the child and on the antecedent and consequent behaviors by members of the family. You might collect the information by means of (a) a handout such as that illustrated by Avril's chart, which, incidentally, incorporates a parallel

Figure 3a. Handout ABC Chart

CHART: *Avril's*   DATE: *4/7*   WEEK: *2*

OBSERVER: *Mother*   CODE:

BEHAVIOR: <u>Defiance</u> = defined by situations when Avril refuses to obey (despite warning) a request/command :   (i) to do something   (D)
                                                  (ii) not to do something   (T)

                  <u>Tantrum</u> = Avril screams / kicks / shouts

ANTECEDENT EVENTS (BEFORE)	BEHAVIOR	CONSEQUENT EVENTS (AFTER)
Avril asked for a chocolate at the checkout counter; I said "No." She grabbed one. I put it back. She snatched it. I put it back.	(D)	Avril ran away and climbed on a display counter (see below). She only came down when a shop assistant offered her a chocolate.
I told her off when we got home.	(T)	I went to the bathroom with a magazine. The noise subsided.

Figure 3b.   *Mrs Hayes' Rating Scale:* My anxiety level when Avril defies me in front of other people

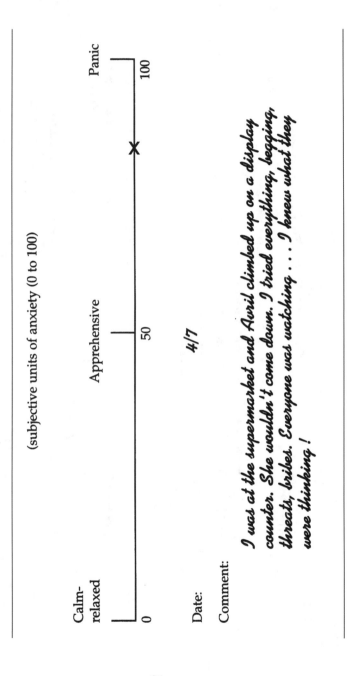

(subjective units of anxiety (0 to 100))

Calm-
relaxed

0

Apprehensive

50

Panic

100

X

Date: 4/7

Comment:

I was at the supermarket and Avril climbed up on a display counter. She wouldn't come down. I tried everything, begging, threats, bribes. Everyone was watching . . . I knew what they were thinking!

Figure 3c. ABC diary

Time	Antecedent: What happens beforehand?	Client Behavior	Consequences: What happens next?
9 p.m.	Mother asks Avril to put her toys away.	Avril takes no notice.	Mother tidies them up.
9:30 p.m.	Father tells Avril to go to bed.	Avril says "I don't want to, just give me a little while more."	There is a debate. 1. Father tells her it is late (she ignores). 2. Mother pleads. Avril argues. There is a heated exchange. 1. Mother scolds. 2. Father shouts. Avril is given 10 more minutes.

measure (b) of the mother's reactions, or (c) a simple diary record with the kind of headings illustrated there.

You will have to ask, observe, and possibly role-play, over a series of interviews and home visits in order to know which events tend to follow which, in what circumstances.

You might ask parents to describe a "typical day" in the life of the family – for example, who does what, when, how ... to whom or with whom ... with what consequences. (Chapter 5 contains an example of a questionnaire/rating scale dealing with family functioning and family difficulties.) The typical day tends to highlight particular times and situations in which there is family friction.

Step 7.	**Establish problem priorities.**
	Those workers with mandatory obligations will doubtless have their own guidelines on priorities. But do ask clients what their greatest worry is, what their top priorities are for bringing about change.
	Your and their hierarchy of tasks might be influenced by the following considerations with regard to the problem(s):
	• their annoyance value;
	• their actual/potential dangerousness;
	• their interference with the life of the family or its individual members;
	• their accessibility to change (improvement) and an intervention;
	• their frequency, intensity, and magnitude;
	• their disabling implications;
	• the "costs" of change in terms of resources (time, money, etc.) and other people's well-being;
	• the ethical acceptability of the desired outcome; and
	• the availability of the necessary skills resources on your part or the part of your agency to provide help.

Summary and Comment

In this chapter we have asked the vital "what" question that is the beginning point of any assessment of a family and its problems. The first seven steps of this process were set out. This phase of your investigation should take two or three interviews/observation sessions. The need to be specific and precise was emphasized.

Start where the client is. Without necessarily accepting his or her (or their) assumptions, allow them the opportunity to describe the problem in their own terms. The client may see the difficulties as being the child's alone. Don't challenge this view immediately. Wait until you have your data, then extend the agenda to include parental and other factors.

Working with families requires a particular perspective or systems approach. It is essential to take account of the interdependence of family members and the fact that what happens to one person is likely to affect the others. This focus on the family as a system requires an understanding of group processes as well as individual influences for the assessment of child and family problems.

CHAPTER 3

Taking Account of the Family

The "Why" Question

By this stage you should have enough information from your initial assessment and data gathering to know whether the problems are sufficiently salient and serious for you to continue the assessment. It may be possible to move on and seek answers to the *why* questions (see Herbert, 1994; 1998a), in the form of explanatory hypotheses, of the causes of these problems. In working with children and their families, important and early action toward an immediate problem solution needs to be offered if possible. For example, in situations of needed resources, can those resources such as income or free access to child care, be found? The child could be out of school because the family has not provided or allowed necessary immunization for school admission. If problems troubling families are readily resolvable from a professional perspective, referral and education for obtaining needed services and resources are valuable intervention activities on your part. If intervention is not so immediate and the problem so readily solvable, has your assessment thus far helped determine if the family is willing to agree, or establish a contract, to continue in treatment and work toward problem resolution? Finally, is intervention, based on your assessment, within your range of expertise? Are there alternative treatment resources that would be more helpful to your client? Your professional ethical judgment enters the decision of "where to from here" based upon your encountering the family and assessing the problems they are troubled by.

Families, not unlike the members within them, experience evolution and change throughout the various stages, or cycles of family life. It is important to always bear in mind that movement, change, and transition are quintessential to the development of children, and, indeed, adults; the same can be said of family life. Both individuals and families have their life cycles and life tasks in their development through the life cycles of families and their members (Carter and McGoldrick, 1989; Janzen and Harris, 1997).

The birth of a first child to a couple makes parents of them and transforms their partnership into a family. While their children are growing up and changing, parents too are facing shifts in their own personal development, from youthful maturity to early middle-age. We cannot consider children or adolescents and their problems without considering the manner in which they interact with their parents, who are not without their own preoccupations and anxieties. Let us take an example of parents who are thirty years old and upward when their first child reaches puberty. Insensitive offspring would call this middle-age. Delayed child bearing provides young adults an extended time for career preparation and for establishing their lives as a couple before including a child in their family. For couples who delay having children into their thirties, their children will reach their "teens" when they are in their forties or fifties. These couples may view their middle years as the "prime of life." But what do the teenagers make of them in their thirties, forties, or fifties? For some, their parents' generation seems to have lost its zest for living or to be boring; while for others, the distance between generations seems to have little bearing.

On the other hand, children born of teen parent(s) will likely be reared, at least in their early years, by parents who struggle to work, pay bills, find better jobs, and enroll in various degree and training programs. Life circumstances of families affect children whether it be age of parenthood, income, employment, rural versus urban lifestyles, extended family relationships, physical and mental illness or disabilities, or marital changes such as divorce or remarriage (Helton and Jackson, 1997; Mason, et al., 1998).

The point of all this is that a "family life map" constructed by you and your client family can illuminate interesting connections. It may indicate why confrontations occur between members of the family who face different life tasks (see Figure 4, p. 45) and life events. A decision by one to make a change in his or her lifestyle can affect the entire family. Just as a family responds and adjusts to life events and decisions for change by its members, it also must respond to unexpected events or crises that may be so powerful as to cause the family to need help with finding new ways of coping or of identifying alternative ways of functioning, particularly in the face of great losses such as death, job loss, debilitating illnesses, and even catastrophic national and community disasters. There are many major life events that frequently cause families to seek help.

Life-Event Information

Common and often overwhelming life events confronting families call for careful assessment and information gathering. These events are potentially disruptive and stress producing and can have long-term impact on a family's approach to problem solving, coping, and communication. It is important to identify major events that impinge at present or that had a potentially disruptive influence in the past on the lives of your client family and its members. The following list identifies some of the major, yet common, life events that occur in families.

- death of a spouse;
- divorce;
- marital separation;
- detention in jail or other institution;
- death of a close family member;
- major personal injury or illness;
- marriage;
- marital reconciliation;
- retirement from work;
- major change in the health or behavior of a family member;
- pregnancy;
- sexual difficulties;
- gaining a new family member (e.g. through birth, adoption);
- major change in responsibilities at work (e.g. promotion, demotion, lateral transfer);
- son or daughter leaving home (e.g. marriage, attending college, etc.); and
- in-law troubles.

Rutter's Family Adversity Index (Rutter and Quinton, 1977) demonstrates that psychiatric disorder rises in terms of risk with each increase in the adversity score on the following items:

Item 1.   Father an unskilled worker;

Item 2.   Overcrowding: at least 4 children or more than one person per room;

Item 3.   Persisting marital discord or one-parent family situation;

Item 4.   Maternal depression or neurosis;

Item 5.   Delinquency in the father;

Item 6.   Institutional care of the child exceeding one week in duration (see Blanz, *et al.*, 1991, for experimental data).

Families with teenagers frequently seek help as each seeks to accomplish life tasks appropriate for his or her age and development. It is these mature families struggling with adjustments and conflicts rather than stress related to unexpected crises or devastating life events that sometimes challenge even experienced professionals.

Parents sometimes create their own problems by trying to live through their children, relying mainly on vicarious satisfactions. In this context, it is commonly asserted that middle age is a more difficult phase of life for women than men. The changes in her life are in many ways more obvious. The children are becoming less dependent, if not totally independent, of her; and until this period of her life her maternal interests may have been uppermost in her life. Although her concern continues, her direct role as a mother is coming to an end. But we must not exaggerate the "empty nest" phenomenon. Among middle-aged people whose younger child is about to leave high school, most women do mention the approaching departure of the youngest child as a forthcoming change but do not consciously believe that it will be a difficult time for them. Most men ignore the imminent event in their conversations with researchers, their attention being already directed to their own retirement in the future.

Marriages are likely to be undergoing greater strain at this juncture than at any time since the initial impact of the intimacy of living together when the couple first set up home. This is not to say the relationship is necessarily poor or terminal; but there may be special marital stresses. Coping with turbulent young-sters is difficult especially if a person is not getting full support from his or her partner. Difficulties in the marriage may become more exposed, more abrasive, if offspring are rebelling, getting into serious trouble, or playing one parent off against the other.

This age group has been referred to as the "middle genera-tion" because their own parents are usually alive, and they are likely to feel obligations to the younger generation and the older one. Some parents feel trapped by the needs of aging parents and demanding teenagers and wonder where those chances of "doing their own thing" have gone.

All or part of these life events may or may not be present for some or all of your client family members. One of the strengths of a good assessment is that not only is the presence or absence of these life events determined for your client family members, the "worry index," the degree to which these events were and/or continue to be a source of stress and worry, is identified. Families can identify those stressors they cannot change, those they can change, and those that are becoming less stressful without action on their part. It is important to identify life events and life tasks for families so that expectations are devel-opmentally appropriate for the members as well as the family as a whole.

Step 8.	**Work out a family life map.** Your client's family life map will be con-structed with the family and will include data mapping accomplishments, or lack thereof, for life tasks and life events for each member of the family. Your client's family map might look something like Figure 4.

44

Figure 4. A family life map: Transitional stages of life

TIM: 22 months	ANNE: age 10 years	PETER: age 14	MOTHER: age 38	FATHER: age 45	GRANNY: age 66
LIFE TASKS	*LIFE TASKS*	*LIFE TASKS*	*LIFE TASKS*	*LIFE TASKS*	*LIFE TASKS*
• Develop motor skills	• Cope with academic demands at school (underachieving)	• Adjust to physical changes of puberty	• Review her life and commitments	• Review commitments in mid-life	• Deal with increasing dependence on others
• Develop self-control	• Developing her sense of self	• Adjust to sexual awareness	• Adjust to loss of youth and (in her perception) "looks"	• Develop new phase in relationship with wife	• Come to terms with old age/death
• Elaborate vocabulary	• Learn to be part of a team	• Cope with the opposite sex (shyness)	• Cope with an adolescent as a patient and caring parent	• Face physical changes—some limitations on athletic/sexual activity	• Cope with loss of peers
• Explore his world—make "discoveries"		• Deepen friendships (intimacy)			
LIFE EVENTS	*LIFE EVENTS*	*LIFE EVENTS*	*LIFE EVENTS*	*LIFE EVENTS*	*LIFE EVENTS*
• Parents insist on obedience now	• Afraid to go to school (cannot manage math)	• Worried about his skin (acne) and size of his penis	• Coping with late child—an active toddler	• Threat of being laid off	• Poor health
• Adjust to temporary separations when mother works	• Bullied by a girl in her class	• Has a girlfriend—his first	• Has taken part-time job to relieve feeling trapped	• High blood pressure	• Gave up home when bereaved (may have made a mistake!)
• Not the center of attention and "uncritical" deference	• Jealous of attention Tim gets (calls him a spoiled brat)	• Upset by his parents' quarrels	• Feels guilty	• Worried about drifting apart from his wife	• Enjoys the little one, but
	• Worried about father's health	• Complains that his mother is always watching him	• Bouts of depression	• Had a brief affair	• Feels "claustrophobic" with all the activity/squabbles
			• No longer enjoys sex	• Feels unattractive	
TODDLERHOOD	PREPUBESCENCE	ADOLESCENCE	← MIDLIFE →		RETIREMENT

45

The Family as a Dynamic Organization

The family is a dynamic institution, that is to say susceptible to change in several ways. The family is more than the sum of its parts, more than the static aggregate of the individual personalities who make up its membership. It has, in a sense, a life of its own. The members interact in many subtle ways that give a particular "feel" or atmosphere to a family; they have different and changing roles that in turn change the "personality" of the family as time goes by; they have their successes and failures that reflect on the family; alliances form, dissolve, and reform. The family thus has its own life cycle from "infancy" to "old age" with associated changes in its size, "shape," and function. It also has its pool of skills. The all-important transmission of culture cannot be inflexible as would be a genetic code determining our physical equipment. But nor can it be left to chance. The welfare of the individual and the continuity of the culture depend upon there being a satisfactory means of socializing the new generation into society's mores, attitudes, and skills, and to ensure that they, in turn, will satisfactorily transmit the culture. The family plays a major role in this important socialization process, thus preparing children to transmit cultural traditions and societal mores to future generations.

Theories of Family Life

Defining interactions and development of families is approached from a variety of perspectives, and each perspective informs its intervention. In other words, what we believe about families shapes how we work with families. Selected and widely used models of family therapy vary in the theoretical framework embraced and interventions applied. There is a structural school which has its roots in the work of Salvador Minuchin and his colleagues, originating in a residential institution for ghetto boys in New York (Minuchin, 1974). Strategic family therapy has its origins in the Palo Alto research group led by Gregory Bateson — working, inter alia, on family communication as it affected schizophrenics (e.g. Bateson, *et al.*, 1956). Humanistic, existential therapies of the 1960s, such as Gestalt therapy, psychodrama, client-centered therapy and the encounter group movement, influenced the theory and methods of various experiential family therapies—challenging the positivist tenets of the more problem-focused schools of family therapy. Behavioral family therapy found its intellectual roots in Social Learning Theory (Patterson, 1982). Psychoanalytic and object relations perspectives are derived from psychoanalytic theory, but draw upon other principles as well. A leading exponent is Nathan Ackerman (1958) who founded the Family Institution, New York.

The intergenerational perspective, which looks beyond the immediate family circle and enlists the cooperation of others in resolving the family's distress, is associated with the names of pioneers such as Murray Bowen (1978) and Virginia Satir (1983). Satir focused on the interaction of family members and involved the entire family in assessment and treatment. Salvador Minuchin based structural family therapy on family systems, their transactions and changes, and intervened through changing transactions and reorganizing relationships of members in the family with respect to the strengths and contributions of each member and of the family as a system. Individual, subsystem, and family boundaries are important in the realigning and joining techniques of this approach (Minuchin, 1974; Minuchin and Fishman, 1981).

A widely used approach to understanding and helping families in the strategic family approach focuses on the world view or the conceptual frames of reference of families and their members in terms of how they see themselves and alternatives in the context of their lives. Strategic family therapists see dysfunctional behaviors and coping efforts as symptoms in response to the context of families' lives. The question of "why" is not as important as "what" is going on in the hierarchy of the family, in their systems of power and control, and in how the family is organized and can be restructured. Strategic family therapy is directive and teaches clients to take control of behavior including violent and angry behaviors and to forgive themselves and others close to them (Haley, 1987; Madanes, 1981, 1984, 1990).

Solution-focused family treatment focuses on solutions, not problems. Problems are defined and viewed as experiences that have a purpose and then goals for new solutions are defined. Clients are helped to value and explore experiences, take action toward solutions, and explore ideas and beliefs through their own language and stories of themselves and their experiences. There is no singular right solution but a range of solutions around which action and anticipation of future success can occur (O'Hanlon, 1993; O'Hanlon and Weiner-Davis, 1989). Berg (1994) applies solution-focused intervention to families and children who are clients of child welfare services. Intervention is relatively brief, recognizes change in families and individuals in families, and is directive in helping families find solutions and create new solutions for those previous behaviors or responses that work less well.

Having its roots in behavioral theory, the social learning model is a useful approach to understanding how families function and to helping families change behaviors (Horne, 1991; Horne and Sayger, 1990; Janzen and Harris, 1997). Learning occurs in the environment families create for themselves. There, behaviors occur and are accepted, reinforced and established, are ignored, or are unaccepted and sometimes punished. This process shapes and reinforces behaviors within the culture of the family and its process of development. As such, this learning process occurs in response to interactions and relationships in the family and is not generally a planned nor consistent process.

In the social learning model, behaviors are approached as learned through cognitive processes involving satisfaction and reinforcement. The social learning approach recognizes the social context of behaviors, relationships that reward behaviors, and the cognitive and problem-solving capacities that enable families to normalize problems and set about structuring their environment to successfully change behaviors and alleviate problems in family functioning (Goldenberg and Goldenberg, 1991).

Family members establish functional and dysfunctional behaviors in their relationships as they interact and cope in their daily lives. Behaviors that trouble families are often the impetus that serves to cause families to seek help with family functioning. When they do seek help, generally the behavior of a family member is presented as the problem to be treated. For example, families seek help with problem behaviors such as violent behavior of a parent, hyperactive or uncontrolled behavior of a child, an eating disorder of an adolescent, or conflict with a marital partner.

The systems perspective provides a framework for understanding family functioning and relationships within the family system and community and social systems in the family's environment. Unhappiness within families produces unhappy members, all of whom are affected and involved in the particular problem, and all of whom need to be involved in improving the unhappiness or problem. It is within the functioning and life cycle of families that children develop, experience stages of their biological, social, and emotional development, and are greatly impacted by their experiences in their families. From infancy through young adulthood, children learn to behave, develop an image of themselves, and establish the map for their world view as adults. Throughout life cycles of families, children, and adults, systems and systems constructs play a major role in individual development and understanding human relationships (Carter and McGoldrick, 1989).

Major theories of family functioning and human behavior are reviewed by Herbert (1998b), Vetere and Gale (1987), and Zastrow and Kirst-Ashman (1997). Some concepts important in working with children and their family system that you will need to understand and perhaps explore in the literature include:

- *Cohesion*, which reflects the transactions—the emotional attachments of members—and their individual autonomy. It is at its highest in enmeshed (closely interrelated, mutually involved) families and at its lowest in disengaged (unattached) families.
- *Boundaries*, which delineate the components belonging to the system and those belonging to the environment; they are defined by rules which specify individual's roles, what subsystem he or she belongs to, and the appropriate behavior which such membership entails. Boundaries can be clear, where they are defined by easily recognized and acceptable rules; diffuse, where they are ambiguous and

chaotic because rules are unstable or absent; or rigid, if they are inflexible and unadaptable.

- *Adaptability,* which indicates that a family can modify its roles and relationships in response to influence for change.
- *Homeostasis,* which is a term that describes the "steady state" of the "organism" (for our purposes the family)— indicating that the various subsystems are in balance and the whole system is in harmony with the environment. To achieve and maintain homeostasis in the face of change and stress, a system must be open.
- *Open,* which means that family members have a high level of exchange with the outside community, as compared with systems that are closed and take in little new information or energy.
- *Closed,* which have very little exchange with the community outside their boundaries.
- *Feedback* processes are believed to characterize social systems and reflect the ability of the family to "recognize" its own output as input at some later stage. For example, the family that is functioning well is capable of monitoring its progress toward family goals and correcting or modifying its actions to bring itself back on track, if necessary.

All families are different in their own ways; nevertheless, certain dynamics and problem areas occur in the lives of many families. Families in need of professional help often have the commonality of similar problem areas. In the life of a professional, rarely will a client family seek help to celebrate their successes. Instead, it is the configurations of problems and stress that cause stress in the lives of families and their members for which professional intervention is sought. Let us look at the all too common problem of family violence, a problem area where family cohesion is often minimal and boundaries are marked by either extreme rigidity or excessive diffuseness. Victims of family violence are usually those members most unable to protect themselves—sometimes the elderly member, the mother, and all too frequently, the children.

Family Violence

The image of the family as a nurturant organization and a haven of safety is shattered more often than we care to think, when it erupts with violence. The point has been made by experienced workers that people are more likely to be killed, physically assaulted, hit, beaten, or slapped in their own homes by other family members than anywhere else or by anyone else in our society. Three groups of people are particularly vulnerable: children, women, and the elderly. It is not good enough to categorize the perpetrators of such awful deeds as degenerates, drunks, psychopaths, or mental cases. Such categorization simply applies known labels to unacceptable behavior. Some labels even excuse violent action by implying that the perpetrator is not accountable for uncontrollable behavior.

The evidence suggests that many diverse factors, including social and psychological factors, contribute to family violence. We consider these in Chapter 4. Various forms of physical abuse are obvious and easily assessed or diagnosed if seen by a physician. Other forms, equally disabling for the victim, include psychological and emotional abuse and neglect. Children seen with unexplained injuries and old and healed cuts and fractures that have gone untreated are likely victims of physical abuse. Abuse is willful and harmful action toward the victim while neglect is more likely to be a lack of care and a problem of omission. Although the problems of abuse and neglect may both go on over time, neglect is likely to go undetected and unreported much longer. Abuse and neglect of children are commonly referred to as child maltreatment, a problem that occurs in the social, cultural, and family context of the lives of children. Having a multi-causal origin, child maltreatment is a serious problem in the lives of families and has long-term consequences for victims. Common categories of abuse and neglect are presented by Browne and Herbert (1997), Faller, *et al.* (1981), and Tower (1996).

Abuse

- Physical abuse is the infliction of a range of physical injuries to a child and can include bruises, cuts, burns, scalds, injuries to bones and joints including fractures, and serious internal injuries to various organs of the body, head, and brain. Failure to thrive, particularly when food and water are withheld, is physical abuse.

- Emotional abuse is the infliction of psychological and emotional assault, including threats of serious physical or sexual harm, scapegoating, confinement, disregard, yelling, and punitive communication. Emotionally abused children often present symptoms such as bed wetting, aggressive or bizarre behavior, difficulty in forming relationships, poor self-esteem, and problems in school.
- Sexual abuse is the sexual assault and misuse of children by adults, siblings, or parents and is sometimes difficult to diagnose but may include genital infections, bruises and lacerations, pregnancy, and bloody or infectious discharges. Children exposed to sexual abuse are often more familiar with sexual and physical information than is typical for their age and development, display excessive masturbation, and sometimes are involved in sexual behaviors as the perpetrator. Exploitation of children for personal satisfaction or for monetary gain, such as pornographic literature or movies with sexually explicit content involving children, is sexual abuse.

Neglect

- Physical neglect is the failure to provide a safe and nurturing home for a child and may include a failure to feed, shelter, clothe, and protect from harm. Failure to thrive may be due to physical and/or emotional neglect.
- Emotional neglect is the failure to nurture the psychological, social, and emotional aspects of a child's life and may involve an absence of love, affection, attention, intellectual and emotional stimulation, social interaction, and warmth related to a lack of cuddling and demonstration of love and affection.
- Supervisory neglect is the failure to provide supervision to assure safety including: protection, not being left alone for periods of time inappropriate for age and development, and not being abandoned.

- Medical neglect is the failure to provide medical care including immediate and appropriate care for critical injuries or illnesses, immunizations, and medical treatment when needed.
- Educational neglect is the failure to provide school enrollment and attendance on a regular and timely basis so that the child is appropriately on time, in school when not ill, and provided with necessary clothing and materials for school. Changing unwanted behaviors, or developing skills of interacting and relating, where skills are faulty or absent, usually requires the participation, and the willingness to change, of parents and, sometimes, the entire family. To this end one might say that every family makes use of its combined store of skills so that members can usefully share and learn from each other. Broadly speaking these skills fall into seven categories: relationship, social, communication, problem solving, coping, study, and work skills.

Parenting skills include several of these categories (see Chapter 9); deficits in parental abilities can lead to problems in the offspring—your analysis is by this time beginning to move toward a formulation of why things are going wrong for this family. The *what* question merges into a *why* question, the answers to which are the subject of the next step.

Taking Account of the Child

Children in Need (see Herbert, 1993)

Children "in need" are assessed as such in terms of their (a) physical well-being and physical care, (b) mental health, (c) social and intellectual development, (d) emotional and behavioral development. It is noted that a child's health and/or development may be significantly harmed by parents or caregivers who neglect or who overprotect because of the childs' behavior. In children, disability refers to the presence in the child of visual impairment, hearing impairment, serious communication difficulties, substantial handicap stemming from illness, injury or congenital conditions. In the United Kingdom these terms are defined in The Children Act, 1989.

The Adoption and Safe Families Act, 1997 calls for safe and permanent homes for children in the United States. This Act provides for working with biological as well as foster or adoptive parents to assure that every child lives in the most permanent and least restrictive home possible, i.e. ranging from the child's biological home through relative, adoptive, foster to group home if need be. Child Abuse Prevention and Treatment Act Amendments of 1996 (P.L. 104-235) identifies four major types of maltreatment: physical abuse, neglect, sexual abuse, and emotional abuse and standards for appropriate nutrition, hydration, and medication. Child well-being includes the provision of shelter, medical care, and safety.

Whether a child is "significantly at risk" is usually determined by a child protection case conference. Some children may be at risk and in need, although there is no evidence that they are not achieving or maintaining a reasonable standard of health and development. We can never overestimate the difficulties faced by social and health practitioners, particularly social workers and home health visitors, in making the agonizing decisions inherent in the protective roles called for by the nature of their jobs. They have to interpret complex terms, and balance the needs and safety of children and the needs and rights of parents. Theirs is only too often a situation in which they are blamed when things go tragically amiss, and unacknowledged when things go well and children and families are protected and supported.

When is a Child Being Harmed?

At what point can it be said that a child is actually being *harmed* to a significant extent by the neglect of needs or the presence of unskilled, insensitive or inexperienced parenting? After all, it is not the cases of explicitly malicious abuse or extreme neglect that create the agonizing debates about what constitutes harm. Harm may or may not be easily determined. It is the more subtle and ambiguous consequences for the child's well-being that flow from parental ignorance, inexperience, emotional inadequacies or lack of resourcefulness, that evade confident classification. The professional may have a nagging concern about a child who is failing to thrive or cope, and/or the parents who may be ignorant or unwilling to face up to possible harm to their child because of the state of his or her health or development. *At least* s/he must have reasonable cause to suspect that the child is suffering, or is likely to suffer, significant harm. Infants and children—if they are to survive—must also acquire vast amounts of information about the environment they inhabit.

For example, the needs of children who are potentially at risk (if not responded to consistently and appropriately) are of two major types:

- *survival* functions such as the need for food, shelter and physical care; and
- *psychosocial* functions, including the child's requirements of love, security, attention, new experiences, acceptance, education, praise, recognition and belongingness.

Assessment Methods Criteria (see Jordan and Franklin, 1995)

If an assessment of these matters is to be trusted, then the methods or indicators used, and their application, should meet certain criteria:

- Appropriate coverage—breadth and specificity: observations, for example, should be of a *representative* sample of the client's behavior occurring in specified situations.
- Indicators or measures that are fair: this point is related to the one above. The assessment should not apply to a biased or narrow aspect of the clients' activities or attitudes. Nor should one use tests or questions that are culture-bound (ethnocentric) and which therefore discriminate unfairly against particular persons.
- Accurate indicators or measures: this means that they should be reliable (and, if circumstances allow, repeatable). They should also be translated into precise statements and descriptions as opposed to vague, global terminology.
- Indicators or measures that are relevant: relevance is critical if assessments are to be valid. In other words, assessments

should measure or indicate what they purport to measure/indicate.

- Practical to use: There is little point in using unwieldy, time-consuming, esoteric methods.
- Ethical: This is a *sine qua non* of all one's practice.

Taking Account of the Parents

One of the main objectives of training and education is the preparation of children for their future. It is doubtful whether any child—in our far from ideal world—has all of his or her individual needs satisfied by parents. This, in part, is why the term "good enough parenting" has entered the professional vocabulary. To quote Bruno Bettelheim:

> *In order to raise a child well one ought not to try to be a perfect parent, as much as one should not expect one's child to be, or become, a perfect individual. Perfection is not within the grasp of ordinary human beings....But it is quite possible to be a good enough parent...*
> (Bettelheim, A Good Enough Parent, 1987).

It is important to marshal rational arguments for choosing particular judgments and decisions, not personal sentiment or prejudice. Professionals carrying out an assessment need a sound empirical knowledge base for their recommendations.

Step 9.	**Make an assessment of your client's skills (incentives, resources).** Parenting is a complex series of skills, part common sense, part intuition, and part empathy, that is, the ability to see things from another's point of view.

Parents can be trained in many of the necessary skills of child care and behavior management; the latter is a major theme of this book. Although not so easy, those attachments and feelings that come so readily to most parents and children, but which are absent or distorted in some, can be encouraged.

Ask your client to go through the skills listed in Table 3 with you. He or she may be pleasantly surprised at how many they

Table 3. A List of Parenting Skills

I and my child	*I and significant others*
Skills I need to relate effectively to him/her	Skills I need to relate effectively to others (e.g. my partner, teachers, friends) involved with my child
• How to communicate clearly • How to "listen" carefully so as to understand • How to develop my relationship • How to give help and care and protection without "going over the top" • How to teach and discipline • How to show and receive affection • How to manage/resolve conflict • How to give and receive feedback • How to maintain a balance between extremes (e.g. loving without being possessive) • How to negotiate sensible compromises • How to set limits—reasonable ones, and stick to them	• How to be reasonably objective about others • How not to be possessive • How to be assertive (without being intrusive or bossy) • How to influence crucial people and systems (e.g. school) • How to work in groups (e.g. parents' groups, pressure groups) • How to express my feelings clearly and constructively • How to inspire confidence and strength in others • How to see my child's friends from his/her point of view • How to resist/cope with jealousy

(Adapted from B. Hopson and M. Scally. 1980.)

57

can claim. Unless your clients know that they possess certain skills they may not be able to make the most constructive use of them. It is important not to demoralize clients with this exercise; not all of them are pertinent for the particular individual. There may have been little or no opportunity to develop some of them.

Now do something similar for the child or teenager. Look for positives in the child's situation: what is going well in the situation you are concerned about at present with regard to the child or teenager? How does this young person contribute to your family life? What are his/her good points? You might draw up a balance sheet for attributes perceived by parents as on the credit or debit side. You may find it useful to ask the youngster to carry out the same exercise with regard to himself/herself.

| *Step 10* | **(a). Ask your clients (parents) what their goals (ambitions, plans) are for their child.** |

In the case of children, change and development must have some point—a destination and thus a direction. Only parents and children can decide on their goals and aspirations although your counsel, based on professional knowledge and experience, should play a part.

| *Step 10* | **(b). Ask your clients what their goals are for themselves; in other words, their self-oriented goals.** |

We have been discussing goals which involve children and the interactions between parents and children. But what of goals involving adults in their own right, where you may have to counsel them? A mother may wish to increase her self-confidence and banish her recurrent bouts of depression. A father may ask for help in controlling his temper and reducing his irritability. A teenage brother or sister may desire to play a greater part in family decision-making.

We have now reached Phase III of the flow chart (Chapter 2); it is good practice to have a pre-intervention record of the extensiveness of the client's problems based upon a week or two of observations and self-reports. This baseline allows you to evaluate any changes that occur before and after intervention. Baseline data provide the standard against which to measure the effect of your intervention.

Baseline Data Collection (further one or two interviews, preferably including home visit[s]).

From this baseline you collect information about the extent and precise circumstances of the problematic interactions. You show your client(s) how to observe behavior so that, in a sense, you can observe things through their eyes during the time you cannot be with them.

Until now the main source of information has been the interview—a systematic approach to obtaining information about the problem, its nature, frequency, antecedents, consequences, etc. It may have been conducted at the office or in the client's home. Next, the baseline data collected by interview are checked, supplemented, and quantified by:

- direct observation of the client in natural settings, for example, home, school, youth clubs;
- direct observation in other settings, for example, office, reception center, and so forth;
- self-recordings by the client (diaries, activity charts, self-ratings) in his/her day-to-day life or special situations;
- use of questionnaires, rating scales, and the like, completed by the client or others; use of audio or video cassette recordings.

Summary and Comment

We have carried forward the analysis of the dynamic interactions within the family in this chapter. By the end of Phase II of the assessment you should be in a position to decide whether the problems are sufficiently serious to continue on to the collection of baseline data. If not, you need to advise parents why you do not regard a further assessment or intervention as necessary. Perhaps the child's problems are normal for his/her age and situation. Perhaps parents have exaggerated because of their personal anxieties or ignorance of child development. Of course, you cannot simply dismiss parents with a philosophical "Don't worry" statement. They may require information about child behavior and development, or some understanding on how to manage the child's not unusual but worrying fears or tantrums or bed wetting. Knowledge of age-appropriate behavior is obviously vital for the professional and information necessary for parents.

We have seen that many of the problems affecting parents and their children are the problem of the family, as a family, and need to be construed as such. Problems within the family with which you are likely to deal are those involving relationships (e.g. sibling rivalry and jealousy, parental overprotection, marital discord); lack of knowledge (e.g. ignorance of what to expect of children at different ages); disagreements over the sharing of finite resources (such as money, time, attention); conflict (over policies such as rules, discipline, routines). Helping parents to resolve conflicts with adolescents is a valuable contribution to happier family life, as is the reduction of aggravation brought about by planning of "around the clock" rules and routines for the toddler who needs help with activities such as dressing, meals, visiting, shopping, and going to bed.

Among the most serious problems you might be called on to deal with is violence within the family. Physical and emotional abuse are described, together with a range of family dysfunctions.

CHAPTER 4

Formulating the "Why" Question

In Stages 2 and 3 of the ASPIRE procedure, the formulation of an intervention plan involving the choice of methods/techniques for bringing about change, is a process that flows from the assessment of the determinants of the problem/s. In an ideal world this formulation would inform the choice of a therapeutic strategy (the "how" question which we return to in Part III) or some broader based community intervention. Only too often the assessment data, like the occupants of Procrustes' bed, are made to fit the favored therapeutic model. The Rigorous Evaluation requirement in the ASPIRE procedure is that the specificity of goal-setting and requirement of monitoring change, allow the practitioner to judge fairly early in the intervention whether the program is on the right track or not (see Herbert, 1987a; Hudson and McDonald, 1986; Jordan and Franklin, 1995; and Sutton, 1994). This evaluation requirement is one of the strengths of the ASPIRE model. There is an implied suggestion that a particular approach can be applied to all problems. Sadly, faith, rather than evidence, is mostly what is on offer to support the more Panglossian prospectuses.

Some parents (and, indeed, professionals) dwell on the past when they look for the why's and wherefore's of their offspring's difficulties. It is important to maintain a balance between past and present when trying to find reasons or causes for current behavior. The past cannot be changed, although you might "liberate" some from the past by resolving or changing present unhealthy attitudes which are rooted there. In any event, it is only in rare instances that current problems can be traced to specific past experiences with any degree of confidence.

Yet, when things go wrong, our society gets an irresistible urge to find something or someone to blame. And when they go wrong with children, or the relationships between parents and their children, the finger is often pointed at the mother. The literature on childhood psychological problems is full of over-protective, dominating, or rejecting mothers.

But is it really all so one-sided? What are fathers doing during these early years of their children's lives? The cynic might think that fathers were remote figures because it is mothers who generally bring the children to the office or clinic and are interviewed.

More surprising is the relatively neglected role of the child in all these unhappy events. Is it just a one-way process, with awful or stupid things being done to a passive infant? Certainly by encouraging some activities and discouraging others, parents influence their children's behavior and personality. But in all sorts of subtle ways, their behavior is also shaped by the child. In the crucial business of growing up, there is a two-way traffic in the relationship between parents and child.

Most current theories about the problems of, for example, child abuse place the sole emphasis on parental and, in particular, maternal psychopathology and environmental factors. The role the child can unwittingly play in his or her tragic predicament is usually overlooked. Yet research suggests that there are children who, from birth, show characteristics that make them not only difficult to rear but also difficult to love.

It is commonly known that among all the allegedly harmful factors blamed for this or that problem, whether adverse parental characteristics, family conflicts, or the like, it is possible to identify a significant number of children who developed without serious problems, despite being subjected to these influences. Those practitioners who are behaviorally oriented will lose little sleep over the doubts and uncertainties about the precursors of psychological problems—the tenuousness of the link between conditions of the child's life including home and school circumstances far removed in time from present manifestations of troublesome behavior. This is because human actions, whether simple or elaborate, normal or abnormal, are brought about by many influences rather than a single factor. And whatever the influence of personality traits, attitudes, and ideas, shaped over years of learning and development, the young person's day-to-day actions are powerfully controlled by current events, such as opportunities and temptations and the favorable outcomes, for example, reinforcements, to which these actions give rise.

Such observations give rise to a critical issue concerning the way you work: the theoretical perspective you adopt, or the particular model of human behavior that informs your practice. In order to help parents and their children effectively, you need to be clear about your underlying assumptions, as to how and why such individuals behave in the way they do (see Herbert, 1998a, 1998b, 1998c; Robins and Rutter, 1990). In what way do you make sense of your clients and predict or anticipate how they are likely to respond to your intervention?

Formulating Causes in the Case of Avril Hayes

You will soon detect the predominant model underlying our formulation of the causes of Avril's and her parents' difficulties. We had looked for patterns of antecedent and consequent stimuli which might be precipitating and maintaining the problem behavior. We also examined other situations in which the child's behavior differed from that in the "problematic" situations, for example, evidence of pro-social behavior and the settings in which it took place.

The case of Avril was thought to be one largely but by no means exclusively of faulty training and learning. For complex reasons that reach back to Avril's conception and birth, Mrs Hayes had become trapped in a pattern of behavior in which she unwittingly "encouraged" the very behaviors she wished to eliminate in the child's repertoire. Avril's demands, with few exceptions, for being waited on, attention, and so on, were acceded to following her display of tantrums and disruptive behaviors. The invariable outcome in the case of defiant actions was to increase the interaction between Avril and her mother. The resulting attention was reinforcing these non-compliant actions. It was quite straightforward to identify favorable consequences. To take but one example, she was being allowed to veto activities she did not like. Conversely, in all examples of misbehavior, there were no really negative or unfavorable consequences which might serve to diminish the behaviors.

With regard to the cues for the performance of problem behaviors, the most significant of these were the presence and actions of Mrs Hayes. The currency of her commands and threats had been debased; Avril did not trust her words. She had learned that her wishes for her mother's undivided attention, and "obedience" to her commands, were likely to be met if she persisted long enough or escalated her coercive behaviors.

Essentially she had learned that certain antisocial behaviors were guaranteed to produce "payoffs." This lesson, applied in the school situation, could have aversive consequences for her and reduce her ability to learn. It was our opinion that they had affected her social development adversely—her manner was babyish and frustrating. From the point of view of other members of the family, Avril's egocentric, monopolistic, and immature behavior was undoubtedly undermining their well-being. Her sister was beginning to imitate some of her behaviors. As her parents saw things, they had endeavored to provide the best that they could for Avril and yet they were faced with a situation in which they no longer enjoyed their child. They increasingly quarreled over how to deal with the situation. These considerations, among others, contributed to the decision that an intervention was required.

She was certainly receiving a large amount of attention including physical proximity and verbal exchanges, but much of it took a negative form. It was precisely because of the endless rounds of disputations between parents and child that Avril was precluded from much of the usual range of symbolic rewards or social reinforcers which belong to happy and meaningful family communications. Avril, as a volatile, demanding child, had made constant assaults on Mrs Hayes' self-doubts. This is how her mother described the situation:

As time went by, Avril had developed into a despot. She shows a general aggression, a degree of wilfulness, and various other unacceptable behaviors. She whines, clings like a limpet, is insecure, and worst of all for me, incessantly disobedient. ... The situation over the years has deteriorated, compounded by an increasing tiredness on my part. This gradually deepened into general depression for which my doctor prescribed drugs. They didn't help; in fact feeling slightly drunk and rudderless made coping even more difficult. I was tearful, tense, often unreasonably angry, erratic and emotional, and then silent and with-drawn in turns. The tension in the house was painful. All the time her behavior has gotten worse. We were trapped in a vicious circle. Life was so miserable for me at this time that when I think back I can still feel the emptiness inside, the feeling of isolation, the constant fear that I would totally lose control and hurt her. I was really desperate. It was an effort to go out, even to go shopping. I looked awful, felt awful. Sometimes the loathing for Avril spilled over and I would find myself wanting to tell her, "Go away out of my life, I hate you. You've ruined my life." Sometimes I would start then have to bite back the words, remembering that I did love her. Afterwards I would feel consumed with guilt that I could even think of these things. And overall was this dreadful sense of failure. Failure as a mother and failure as a wife, even failure as a woman. I have never been so close to a total breakdown.

As Mrs Hayes appeared to bear the brunt of most of Avril's misbehavior, it might be concluded that her father was able to exercise control over her. This was not so; in fact, Mr Hayes' small part in this analysis of the problem situation reflects his minimizing of the contact he had with Avril—much to his wife's annoyance.

Having attempted to identify the conditions controlling the problem behavior, the next task was to try to explain their origins. The importance of this is not so much to help the client achieve insight, although awareness may facilitate change, but rather to discover to what extent the original "causal" factors continue to influence the current controlling conditions. Avril's developmental history was analyzed in order to seek any possible contribution to the problem by somatic or other factors. Physical conditions might produce problem behavior directly or might contribute to it indirectly through the reaction of children and/or their parents to any disability.

You may remember that Avril, from early in life, had been a difficult and overactive child, and that from the day of her birth she would cry day and night. The nights were particularly difficult. Mrs Hayes spent most of them nursing her. Being of such a commanding temperament, Avril learned from early on the strategy of how to gain attention from her mother and the rest of the family. The parents always intervened when she was

crying, shouting, screaming; when she was frustrated, disobedient, and aggressive, they often obeyed her commands for the
sake of peace, to save time, or to avoid embarrassment. A
variety of situations and settings became cues for verbal disputes and other forms of coercion by Avril. Her difficult
behaviors escalated at supermarkets, friends' homes, car
drives, and the like. Here the parents were constrained even
more than usual in responding to her oppositional behavior.
The following is a summary.

Avril appeared to be a child who displayed a range of
extreme behaviors almost from birth; these have been shown to
be closely linked with the development of maladaptive behaviors at a later age. In addition, her mother's ability to cope had
been considerably reduced in a number of ways. First, Mrs
Hayes had been handicapped by her fatigue and depression
and in particular by the fiercely protective and even defensive
attitude she had toward this "unwanted" child who had turned
out to be so difficult. This, together with a philosophy of child
rearing which was a reaction to her parents' methods, had considerably limited her choice of disciplinary procedures.

Clearly, the number of times the word "learning" appears in
the formulation is numerous. The social learning model will be
drawn on as a theoretical model to understand and intervene
with Avril and with the Hayes family as a unit.

Theoretical Approaches to Understanding Behavior

Social Learning Model

It is hypothesized that a major proportion of a child's behavior is
learned, maintained, and regulated by its effects upon the
natural environment and the feedback received with regard to
these consequences. Behavior does not occur in a vacuum; nor is
it a passive process. It is a result of a complex transaction
between the individual, with his or her inborn strengths and
weaknesses, acting and reacting with an environment that sometimes encourages and sometimes discourages certain actions.

An important feature of the social learning model is the
acknowledgment of the active role of cognitive variables, such

as, complex interpretive, thinking processes, in the way we learn. The part played by understanding in learning is significant. Not all learning, for example, to walk, to ride a bike, involves understanding, but much learning involves knowing rather than simply doing. Stimuli have meaning to the learner, who acquires knowledge of the situation which can be used in adapting to it. The emphasis, therefore, is on awareness in learning (Goldenberg and Goldenberg, 1991; Horne, 1991).

Many problems in adults as well as children are the consequences of failures or distortions of learning. The laws of learning that apply to the acquisition and change of normal socially approved behavior are assumed to be relevant to the understanding of self-defeating and/or socially disapproved actions. More specifically, the behavior problems of childhood are in large part due to the child's learning inappropriate responses; they are also the consequences of the child's failure to learn the appropriate behavior.

With all forms of learning the very processes which help the child adapt to life can, under certain circumstances, contribute to maladaptation. An immature child who learns by imitating an adult (observational learning) will not necessarily comprehend when it is undesirable (deviant) behavior that is being modeled. Mrs Hayes is a good example of a parent who does not always realize that she is reinforcing unwanted behavior by attending to it (instrumental or operant conditioning). If the consequences of a behavior are rewarding or favorable to a child, that behavior is likely to increase in strength. For example, it may become more frequent. Put another way: if Pat does something, and as a result of his action something pleasant happens to him, then he is more likely to do the same thing in similar circumstances in the future. When psychologists refer to this pleasant outcome as the positive reinforcement of behavior, they have in mind several kinds of reinforcers. Tangible rewards include sweets, treats, pocket money; social rewards include attention, a smile, a pat on the back, a word of encouragement; and self-reinforcers include the ones that come from within that are non-tangible, like self-praise, self-approval, or a sense of pleasure.

Behaving in a manner that avoids an unpleasant outcome leads to the reinforcement of behavior, thus making it more likely to recur in similar circumstances. If a young girl does something her parents do not like, such as losing her temper too easily, they may increase her ability to think first and hold her temper by penalizing her consistently for failing to do so. In this way they are providing what is called negative reinforcement. She avoids punishment by appropriate actions. They may not have to apply the penalty if she believes their threat because of their record of keeping their word. Consistency and persistence are watchwords in early learning, especially with certain volatile children, particularly children who display hyperactivity.

The reason we look at the "A" term (antecedents to problem behavior/confrontation) in the "ABC" sequence, referred to in Chapter 2, is that it seems that the antecedents of a behavior, its cues or triggers, are very important. If you think about and watch the settings of your client's behavior, it may be that the child behaves in a non-compliant way, or has a tantrum on some occasions but not on others; that is, some situations seem to act as cues to behave in a particular way (see Figure 5).

People tend to tailor their behavior to the particular places and the different persons with whom they find themselves. In the case of children, this chameleon capacity often leads to misunderstandings between home and school with each blaming the other when more often than not they are difficult in the one setting but not the other.

The so-called operant conditioning rule is of great significance in social development. Fortunately, as we have seen already, there is a basic "preparedness" on the part of most infants to be trained—that is, a bias toward all things social. The baby responds to the mother's friendly (baby talk) overtures in a sociable manner that produces in her a happy and sociable reaction. The baby also initiates social encounters with vocalizations or smiles directed to the mother which cause her in turn to smile back and to talk, tickle, or touch. In this way she elicits further responses from the baby. A chain of mutually rewarding interactions is thus initiated on many occasions.

Figure 5. Layout for a preliminary analysis of a problematic classroom situation

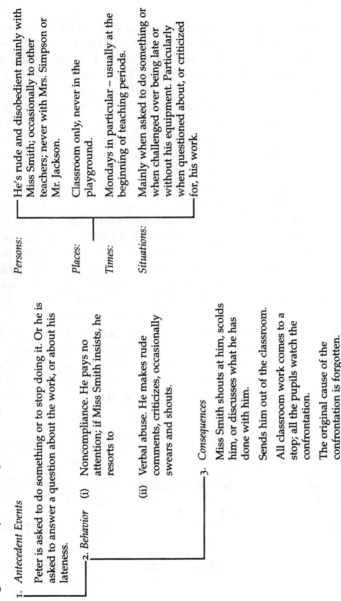

1. *Antecedent Events*

Peter is asked to do something or to stop doing it. Or he is asked to answer a question about the work, or about his lateness.

2. *Behavior* (i) Noncompliance. He pays no attention; if Miss Smith insists, he resorts to

(ii) Verbal abuse. He makes rude comments, criticizes, occasionally swears and shouts.

3. *Consequences*

Miss Smith shouts at him, scolds him, or discusses what he has done with him.

Sends him out of the classroom.

All classroom work comes to a stop; all the pupils watch the confrontation.

The original cause of the confrontation is forgotten.

Persons: He's rude and disobedient mainly with Miss Smith; occasionally to other teachers; never with Mrs. Simpson or Mr. Jackson.

Places: Classroom only, never in the playground.

Times: Mondays in particular – usually at the beginning of teaching periods.

Situations: Mainly when asked to do something or when challenged over being late or without his equipment. Particularly when questioned about, or criticized for, his work.

(From Herbert, 1987, with permission.)

69

Parents and children learn about and nurture each other in the course of these interactions.

Learning to be skillful and social. Learning is the key to our understanding of the process of socialization. Parents and teachers teach children skills and guide them toward pro-social actions and away from antisocial activities. There seems to be a fair amount of latitude in learning conditions for those children with intact central nervous systems, healthy bodies, and relatively unvolcanic temperaments. They acquire an understanding of and willingness to abide by society's conventions, despite parental inconsistency, contradictory demands or double-binds, and ambiguous rules. For them, parental inexperience or poor judgment seems no more than a minor hindrance in the business of growing up.

The welfare of the individual and the continuity of the culture depend upon society's having a satisfactory means of indoctrinating the new generation into its mores, attitudes, and skills and to ensure that they, in turn, will satisfactorily transmit the culture. The family plays a major role in indoctrinating and training the child for life. All parents are informal learning theorists and all are in the business of changing behavior.

They use various techniques to teach, influence, and change the child in their care. Among those used are material and psychological rewards, praise and encouragement, giving or withholding approval, and other psychological punishments such as reproof or disapproval. At its simplest level this process is as follows:

Acceptable behavior	+ Reinforcement	= More acceptable behavior
Acceptable behavior	+ No reinforcement	= Less acceptable behavior
Unacceptable behavior	+ Reinforcement	= More unacceptable behavior
Unacceptable behavior	+ No reinforcement	= Less unacceptable behavior

Of course parents also give direct instructions, set an example or model desired actions, and provide explanations of rules, that is, inductive methods. When the family fails in providing appropriate and consistent socialization experiences the child seems to be particularly vulnerable to the development of anti-social conduct and delinquent disorders (see Chapter 6). Typically children with persistent antisocial problems come from families where there is discord and quarreling; where affection is lacking; where discipline is inconsistent, ineffective, and either extremely severe or lax.

Relationships. Many relationships can be understood in part in terms of social learning principles. Adults initiate and prolong relationships of intimacy in close friendships, courtship, mar-riage, and cohabitation as long as those relationships are reasonably satisfactory with regard to what are called their "rewards" and "costs." It may seem crass to think of human relationships in terms of what are reminiscent of economic exchanges and bargains. Nevertheless, for example, in marital interaction a social exchange model not only helps us to assess what is going wrong with a partnership, but also to do some-thing about it.

In this model, marital discord is thought of as a function of prevailing rates of reinforcement (satisfaction) and punishment (dissatisfaction). Individuals, it is assumed, try to maximize sat-isfaction or positive rewards arising from the partnership while minimizing the dissatisfaction or the negatives generated by the marriage. We shall return to the use of notions of behavior exchange to bring about behavior change in adults and young people in Chapter 11.

The social learning approach is certainly one approach to working with Avril and her family and is the preferred approach for this particular case in the practice experience and expertise of the authors. Nevertheless, there are a variety of approaches that offer explanations and interventions for working with children and their families. These various approaches or theories provide a way to view the situation in terms of other explanations and possible solutions. It is impor-tant to consider a range of theories and to be able to evaluate the validity, utility and application of various theoretical perspectives for their use in working with particular cases or problems. Being able to select and apply the theoretical framework most appropriate in a particular practice context requires familiarity with the theory, the research supporting it, its application, and the outcomes expected from such application. More than one theoretical approach to working with Avril is appropriate and it is the responsibility of the practitioner to make an informal and ethical decision on how to proceed with intervention based upon information gathered from assessing the problem presented. Several theoretical frameworks are briefly presented for the purpose of broadening the scope of potential interventions in this case.

Medical Model

The medical model provides explanations of human problems in terms of disease or other physical processes. Such explanations have been questioned by social workers and clinical psychologists. But a critical exercise that rightly rejects pathological explanations of actions and feelings (where inappropriate) has been taken to an extreme and these are often neglected in cases where it is essential to consider the contributory influence of physical factors, for example, in cases of bed wetting and soiling. The tendency to "throw the baby out with the bath water" is sadly a common one in the helping professions. The medical model addresses a problem to be treated and, therefore, fails to treat the whole person (Payne, 1991).

Physical or medical explanations may encompass, for example, infections, that is, as they affect bladder incontinence, and physical disabilities in so far as they affect learning, and thus achievement and self-esteem. The concept of brain damage is a popular explanatory notion for hyperactive, conduct-disordered patterns of behavior. And it is a good example of the misuse of a medical explanation. Being tautologies or renaming in most instances, they tell us very little about the child and only too often are therapeutically pessimistic. For example, parents and teachers are sometimes told that a particular child's difficulties at home and at school are a result of brain damage, suffered perhaps as early as at birth. This is no more helpful than for a general practitioner to tell a mother her child is physically ill when she takes him along for a diagnosis of a bodily malaise. Certainly no program of rehabilitation, either remedial teaching or treatment, could be planned on the basis of such a vague diagnosis as brain damage. What is needed, in describing children, is not a meaningless label but precise information, with practical implications, about their specific physical and intellectual problems, and also about any emotional and social difficulties that have a bearing on their ability to learn and adapt to life's challenges. Unfortunately, some social workers and educators have thrown the "baby out with the bathwater" in their wholesale rejection of medical expertise, despite its proven value in association with psychosocial inputs, especially, in areas such as hyperactivity, anorexia and the incontinence disorders.

Psychometric Model

This model places a person high or low or somewhere in between on what is called an intelligence quotient (IQ). The average is 100. Avril's IQ of 140 is extremely high. Her score is equaled or bettered by only one or two percent of children of her age. By the way, this important information came as a shock to her parents who had now to reconstrue their somehow "subnormal" child.

One of the drawbacks of the psychometric model and the medical model is the tendency to classify individuals in terms of what they cannot do or what they do not have. Negative assumptions and conclusions can become recipes for pessimistic inaction. Nevertheless, both have important roles to play. An example of the use of psychometric instruments as a relatively unintrusive means of assessing child sexual abuse, but one fraught with conceptual and practical difficulties, is described by Babiker and Herbert (1998).

Personal Construct Model

Personal Construct Theory has a particular bearing on practice theories. Even the most theoretical social worker has attitudes.

These attitudes (or theories) have, inter alia, a knowledge function that gives meaning to the world we live in. They provide a frame of reference with which people can make interpretations of life, and they are an economical way of putting together a variety of facts and creating a model for action. The fact is that all individuals are concerned to anticipate or predict what happens to them and around them. If you are able to make sense of your world you can then make the necessary adaptations to changing circumstances. To this end each and every individual constructs in his or her thought processes a model of events. This model is like a figurative set of goggles through which the individual construes life and its events and inhabitants. On the basis of this construing or interpreting, he or she is able to take appropriate or inappropriate actions. Inappropriate actions are generally in response to one's faulty constructs.

The theorist of this model, George Kelly (1955), uses the metaphor "man the scientist" to illustrate his contention that individuals are constantly trying to understand and predict or anticipate events. The term "personal construct system" illustrates an important dimension of his theory. The term "personal" underlines the fact that every individual lives in a unique world. People may resemble one another in their construing processes, but essentially no one is a carbon copy of another. Every person lives in a world that is unique to him or her because it is idiosyncratically interpreted and experienced. For example, the way thought-disordered schizophrenic people see their world depends on the way they have arranged their hierarchy of constructs and the importance they attach to them.

Thus, Kelly provides one answer to the age-old question of why two people react very differently to the same situation; the two people are not in the same situation, it only looks the same from the perspective of a third observer. The situation may be very dissimilar from the point of view of each individual's construing system. Each may be reacting meaningfully in terms of his/her own situation as he/she interprets it. Psychological constructs guide behavior we observe; thus, changed or new constructs bring new behaviors as well (Payne, 1991).

Parents evolve a construct system to make sense of the world of children and family life. Parents bring constructs from their family of origin and elaborate with more recent experiences of actual parenting. These constructs give meanings to their offspring's behavior and facilitate mutually satisfactory interactions. Sadly some construct systems lead or mislead parents into confrontations with their babies. If the crying of a very young baby is construed as willful naughtiness and smacking is construed as an appropriate training method or punishment for dealing with naughtiness, a problematic and potentially dangerous situation might arise.

The child, too, actively seeks to make sense of his or her world. It is an important part of your assessment to tease out how the child views those parts of the world that are salient to your quest for understanding. There are techniques such as repertory grids for identifying child and adult construct systems (see Bannister and Fransella, 1980).

There are also active role-play methods for helping clients to test out the way they perceive their world. Role play is helpful in identifying positive and useful perceptions and behaviors as well as self-defeating and misconstrued perceptions and behaviors. They are useful for those who have low self-esteem and feel persecuted and socially isolated (see the case of Avril's mother, Chapter 8). These are the steps you take:

- The person is encouraged to try out or explore patterns of behavior contrasted to his/her own. This is based on a carefully scripted role sketch worked out with clients and derived from a compromise between what they are actually like and what they would like to be like.
- They are invited to practice these patterns in everyday life.
- They gain some experience from practice of how the environment can differ in appearance and "feel" and how it reacts when they behave in a different manner.
- Practice generates new and more effective skills that can be supplemented by novel experience from the feedback they have received.
- The expectation is that by receiving new and helpful forms of feedback from the environment they will change the self-defeating attitudes that control their behavior.

Psychodynamic Model

Psychoanalysis is one of the most controversial systems introduced to professional social work practice (Yelloly, 1980). Many psychologists, psychiatrists, and social workers are now questioning the place of psychoanalysis in these helping professions. There is no questioning of the status of Sigmund Freud (1974), the founder of psychoanalysis. Freud's thinking has been more pervasive than that of almost any other researcher; many of his discoveries are today's "clichés."

From psychoanalysis comes an accent on the one-to-one (dyadic) helping situation, on long-term intensive casework, and a choice of methods involving the development of insight. What have come to be called psychoanalytically or, more popularly, psychodynamically based theories represent a significant ideological strand in social work.

Many social workers describe their orientation as being psychodynamic. The term encompasses theories of personality and therapies which assume the existence of unconscious mental processes, which concern themselves with the elucidation of motives, and which assume the significance of transference relationships, such as the transfer on to the therapist of attitudes and feelings attaching to significant others. It is the *verstehende* (understanding) aspect of psychoanalytically based theories rather than the application of analytic treatment techniques which has contributed to social work practice.

It is sometimes argued that the interpretive-insight approach promotes excessive self-absorption and diverts attention from groups and structures as causes and remedies for psychosocial problems. Still, a psychodynamic perspective on psychosocial issues might be essential in social work because it is one of many ways by which meanings in exceedingly complex situations can be grasped (see Rycroft, 1970).

A good example of this is the psychodynamic theory of ego defense mechanisms. The construct ego or self is seen by contemporary psychodynamic theorists as the central integrating aspect of the person, and any threat to its valuation and function is a vital threat to the very being of the individual. As a result, a variety of "devices or coping mechanisms" are gradually accumulated by the self so as to soften anxieties and failures and protect the integrity of the ego by increasing the feeling of personal worth (Arlow, 1995). There is evidence that all of us learn to use strategies such as these. It is when we use them inappropriately or to excess, with too great intensity, or too inflexibly that they become maladaptive. The trouble is that they involve a certain amount of self-deception and distortion of reality and may prevent, by a sort of short-circuiting, the realistic and painstaking solution of problems.

To a very great extent we are unaware or unconscious of our use of these strategies. One of the purposes of adopting particular strategies is to reduce tension. The minimizing of immediate discomfort reinforces their use. An individual makes choices and carries out actions which will reduce and, if possible, avoid anxiety, pain, or any other distress.

Let us look at some of our psychological strategies.

Emotional insulation (isolation, dissociation). In all these defensive strategies the individual reduces the tensions of need and anxiety by withdrawing into a shell of numbness and passivity, also by lowering expectations, by remaining emotionally uninvolved and detached. Apathy and defeated resignation may be the extreme reactions to stress and frustration of long duration. Cynicism is often adopted, particularly by adolescents, as a means of protection from the pain of seeing idealistic hopes disillusioned.

Displacement. Displacement is a defensive strategy that involves a shift of emotions or of an intended action from the person toward whom it was originally intended onto another person or object. An example could be a child who is a nuisance because she pinches, bites, and scratches her playmates at school and harasses the teacher in a variety of ingenious ways. Investigation might reveal that the fault lies in part in the playground situation at school but also has its roots in the home situation.

Projection. When feelings arising from within ourselves are unjustifiably attributed to others, such behavior is called projection. It helps us to avoid conflict over our own barely conscious or acknowledged feelings and impulses by finding scapegoats and ascribing these obnoxious, intolerable, and therefore unacceptable ideas to them. By disowning these tendencies we protect ourselves from anxiety. Thus the individual who feels hateful jealousy and hostility to his wife may deny feelings to himself but complain bitterly that his wife is unpleasant to him and rejects him.

Rationalization. Rationalization is a technique that helps us to justify what we do and to accept the disappointments arising from unattainable goals. The "ego" uses rationalization to modify otherwise unacceptable impulses, needs, feelings, and motives into ones that are consciously tolerable and acceptable. Rationalization helps to reduce cognitive dissonance. In simple terms, this means that when there is a discrepancy between behaviors and thoughts (cognition), psychological distress is caused. This distress will persist until the behaviors and cognition are made harmonious again.

Common rationalizations explain away the unacceptable and sometimes make the incompatible bittersweet. In the former we justify failure to obtain something that is desirable on the grounds that it was not really worthwhile after all. In the attitude we mollify ourselves for an undesirable outcome by saying that it was for our own good.

Fantasy. Fantasy is one of the favorite tactics of children. In order to cope with stressful circumstances we not only deny unpleasant reality, but we create the sort of world of fantasy we would like to inhabit. Incidentally, fantasy also provides children with the opportunity to rehearse in imagination the solutions to their problems without entailing the risks of the real situation. Fantasy can be productive in such cases. Nonproductive fantasy is the too-persistent indulgence in a wish-fulfilling kind of mental activity. It compensates for lack of achievement. "Walter Mitty" fantasies allow a person to be the conquering hero he or she would like to be. People may also explain away their failures and inadequacies by what are called "suffering hero" fantasies—seeing themselves as misunderstood, "put-upon," but nobly courageous victims. In this way the individual retains his or her self-esteem. Fantasy solutions gloss over unpleasant reality. Children who daydream a lot are frequently trying to compensate for or escape from unacceptable environmental realities.

Reaction formation. Reaction formation is a method of defense whereby individuals suppress their desires and then adopt conscious attitudes and behavior patterns that are quite opposed to the unconscious wishes. Reaction formation is extreme and intolerant in its manifestations. Those who devote all their time to the obsessive condemnation of sexual license in others may well be having trouble in coping with their own sexual inclinations. In children, a "don't care" independent attitude may well mask a craving for nurturance and a need for dependency.

Defensive strategies or defense mechanisms are not without some experimental confirmation. The mention of psychoanalytic or psychodynamic theory is a reminder to us that its tenets are not wholly antagonistic to behavioral theory, although many would claim that they are. The psychodynamic approach to problem development stresses the "understanding" and historical element more than does the behavioral approach, which emphasizes explanations of behavior in the here and now. Nevertheless, the specification of reinforcers, the "C" term in the ABC analysis, is one in which some theorists would see a potentially useful borrowing from Freudian ideas (Wachtel, 1997).

Human beings old enough to have acquired even a rudimentary self-image demonstrate a need to perceive themselves in at least a moderately favorable light. A reasonable agreement between the self-concept ("myself as I am") and the concept of the ideal self ("myself as I would like to be") is one of the most important conditions for personal happiness and for satisfaction in life. Marked discrepancies arouse anxiety and can be indicative of psychological problems.

You might ask the client to write an account (or talk it out) on the theme "Myself as I am" and another entitled "Myself as I would like to be." Compare them and discuss the points of mismatch with the client. It could be a help in setting realistic and meaningful goals.

There are sometimes heated debates about the status and, indeed, viability, of psychoanalysis. There is wide disagreement among distinguished thinkers as to whether it is a science, a myth, a theory, a therapy, or a premature synthesis (see Ferris, 1998; Wachtel, 1997).

Charles Rycroft, an eminent psychoanalyst, believes that the controversy between psychoanalysts and critics like Hans Eysenck is not a meaningful one. Freud's work was really semantic, but owing to his scientific training and allegiance he formulated his findings in the inappropriate conceptual framework of the physical sciences. As Rycroft (1970) puts it:

> *If psychoanalysis is recognized as a semantic theory not a causal one, its theory can start where its practice does—in the consulting room, where a patient who is suffering from something in himself which he does not understand confronts an analyst with some kind of knowledge of the unconscious—i.e. who knows something of the way in which repudiated wishes, thoughts, feelings, and memories can translate themselves into symptoms, fantasies, and dreams, and who knows as it were, the grammar and syntax of such translations and is therefore in a position to interpret them again into the communal language of consciousness. It seems to me that it makes better sense to say that the analyst makes excursions into historical research in order to understand something which is interfering with his present communications with the patient (in the same way as a translator might turn to history to elucidate an obscure text) than to say that he makes contact with the patient in order to gain access to biographical data. (Lee and Herbert, 1970)*

If evaluated carefully and critically, the writings of psychoanalysts can open "mental doors" for social workers to dimensions of experience that are not readily accessible to ordinary common sense. It is assumed that this insight will give them greater control over their behavior. Many of our motives are unconscious, and it is impossible to come to terms with an "invisible enemy." The therapist tries to make the invisible visible, the unconscious conscious, so that reality can be grappled with.

It would be mostly safe to say that all insight therapies are "talking" therapies. The patient or client does a lot of talking about his or her personal life, early history, personal relation-

ships, work, ambitions, fears, and worries. The psychotherapist, to a greater or lesser extent, also verbally offers
interpretations of the patient's conflicts and problems, reassurance, and sometimes advice in order to direct the person's
thoughts and actions into potentially fruitful channels. If the
child is very young, conventional psychotherapy is inappropriate. Children are not always able to put their anxieties into
words. They are not always interested in exploring their past
life. They are too close to the episodes that are thought by psychoanalysts to be crucial in the development of dysfunctional
behaviors to enjoy talking about them. They will not always
free-associate. The main problem is that the motivation to participate in analysis is missing because children are often
brought for therapy against their will.

Play as communication. Play makes use of children's families
and natural mode of expression—play with dolls, miniatures,
puppets, paint, water, and sand—in a special playroom. This
provides a background for the therapist to discuss their problems with them (Webb, 1991).

Theories of the importance of play in childhood go a long
way back. The first person to advocate studying the play of
children in order to understand and educate them was Jean
Jacques Rousseau. There have been several theories put
forward to explain the meaning and utility of play in childhood; they generally emphasize its function as a means of
preparation for the future, as a natural process of learning, and
as a means of release from tensions and of excess physical ener-
gies. In many ways play, for children, is life itself. They use it in
order to develop their personality and their ability to get on
with other children.

Sigmund Freud's daughter, Anna Freud (1946), used children's play in a manner analogous to the use of dreams with
adults. Play was analyzed so as to uncover unconscious conflicts. This involved the interpretation of the symbolic
meanings, the unconscious motivation underlying drawing,
painting, games, and other forms of imaginative play. She
transposed classical psychoanalytic theory into a system of
child analysis.

There have been several offshoots of psychoanalytical play therapy and also systems of play therapy which are not in this mold at all. The active forms of play therapy have much in common with the desensitization techniques used in behavior therapy. Other forms of play therapy—relationship therapy, cognitive behavioral play therapy (Knell, 1998) and non-directive therapy (Axline, 1947)—have evolved and continue to be used. We return to this topic in Chapter 9.

Family Process Model

The family process prospective, exemplified by the model of intervention known as family therapy, shifts the focus for understanding problems and dealing with them from the individual's behavior to his/her relationships with the family. In this view, many problems have their source in family behavior patterns that are faulty or self-defeating, that is, dysfunctional in different ways.

Family therapy and family-oriented behavioral work are commonly but certainly not exclusively used when children present problems. Like other psychological therapies, these approaches are made up of several variations on a theme—the theme here being that the family is more than the sum of its parts and vital to work with in its own right. Some of the many techniques focus specifically on presenting problems, dealing with current events, while others grapple with the question of how the family history has influenced the family unit.

The process model of working with families calls for joining the therapist and the family together in the process of change and focusing on interactions and transactions. The intent of the process model is to utilize these interactions and transactions to move toward healthier exchanges, thus increasing processes characteristic of wellness versus those processes reflective of dysfunctions and problems in the family system (Satir, 1982). Satir calls for the therapist to lead and facilitate but to avoid "taking charge" or directing family members. The process model calls for all members of a family system to be involved in the treatment process, including significant others who are intrinsic parts of the family system. Techniques include interventions such as family sculpting, visualizations, empty chair, role playing, hugging, apologizing, forgiving, and expressing feedback from emotions experienced (Bowen, 1978; Minuchin and Fishman, 1981; Satir, 1982).

Empirical Research Model

A typical approach to the understanding of family problems is the accumulation of data on the basis of studies—clinical and experimental research—of particular topics. A matter of particular concern to us is family violence, initially presented in Chapter 3. This illustrates the value of the empirical research model, especially where no theoretical model fits neatly.

The various forms of family violence—physical, sexual, and emotional abuse—perpetrated on children, spouses, or the elderly, have been the subject of much research but require further study and certainly cannot be fitted into any simple theoretical model (see Browne and Herbert, 1997). Correlations on abuse abound in the social work and empirical clinical literature. However it is important to remember that a correlation does not necessarily imply causation. A correlation is sometimes found between criminality, alcoholism, drug abuse, and low intelligence and the various forms of family violence. Obviously there are many people who drink heavily or have criminal records but never abuse children, wives, or grandparents. Causation is a difficult concept; some factors may set the stage or predispose a person toward abusive behaviors. The childhood experience of being abused oneself may lead to abusive behavior to one's children or spouse. Other episodes of abuse, trauma, and personal indignities may trigger particular incidents of assault.

Multifactorial causation occurs with the problem of family violence, as in so many other areas of family dysfunction. The majority of child abusers are under 20 to 30 years of age, most wife abusers are between 20 and 30, while most abusers of the elderly are between 40 and 50 and above. Both sexes are implicated in family violence. Unemployment, low income, and extramarital problems are stresses that can contribute to family violence.

Those who are abused tend to have one or more of the following attributes:

- a poor relationship with the abuser;
- a relationship of dependency;
- physically weaker than the abuser;
- emotional and social isolation; or
- ill-health/disability.

In some families all forms of violence take place; in others it is one category. In some homes violence is accepted as the "norm." Abusing families are particularly distinguished from non-abusing families by their lack of affectionate relationships, and by the abuse of power by the strong over the weak; for example, children, the frail elderly, and others are susceptible to being scapegoated for frustration experienced by the abuser.

The influence of psychosocial factors, drawn from the empirical research literature, indicate the potency, for good or ill, of family relationships and make it imperative that you observe all the family together as well as individually and that you tease out their perceptions of each other. Look carefully at:

- their attitudes;
- their perceptions;
- their expectations;
- their actions; and
- their feelings toward each other.

Check on their knowledge of child development and of aging processes. Detailed and rigorous observation and monitoring are vital where high-risk families are brought to your notice (see Appendix 2, Treatment Options in Cases of Child Abuse and Neglect).

Summary and Comment

We have looked briefly at various models used by members of the helping profession in the quest for an understanding of their client's difficulties. The assumptions, attitudes, or constructs held by practitioners also have implications for their choice of intervention. For example, a common assumption underlying many therapeutic endeavors entails a cathartic or hydraulic view of emotion. This assumption is based on the belief that antisocial, unpleasant, and atavistic feelings can be channeled away through a figurative "overflow pipe" leaving behind the loving, cooperative, pro-social human being that exists underneath. The way in which the cathartic purging is administered varies widely, but the principle remains the same. Such an assumption can lead to quite opposite therapeutic advice or procedures in psychotherapy and behavior modification, respectively, especially with regard to aggression.

At present, aggressive children, whatever the reasons for their problems, may be subjected to therapeutic regimes that encourage them to "act out" their hostile behavior. Intervention may be in the form of regression therapy used in some residential establishments or the permissive atmosphere encouraged in some intermediate treatment approaches. Or it may range to models or programs that seek to inhibit such expressions and to encourage alternative pro-social actions. Adherents to regression or psychodynamic theory view the latter course of action as "symptomatic treatment"—tinkering with surface phenomena. They would expect the "real" or "underlying" causes to break out elsewhere (a phenomenon called symptom substitution) as a result of such superficial attempts at battening down emotional "safety hatches."

But the latter social learning group would see this as a self-deluding argument and would accuse the proponents of "acting out" theory of sustaining, by reinforcement, the very behavior they claim to want to remove, and of simply relabeling such problematic behavior with some technical term of doubtful validity—and then calling this the cause. In any event, the answer to such fears is to conduct a comprehensive and rigorous assessment and an ongoing evaluation (plus follow-up) of outcomes for the treated client.

PART II

*Understanding
Development and Change
in Families and Children
(Herbert, 1998a)*

The essence of life is development—hopefully, a forward momentum toward greater maturity and fulfillment—and this presupposes change. These aspects of life apply not only to individuals but also to the families within which they reside. Life is all about change—expected and unexpected, welcome and dreaded. The ramifications of transition and change in family life are vitally important in the assessment of children's problems. Assessing children's problems requires that the practitioner takes into account the ramifications of constant change and continuing transitions in individual and family life that impact family interactions and child development.

The nature, sources and consequences of parents' ideas about development and behavior are vitally important in the assessment of children's development and problems (Goodnow and Collins, 1990). Ideas about physical and psychosocial development inform family response to transition and change in family life and individual development. We need to ask about the causes and consequences of a lack of match in the parents' and children's ideas and expectations that arise from differences in a conceptual level. Smooth interactions require that both parent and child act from the same "script." Mismatches are though to promote conflict.

For a long period there was little or no communication between practitioners in the helping professions and developmental psychologists. Systematic attempts to integrate findings between the clinical and developmental disciplines were first published in the 1970s (e.g. Achenbach, 1974; Herbert, 1974). As they pointed out, the evaluation of normality and abnormality within a developmental framework requires a familiarity with general principles of development, not an easy task given the many and varied theories of child development.

For Cicchetti and his colleagues (Cicchetti, *et al.*, 1983), behavioral adaptation—as represented by problems such as hyperactivity and failure-to-thrive—are most fruitfully construed and formulated as a series of stage- and age-related "tasks." The issue of "competence" is common to all stages and, as the child gets older, his or her self-esteem becomes commensurate with his or her sense of competence. If the child fails to develop skills and social competence, he or she is likely to suffer a sense of inadequacy which has spiraling ramifications. There is evidence, not only of the power of parents to facilitate the child's mastery of developmental tasks or hinder him or her, but to do this unwittingly (Cicchetti, *et al.*, 1983). Often these matters become important themes—for those involved in programs to develop parenting skills where frequently the task of increasing parents' confidence and sense of self-empowerment is set by the parents themselves (e.g. Herbert and Wookey, 1998).

Change is often painful and not infrequently resisted. This tension between adapting to new circumstances (transformation) and resisting change that is a feature of the individual's attempts to maintain some equilibrium in his or her life (homeostasis) is also characteristic of family systems. General systems theory highlights the significance of the concept of organization and adaptability within systems. Within the family, different members may be involved in adapting to very different life circumstances. While a girl is moving toward womanhood and experiencing some of the unwelcome changes of puberty and adolescence, her grandmother who lives in the same house, is adjusting, not to development, but to the dissolution of some of her strength, vigor, and independence. Both are in a stage of transition, and each strives in her own way to come to terms with new realities (Herbert, 1987c).

In Part II, we examine some of the salient features of development and changes in childhood and adolescence, as well as those involved in the adult role of parenting in its various manifestations, such as, adoption, fostering, and single parenting.

CHAPTER 5

Childhood and Adolescence

All sorts of terms or euphemisms have been used to refer to troublesome but common behaviors and to more serious psychological difficulties displayed by children and adolescents. There is the popular expression "maladjusted," and others such as "abnormal", "nervous," "highly strung," "emotionally disturbed," "difficult," to mention but a few. They include a large and mixed bag of problems ranging from depression, anxiety, inhibition, and shyness to non-compliance, destructiveness, stealing, and aggression. In essence, these problems represent exaggerations, deficits, or disabling combinations of feelings, attitudes, and behaviors common at one time or another to many young people. Aggression, shyness, and a combination of low self-esteem and poor concentration are examples of behaviors frequently seen.

There is a distinction between those difficulties which primarily lead to emotional disturbance or distress for the young people themselves, such as, anxiety, shyness, depression, feelings of inferiority and timidity, and those which involve mainly the kinds of antisocial behavior that disrupt the well-being of others, notably those in frequent contact with the young person.

Terms like "normal" and "abnormal" are commonly applied to children as if they are mutually exclusive concepts like hard and soft; the label "abnormal" attached to particular children seems to suggest that they are deviant in some absolute and generalized sense. This is misleading; every child is unique and the most that can be said of any child is that some of his or her actions or attributes are more or less a deviation from a *norm* or social standard.

Assessment of Children

It is obviously very useful to know about the social norms and the norms of development when making an assessment. You might incorporate into the assessment steps (set out in Chapter 2), some of the material included in the following pages because of their direct relevance to children's behavior problems. Thus you might ask the parent(s) to rate the child's difficulties (Table 4) and the trouble spots (situations) in which they occur (Table 5).

In the case of concern about *relationships,* whether child–child, adult–child, or child–adult, draw up a balance sheet of the positives in the relationship and the negatives (see example in Chapter 3). At the most general level, you need to ask of the client: "What are the consequences in the short and long term of his or her *behaviors?*" In the case of parents, "What is their method of child management?"

There are supplementary questions (applicable to parents as well as to the child) to ask. Affirmative answers to several questions like these might well be of significance:

- Does the client get excessively miserable, embarrassed, shy, hostile, anxious, or morbidly guilty?
- Does he/she give vent to anger too easily?
- Is his/her tolerance of frustration low?
- Is he/she inflexible in the face of failure?
- Does he/she find it difficult to cope with novel or difficult situations?
- Does he/she experience difficulty in establishing affectionate, lasting relationships with adults and peers?
- Does he/she fail to learn from experience, such as, from disciplinary situations?
- Does he/she find it impossible to get on with most teachers or other adults in authority?

Your answers to these questions could be important diagnostically because problem behaviors have unfavorable consequences for the youngster and/or those in contact with him or her. Generally speaking, there is an association between intense and prolonged feelings of unhappiness and psychological disorder; there is a loss of a sense of well-being.

Table 4. A Child Behavior Rating Scale for Parents

Behavior Questionnaire

Does your child do any of the following? Tick one of the boxes to indicate how often any of the following happen, if at all. Also indicate whether the behavior is a worry to you.

	0 Never	1 Some-times	2 Often	3 Most of the time	Do you see it as a worrying problem? Yes No
Does your child:					
Have temper tantrums?					
Make threats?					
Physically assault others (hit, push, pinch, pull hair, throw things)?					
Quarrel with others (brothers, sisters, friends, etc.)?					
Damage property (own, others')?					
Disrupt, i.e. interfere with others' activities (interrupting, distracting, etc.)? Bully other children?					
Inconvenience others (e.g. playing music too loud, being late for meals)?					
Tease others in a hurtful manner?					
Abuse others with name-calling, obscenities, etc.?					
Engage in unwanted, inappropriate physical contact (clinging, squeez-ing)?					
Lie about him/herself?					
Lie about others?					
React inappropriately (sulking, with-drawing, angry) if s/he cannot get own way?					
Steal money, shop goods, etc.?					
Masturbate openly?					
Disobey you?					
Expose him/herself?					
Wet the bed?					
Soil him/herself, or pass motions in the wrong place?					
Refuse to go to school (truant)?					
Seem tense, agitated, nervy, restless?					
Appear apathetic, lacking in energy?					
Seem shy?					
Seem depressed?					
Appear fearful, anxious?					
Wander away?					
Make unreasonable demands?					
Whine?					
Appear secretive, furtive, mysterious?					

Table 5. A Situational Rating Scale for Parents

Identifying trouble spots

Alert yourself to the most likely 'trouble spots' in your life (when it comes to discipline) by filling in the questionnaire.

Trouble Spots Questionnaire

My child is disobedient:

	Often	Seldom	Never	It amounts to a real problem for me
At home				Yes/No
Visiting				Yes/No
Shopping (or other public places)				Yes/No
At playschool or school				Yes/No
When out playing				Yes/No

My child gives me trouble:

	Often	Seldom	Never
When getting ready (e.g. dressed) in the morning			
At mealtimes			
When going to bed			
Over staying in bed			
Over watching TV			
During washing/bathing			
When I'm occupied (on the phone/ talking to someone/in the toilet)			
When asked to do something			
When asked to stop doing something			
Over keeping to the general rules			
Doing homework			

Typical problems of childhood. A feature of much problem behavior in childhood is its transitoriness. So mercurial are some of the changes of behavior in response to the rapid growth and the successive challenges of childhood that it is difficult to pinpoint the beginning of serious problems. We know as a result of longitudinal studies of children over many years that, for the most part, children who suffer from emotional problems such as fears, phobias, shyness, and inhibitions, become reasonably well-adjusted adults; they are almost as likely to grow up normal as are children drawn at random from the general population. In a sense these difficulties are the emotional equivalent of growing pains. But that is not to deny that they sometimes persist and reach levels of intensity that cause all-round suffering.

There is another category of difficulties that declines at a rather later stage, and at a slower rate, than most others; for example, over-activity, destructiveness, and tempers. In their severe forms these and other types of aggressive, antisocial behaviors constitute a constellation of problems referred to as "conduct disorders." They involve physical and verbal aggressiveness, disruptiveness, irresponsibility, non-compliance, and poor personal relationships; along with delinquent activities, early drug and alcohol use, and substance abuse. Kernberg and Chazan (1991) point out that conduct-disordered children lack feeling awareness and act quickly and impulsively rather than expressing their needs and feelings verbally. They exhibit impulsive and aggressive behaviors along with poor self-esteem and limited social awareness, including structures of authority and social organization. Efforts to cope generally end with frequent failure and intense frustration. This behavior pattern is notable for the fundamental inability or unwillingness on the part of the youth to adhere to the rules and codes of conduct prescribed by society at its various levels: family, school, and in the community at large. The problem may become particularly troublesome (disruption in the classroom) and/or serious (delinquency) during adolescence. We deal with it in the next chapter.

It is a useful assessment skill to be able to identify the periods when children are most vulnerable to emotional problems, so as to mobilize resources to help them and their parents through a difficult period (see Herbert, 1998a; Sutton, 1994, 1999). The term "crisis intervention" has been used to describe the expert assistance needed at certain times in people's lives when they not only experience a heightened desire for help but are more susceptible than usual to the influence of others. Children also experience such periods of crisis when, for example, they go to a hospital, endure parental illness, separation or death, cope with the birth of a sibling, or learn to live with a handicapped sibling.

Developmental tasks. A developmental task arises at a certain period in the life of an individual. Successful achievement leads to happiness and success with later tasks while failure leads to unhappiness in the individual, disapproval by society, and difficulty with other tasks. The tasks might be ones such as learning to talk or to control elimination; or they may involve the development of self-control over aggressive and sexual inclinations, acquiring moral attitudes and social skills, adjusting to school life, mastering academic competencies, and becoming self-directed and self-confident. Some are vital psychosocial tasks.

Erik Erikson (1965) has put forward ideas about the interplay of "ego" and "alter" that is so critical in personality development—namely, the achievement of a balance between the poles of recognizing and accommodating the needs of others as opposed to imposing self-centered demands on other people. An extreme lack of balance in reciprocity between itself and others (in either direction) gives rise to unsatisfactory social relationships. Children demand parental support, and they try to limit the restraints parents put upon their pleasures. The balance, therefore, is about a compromise between sometimes incompatible mutual demands.

Erikson's scheme of child development and its tasks is given in Table 1, page 12.

From birth to about four years of age the child needs to develop a sense of trust and, later, a growing autonomy. The major hazards to the development of a perception of a trustworthy and predictable world, in which children initiate their independence-seeking, are social and physical conditions which interfere with their sense of personal adequacy and/or which hinder their acquisition of skills.

Even very young babies exhibit a need to be competent, to master or deal effectively with their own environment. Psychologists consider it to be related to such motives as mastery, curiosity, and achievement. The psychologist Martin Seligman (1975) has this to say:

> *The infant begins a dance with his environment that will last throughout childhood. I believe it is the outcome of this dance that determines his helplessness or mastery. When he makes some response, it can either produce a change in the environment or be independent of what changes occur. At some primitive level, the infant calculates the correlation between response and outcome. If the correlation is zero, helplessness develops. If the correlation is highly positive or highly negative, this means the response is working; and the infant learns either to perform that response more frequently or to refrain from performing it, depending on whether the correlated outcome is good or bad. But over and above this, he learns that responding works, that in general there is synchrony between responses and outcomes. When there is asynchrony and he is helpless, he stops performing the response, and further, he learns that in general responding doesn't matter. Such learning has the same consequences that helplessness has in adults: lack of response initiation, negative cognitive set, and anxiety and depression. But this may be more disastrous for the infant since it is foundational.*

During the next stage, from approximately four to five years, comes a sense of initiative, a period of vigorous reality testing, imitation of adult patterns of behavior and imaginative play. Overly strict discipline, interference, overprotection, and the like can disrupt the successful achievement of these attributes, making for poor spontaneity and uncertain testing and appreciation of realities.

A sense of duty and accomplishments is the next developmental task—from six to 11 years—when the child puts aside much of the fantasy and play-life and undertakes real tasks at school and develops academic and social skills. Excessive demands or competition and personal limitations which lead to persistent failure can make a crisis of this important stage and can result in feelings of inferiority and poor work habits.

95

From 12 to 15 years, children consolidate their sense of identity, clarifying who they are and what their role in life is to be. Society may make for difficulties for the early adolescent by failing to provide clearly defined or valued roles and standards for the young person.

In later adolescence, from 15 to adulthood, a sense of intimacy is desirable—an ability to establish close personal relationships with members of both sexes. The last two stages are described in more detail, in the section on adolescence.

Failure to master previous developmental tasks are thought to hinder the individual in the next psychosocial endeavor.

Underachievement. Perhaps one of the most serious consequences of emotional and behavioral problems is its deleterious effect on children's learning in the classroom and hence their achievement. Even when highly intelligent, those pupils with psychological difficulties tend to have real difficulties in school performance. The greater the number of problems manifested by the child, the poorer, on the whole, is school performance.

Friendlessness. Many of the difficulties which children have to cope with are social ones—the problems of getting along with other youngsters of the same age, with teachers, with their own parents, and also with themselves. Young people need to like themselves, to rely on themselves, and to know themselves. It was Aristotle who suggested that friendly relationships require a certain liking for oneself. Also needed is a degree of self-awareness and social sensitivity. The boy or girl's self-image plays a part in all of this. If it has been endlessly subverted by criticism or rejection they are likely to feel unworthy and inferior and display aggressive or attention-getting behavior betraying defensiveness and overanxiety.

Children who are acceptable to their peers tend to:

- demonstrate sensitivity, responsiveness, and generosity; they help others and give attention, approval, and affection to their peers;
- be confident in their social contacts, active, and friendly;
- see things from the other youngster's point of view;

- be good at resolving day-to-day dilemmas involving person-to-person relationships;
- make others feel accepted and involved, promoting and planning enjoyable group activities; and
- demonstrate empathetic actions. Empathy involves the youngster's capacity to control his or her behavior by considering its effect on the experiences of others, particularly the potential victims of proscribed behavior.

If you are concerned about your client's inability to make or keep friends, carry out a small exercise in "accountancy." Look at things from the other person's point of view. Is your client mature enough to sustain the reciprocity of friendship or is he/she insensitive, too demanding, or disloyal? Is his or her company rewarding enough?

Dealing with unwanted behavior. If an intervention seems likely, encourage parents to think of positive outcomes as well as the reduction of unwanted behaviors. Suggest that they consider their priorities, thinking of their child's behavior as falling into three color codes: green, yellow, and red:

- Green is the "go-ahead" code for the type of behavior they want from their child, the actions which they facilitate by praise and encouragement; for example, sharing toys with another child or eating meals without a fuss. They should include those individual attributes of the child—aspects of his or her personality which make for their uniqueness.
- Yellow is for "caution" behavior, which is not encouraged but is tolerated because the child is still learning and making mistakes; for example, "decorating" the bedroom's walls with finger paints or hurling toys across the room in a moment of fury. Any sort of stress like relocation, illness, or some upset in the family may mean a temporary step backward in the child's behavior.
- Red is definite stop for behavior which needs to be curbed as soon as possible. Obviously anything that could be dangerous for the child or for others has a red code:

running into the road, touching the hot iron, attacking the baby.

Any limits set should be for the child's safety, well-being, and development. Parents should be advised to keep them to essentials. It is crucial to ensure that children know exactly what they are and what is expected of them. Chapter 11 develops this theme of rules and routines.

Puberty: The Gateway to Adolescence

The physical and physiological changes that take place by about the ages of 12 in girls and 14 in boys are due to the action of hormones and are quite dramatic. Beginning in early adolescence and varying among individual children, growth in virtually all parts of the adolescent's body is sharply accelerated. During so-called transitional periods like adolescence, individuals are in the marginal position of having lost an established and accustomed status and of not yet having acquired the new status toward which the factors impelling developmental change are driving them.

Self-discovery. The major task of the adolescent stage according to many contemporary psychologists is the young person's need to shape and consolidate his or her own identity as a unique and mature person. The development of self-identity refers to the core of an individual's character of personality and is thought to be a vital precursor to true intimacy and depth in personal relationships. It begins with teenagers' intense concern for discovering their individual nature and ends when they have established a coherent sense of self and personal identity. This task of becoming a unique person is usually completed between the ages of 18 and 22.

It is important to remember (and to remind parents) that adolescents are individuals and they are as different one from the other in their personal qualities as are children and adults. Their tendency to conform to teenage culture and fashion may present a superficial similarity which the media find convenient to headline, especially when there is a sensational incident involving young people. Social workers and other professionals would do well to encourage parents and other adults to recognize and accept the new challenges, tasks, and needs which preoccupy these sometimes puzzling young adults who are emerging from childhood (see Herbert, 1987c).

Individual and gender differences. Girls' development is roughly two years ahead of boys', and it tends to be so throughout the developmental timetable. There is usually no need for alarm if the child is somewhat early or late. Children vary quite markedly. The gap may be four years or more in the age at which they become pubertal. For girls, that age at which the menstrual cycle makes its first appearance can differ by several years. One may find an early-developed girl at the age of 12 or 13 who is already physically a woman, with fully developed sexual characteristics and destined to grow very little more in height. At about the same age, and therefore in the same classroom and social group, may be a later-developing girl who is just about to begin her growth spurt and who is little more than a child in her physical characteristics. The same conspicuous differences might be seen in boys of 14 or 15. It is obviously simplistic to think about teenagers as a homogeneous group.

Puberty is not just a matter of change in the size and shape of the body. Physiological developments in glandular secretion, particularly those affecting sexual function, occur. Until puberty, males and females have similar quantities of both sex hormones in the bloodstream, with only a slightly greater proportion of the sex-relevant hormone. Thus boys have nearly as much estrogen, the female sex hormone, as androgen. At puberty, however, there is a sharp increase in the secretion of the sex-related hormone. Hormonal changes bring, in their wake, increased sexual arousal; parents will also have to deal with their offspring's increased and, in part, hormone-driven assertiveness.

As we shall see below, adolescent self-centeredness has its basis in the immense physical change taking place at puberty. It also has its roots in the discovery of identity, but there are sometimes disconcerting swings from out-and-out self-admiration (narcissism) to self-hatred and self-deprecation.

How young people perceive themselves depends very much on how others see them; but it depends most of all on how they think others see them—which could, of course, be different from the way in which they are actually perceived. And most particularly children accept into their self-image what they believe to be their parents' view of them, and these views can have consequences over the long term for their behavior. If your client believes that his or her parents' opinion is negative or critical (even if this is not really the case) they may exhibit insecurity and low self-esteem. If people believe things to be real, they are real in their consequences. This applies with force to the delicate area of a person's self-image.

The development of identity doesn't always proceed smoothly. But what evidence we have calls into question Erik Erikson's (1965) belief that adolescents usually suffer a crisis over their identity. Most teenagers actually have a positive self-image; furthermore this view of themselves tends to be fairly stable over the years.

There is a growing altruism and idealism to be seen in many young people. These different facets are gradually integrated into the adolescent personality. Self-esteem is a vital element for healthy adjustment. When there is a large gap between the teenager's self-concept ("myself as I am") and his or her idealized self ("myself as I would like to be"), there are also likely to be anxiety and oversensitiveness in close attendance.

Adolescence

Somewhere between the immaturity of childhood and maturity of adulthood lie the seven or eight years referred to as adolescence. This period serves as a stage of transition from "irresponsibility" to "responsibility" and has been widely, but not universally accepted. It is well known that some cultures, notably preliterate ones, had "rites of passage" that took children directly from their childhood to adult status.

Adolescence is generally categorized as early, middle, and late. Early adolescence may begin as early as nine or ten with physical changes coinciding with exit from elementary education toward teenage activities and behaviors. Middle adolescence begins about age 14 and extends to age 17. The middle adolescent generally withdraws from parents, establishes sexual identity, exhibits mood swings, and engages in sorting through relationships, self-awareness, interests, vocational and educational choices, and periods of narcissism, anger, acting out, and depression. Late adolescence is the bridge to young adulthood and carries on the task of consolidating the mood, feeling, and behavior swings of middle adolescence. In preparation for adulthood, the late adolescent experiences less identity diffusion than earlier and configures personal values and goals (Mishne, 1986).

Some theorists reject the notion of adolescence as a distinct stage of development. They repudiate the idea that at puberty every child somehow takes on a qualitatively different persona or engages in radically different developmental tasks, more or less overnight. Rather the child grows by imperceptible degrees into a teenager, and the adolescent turns by degrees into an adult. Confusion over the boundaries defining adolescence is revealed by the metaphors applied to it: the "in-between stage", and "that no-man's land between childhood and adolescence". Adolescence has also been referred to as a "tunnel" into which young people disappear, displaying certain kinds of characteristics. They are then "lost to sight" for a few years. According to this metaphor you never know what is going to emerge at the other end—a daunting prospect for parents and teachers when they've put so much time, effort, and affection into preparing the children in their care for adulthood. The fact is that many parents await their child's approaching adulthood with a sense of gloomy foreboding. They anticipate the adolescent years as something to be endured rather than enjoyed, to be confronted rather than shared. It is often the case that they are apprehensive that they may "lose" the closeness, the affection, and the degree of parental control they feel to be important in the relationship with their son or daughter. If parents expect the worst they are quite likely to get it—indeed, they contribute unwittingly to a self-fulfilling prophecy. It is generally agreed that adolescence begins in biology (the variable time of onset of puberty) and ends in culture (the even more variable point at which young people are deemed "responsible" and "independent" by society). During the past half-century or so, adolescence in western societies has become a progressively longer span of years, indeed as long as 10 years in duration. This reflects the mixed feelings we have about the decision as to when, in law or social custom, a young person is grown up and responsible enough to drink in a bar, mature enough to manage a bank account, to indulge in sexual intercourse, to get married, to vote, or to be held responsible for a criminal act.

A sheep in wolf's clothing. Parents worry about the imminence of adolescence and small wonder, given that adolescence has such a bad reputation. Adolescence can be traumatic for some young individuals and disruptive for their parents, but it is by no means necessarily so. The growing opinion that adolescence is different from the whole of development which precedes it, and the whole of development that follows it, is of relatively recent origin. Among the early proponents of this view was G. Stanley Hall in his 1904 treatise on the subject: *Adolescence: its psychology and its relationship to physiology, anthropology, sociology, sex, crime, religion and education.* His belief, that adolescence is necessarily a stage of development associated with emotional turmoil and psychic disturbance, was to become so deeply rooted, reinforced by a succession of psychoanalytically orientated writers, that it persists to this day. This "'storm and stress" conceptualization (built on eagerly by journalists in sensational items about feral teenage hooligans and vandals) has filtered down to street level as a veritable "demonological" theory of adolescence. Certainly the psychiatric profession has tended to take a jaundiced view of adolescence. Attention was drawn to neurotic- or psychotic-like features: hysteria, regression, mood swings and disintegration.

Hutter (1938) described adolescence in Alice in Wonderland terms as a period of development "in which normally abnormalities happen so often it is abnormal that everything passes normally." Anna Freud (1954) writing on adolescence in the journal *Psychoanalytic Study of the Child* said it was "abnormal" if a child kept a "steady equilibrium during the adolescent period ... The adolescent manifestations come

close to symptom formation of the neurotic, psychotic disso-
cial order and merge almost imperceptibly into ... almost all
the mental illness." To arrive at a more balanced view of adolescence we have to remember that practitioners tend to see
only individuals who attend social work agencies or clinics.
And adolescents who attend would not be there if they did
not have problems. What is really required is a wide cross-
section of adolescents drawn in large numbers from the
general population. Does such a sample present problems of
sufficient seriousness or in sufficient numbers to give adolescence a "bad name"?

Adolescence, while certainly not immune from its share of
pain for those growing up, is not usually the scourge of folk-
lore. It is something of a sheep, albeit an unruly sheep, in wolf's
clothing. For one thing the problems of growing up do not all
arrive at one and the same time.

The more serious psychological conditions are probably
more common during adolescence than during middle childhood, but the difference is not a very great one. Most
adolescents do not manifest psychiatric disorders.
Nevertheless, some 10 percent to 15 percent of adolescents do
experience significant psychological difficulties. These difficulties, referred to by psychologists as "emotional disorders," are
manifested by about 2.5 percent of pre-adolescent children.
Their prevalence increases somewhat by adolescence, and we
find that boys and girls are about equally prone to them. For
most children (as we saw in the previous chapter) these kinds
of problems manifest themselves briefly and then become
minimal or disappear completely.

This is all very well, but you might well wish to know
whether there are any typical adolescent problems, typical in
the sense that they reflect stresses and strains which differ from
those emerging in childhood, or indeed adult life. We return to
this question later. It is reassuring to realize that although the
rates of unhappy feelings and self-depreciation reach a peak
during adolescence, the majority of teenagers seem generally to
be happy and confident and are not the victims of serious
depression or of other emotional disturbances. In fact,
adolescence does not quite live up to its reputation. This may

help those of your clients who are bracing themselves with trepidation for their child's teenage years.

Striving for independence. By the middle years of adolescence the striving for independence is no longer simply one aspect of a youngster's activities; it is, in a very real sense, an end in itself. It involves striving for psychological freedom from parents, freedom to be one's own person, to have one's own thoughts and feelings, to determine one's own values, and to plan one's own future. It is also about the more mundane freedoms, to find the clothes, companions, and pastimes of one's own choice and to enjoy the privacy of one's own room and belongings. However, there are as many dangers in granting independence to young people by promoting too much freedom too soon as in strongly opposing all signs of it until late adolescence. There is, as seems usual in child development, a "golden mean"—a need to avoid extremes. The reason why adolescent development is relatively unremarkable in the personal disturbance it causes is that there are many strength-giving continuities in this development. The adolescent builds on what has gone before; coping skills developed when younger are not necessarily redundant. Many of the changes of this stage of development represent pluses, not minuses. They take the form of increased capacities of various kinds. It is as well to remember these pluses when considering how much to advise parents to "let go." Cognitive skills in adolescence become more complete and more flexible as new powers of abstraction and logic make problem solving easier than it was in childhood. Social skills increase in range and complexity.

Alienation. The public has been led to believe that "distraction" of teenagers from their parents is almost inevitable, and they may be expecting not to be able to communicate with their children when they get older. Alienation is not, however, a typical pattern. Most adolescents are still attached to their homes in a positive way, and they continue to depend upon the emotional support, goodwill, and approval of their parents. The family continues to be of critical importance; parental concern and supervision are vital during a phase when young-sters are experimenting with life. It does appear that rebelliousness and alienation are more likely in teenagers who, in spite of considerable maturity, remain economically or in other ways, dependent on their parents. Students in higher education are one example. A majority of adolescents share their parents' attitudes toward moral and political issues and are mostly prepared to accept their parents' guidance on acad-emic, career, and personal matters.

Sexuality. Teenagers enjoy the full range of sexual activities earlier than the previous generation. The number of teenage pregnancies has certainly increased markedly, despite innova-tions in contraception. The incidence of AIDS and sexually transmitted diseases among young people has also gone up.

Although adolescents have become more accepting in their attitudes to premarital sex, this does not imply a massive rise in casual sexual relationships. Young people, and particularly girls, continue to emphasize the importance of love and stable emotional attachment in premarital sex, although intended marriage or an engagement is not so often seen as a prerequi-site of such relationships. The emphasis on a stable relationship with one sexual partner at a time is referred to as "serial monogamy." Girls do, however, display more conservative atti-tudes to these issues than boys.

It has been commonly thought that the first experience of sexual intercourse is usually with someone who is already expe-rienced; the first partner is often older and, in the case of the girls, is quite often an adult. Explicit sexual information available to children via television, internet, movies, and magazines increases the level of sexually explicit information for young chil-dren. Schools, communities, counsellors, and families have the responsibility to provide sex education to children, including information on sexually transmitted diseases and contraception.

It is noted that more than ever before, teenagers live in a social context that is increasingly permissive. Teen birth rate in the United States in 1997 averaged 50.2 per 1,000 teens; approx-imately 17 percent of children live in single-parent families (Kids Count Data Book, 1999). It is noted that about one-third of children in the United States live below the poverty line. Other research suggests that about 69 percent of unmarried births are to women over age 20 (Long, *et al.*, 1994). Certainly, a committed relationship has been traditionally thought to be essential for the rearing of children. Many young people today wish such a long-standing commitment to take the form of marriage, but a substantial minority reject such a view. The realities of increasing rates of divorce, single-parenthood, and teenage pregnancy reflect changing family structures as well as the likelihood that many children will be reared outside the traditional, long-lasting family structure of biological parents and children.

Problem Areas

Adolescence has its share of challenges. For parents, their offspring's outbursts of defiance and periods of misery can bring frustration and unhappiness to the family. Wise parents have no wish to emerge as victors of battles of will or confrontations with their children. Rather they choose to win in the task of supporting them in their journey through adolescence to maturity. A realistic, and optimistic view of adolescence, plus a sound knowledge of what is happening physically and emotionally to teenagers, will allow parents to remain rock-solid while their young person finds his or her adult status. Parents can survive, indeed, enjoy adolescence, by letting the occasional waves of discontent, criticism and rebellion break around them—without breaking them. Parental counseling may help in achieving this goal.

Depression (see Kazdin, 1990). In an effort to "normalize" the concept of adolescence, helping professionals have tended to differentiate adolescence into stages of early, middle, and late adolescence because of the different changes and challenges that arise. Various changes and problems are age-related and may challenge the young person, his/her parents and the social worker who becomes involved. It is fairly typical, in the transition from childhood to adulthood, for there to be an upsurge of moodiness and feelings of misery. Adolescents are often tormented by low self-esteem, worries about the future, and fears about such matters as attending school or participating in social activities. These problems are usually relatively mild and might be viewed as normal developmental problems. The milder form of depression may show itself as a lack of physical energy and well-being. In its more severe manifestation, adolescents tend to be irritable and bad-tempered; and, as symptoms worsen, tend to sleep poorly, lack an appetite, and appear dejected, apathetic, and lifeless. Young people who are for whatever reason depressed, feel helpless, sad, and useless and find it sometimes impossible to meet the challenges of everyday life. They cease to strive and to use their full effectiveness in whatever sphere of activity they find themselves. In 1997, the teen violent death rate reached 59.5 per 100,000 teens and included suicide (Kids Count Data Book, 1999).

The checklist below will help you to detect signs of depression in your client:

- a demeanor of unhappiness and misery, more persistent and intense than "the blues," which we all suffer from now and then;
- a marked change in eating and/or sleeping patterns;
- a feeling of helplessness, hopelessness, and self-dislike;
- an inability to concentrate and apply oneself to anything;
- everything (even talking and dressing) seems an effort;
- irritating or aggressive behavior;
- a sudden change in grades or school work;
- a constant search for distractions and new activities;
- dangerous risk taking (e.g. with drugs/alcohol, dangerous driving, delinquent actions).

Depression can be masked in adolescence and thus not easily detected. Another problem is that any item in the list above can occur normally in the adolescent without in any way indicating a depressive disorder. The questions below will help you to judge whether to seek professional psychiatric advice if the answers tend to be in the affirmative:

- Are there several of the signs (listed above) present in the teenager?
- Do they occur frequently?
- Have they persisted for a long time?
- Do they cause extensive suffering to him/her?
- Do they stand in the way of his/her development toward maturity?
- Do they get in the way of his/her relationships with (a) peers, (b) adults?
- Do they cause distress in others?

Suicide and parasuicide (Kazdin, 1990; Wilde, et al., 1992). Feelings of misery and inner turmoil give way, in some adolescents, to such serious moods of depression—such a sense of helplessness and powerlessness and of events being out of control—that they entertain ideas about committing suicide. Suicide rates rise sharply during the teens so that it comes to rank among the half-dozen most common causes of death among older adolescents. The figures are still well below those for adults, and only a minute fraction of the suicide rate in old age. Attempted suicide (parasuicide) is very much a late-adolescent phenomenon, the peak being among 15- to 19-year-olds. There has been a tenfold increase in such incidents since the 1960s among adolescent boys and a fivefold increase for girls. Nevertheless the rate of attempted suicides for adolescent girls far exceeds that for boys. This surge in the statistics lacks empirical verification. It does not seem to be related to drug abuse but may be associated with increased use of alcohol. Parasuicide, particularly among adolescents, is most likely to be linked in some way with the increasing prevalence of marital discord, childhood separations, unemployment and criminality.

Teenagers sometimes have fantasies about their own death which involve their "ending it all" and yet surviving the event by "attending" their own funeral where they are able to savor the grief and guilt displayed by errant parents or boyfriends/girlfriends. These fantasies indicate how, in some adolescents, the finality of death is not fully appreciated, or at least not while in a depressed or hysterical state, and not at the time when the gesture (and often, more than a gesture) of suicide is contemplated. The cliché that suicide is a cry for help is often true. Threats of suicide should not be treated lightly and not dismissed with the words "If s/he really meant it s/he would do it, not threaten to do it." Many individuals who have threatened to commit suicide do in the end carry out their threat. In cases of adolescent depression the disorder may be the outward and visible sign of other covert difficulties.

Schizophrenia (Falloon, et al., 1984). One of the most serious mental health problems associated with adolescence, because it often has its onset during adolescence, is schizophrenia or (more accurately) the schizophrenias. They are a group of psychoses in which there is a fundamental disturbance of personality, a characteristic distortion of thinking, often a sense of being controlled by alien forces, delusions which may be bizarre, disturbed perception, abnormal affect out of keeping with the real situation, and autism. Nevertheless, clear consciousness and intellectual capacity are usually maintained. Wing (1978) suggested that schizophrenia is usually a severe and disabling mental illness, with a lifetime risk rate of about 1 percent in all the populations so far investigated throughout the world. There are two major syndromes: the acute episode, and the chronic syndrome.

The acute episode is characterized by experiences noted below by Schneider (1959), and by delusions and/or hallucinations based upon them. The affected person reports that he or she:

- hears his or her thoughts spoken aloud;
- hears voices commenting on his or her behavior;
- believes that his or her behavior, thinking and bodily functions are influenced by external agents;
- explains these experiences in terms of physical or supernatural forces.

The "negative," or chronic syndrome is characterized (inter alia) by:

- flattening of affect (loss of emotional liveliness);
- loosening of associations in thinking, i.e. making remarks which don't make sense;
- slowness, underactivity, lack of motivation.

There seems to be increasing agreement among researchers that schizophrenia arises from a genetic predisposition interacting with environmental "triggers." Nevertheless, the trigger often appears to be stress related, notably stress associated with poor-quality housing and other pressures of the urban environment; poverty, unemployment and isolation.

There is also an increasing consensus about the key features of schizophrenia. Some of these key features are presented by Falloon, *et al.* (1984). It is suggested that it may be useful to offer this information to families who are uninformed about the nature of the disorder. Helpers should present personally a model of calm behavior in the consultation or discussion session. This is because of the importance of modeling, and because already anxious people are acutely alert to additional sources of threat.

Sometimes, schizophrenically ill people and their families may, through stress, show physical or verbal aggression. It seems to be helpful to control one's own outward behavior and to maintain the impression of personal calm. Helpers can usefully show their recognition of the anxiety being felt by a given individual or members of a family and, by empathizing, convey that this is natural and understandable. It seems to be helpful to people to be able to speak about the anxieties they are coping with. Just listening helps.

Respect and concern to all involved can be demonstrated by paying deferential attention to them. It seems to be helpful to give attention first to the person with the disorder, and then to the family or caregivers. It is important to clarify what people have been told concerning a diagnosis, and while not changing the substance of this in any way, to clarify or correct misunderstandings. It may also be important to correct misinformation, such as schizophrenia is a punishment for certain misdeeds.

There is substantial evidence that high levels of "expressed emotion," especially critical and overprotective remarks, can contribute to early relapse among people with schizophrenia. It is understandable that relatives should feel these emotions, so one of the worker's tasks may be to enable these feelings to be released in a setting where they cannot hurt the client directly. Relatives may then be less likely to vent them upon the person with schizophrenia.

Anorexia nervosa. A problem particularly associated with adolescent girls (it can also occur in prepubertal children) is anorexia nervosa. The anorexic girl deliberately restricts her food intake; indeed, she does not want to eat at all, because she believes she is fat and wishes to lose weight. The word "anorexia" means loss of appetite. However, the absence of hunger or appetite is not a crucial feature of anorexia nervosa. Nevertheless, the teenager will characteristically act as if she has lost her appetite.

Anorexia nervosa is essentially about weight rather than eating. The really central feature of the disorder is a body weight which is abnormally low for the age, height, and sex of the person. There is a further crucial feature: the individual's attitude to her weight. What makes life difficult for would-be helpers is that someone with anorexia nervosa will not always be truthful about her feelings. If she is, she will say that she is ashamed and very frightened of the thoughts of being heavier. She may suffer in various ways through being thin, but compared with gaining weight it is seen as the lesser evil.

Adolescent females experience eating disorders that include anorexia where the intake of food is greatly reduced as well as bulimia, a disorder which is characterized by binges of eating and reducing caloric intake through vomiting, laxative, diuretics, and severe dieting. For these females there is typically preoccupation with images of thin feminine appearance and problems with compliance with authority and with non-assertiveness. Many experience competitive family expectations and report histories of failure to please adults in their lives, typically parents. One study of intervention reports the benefits of structure and support provided through treatment groups. Education about their eating disorder, management or eating behaviors, and learning new improved interpersonal skills and developing self-awareness in relation to others proved to be helpful (Harper and Shillito, 1991).

The acts of eating and fasting are loaded with meaning—personal, familial, cultural, and religious. They also carry the connotations of control and self-mastery, of nurturant love, comfort, sociability, and, indeed, sexuality. The "meaning" of the eating disorder for one anorexic teenager is likely to differ at certain points compared with another. Each must be individually assessed by professionals who are trained and expert in this potentially fatal psychological disorder. Parents need to be alerted to the signs in their teenager of incipient anorexia nervosa: a preoccupation, indeed obsession, with calorie counts, with having control over her diet, loss of weight, cessation of periods, concern over appearance, moodiness, and so on. It is advisable to seek psychiatric or clinical psychological advice early rather than late, if your mental "alarm bells" begin sounding from what you are seeing and hearing from your teenager.

Conduct disorders (Lahey, et al., *1999).* It is quite likely that problems of conduct constitute the most frequent as well as the fastest growing problem area of childhood. The children manifesting these problems in severe form cause themselves and those who are close to them the utmost misery. Antisocial activities tend to disrupt and hinder the acquisition of crucial life skills. Their presence in childhood is predictive of problems of adjustments in later adolescence and adulthood (Greene and Doyle, 1999; Kazdin, 1997). Many evaluative studies of treatment outcomes of conduct-disordered youth have been conducted (Kazdin, 1995; Tremblay, *et al.,* 1992). Overall, about 50 percent of children who have conduct disorder diagnosis grow up to become adults with antisocial problems (Waddell and Offord, 1999).

The conduct disorders represent a heterogeneous dimension of behavior with the common theme of a failure of the individual to conform his or her behavior to expectations of some authority (e.g. parent or teacher) or to societal norms. The behaviors can range from chronic conflicts with authority (e.g. non-compliance, defiance, argumentativeness) to violations of social norms, (e.g. truancy, running away from home) to serious violations of the rights of others (e.g. aggression, vandalism, fire setting, stealing). These behaviors are considered to be indicative of a clinical syndrome (i.e. a conduct disorder) when they are severe, persistent, and lead to significant impairment in a child's psychosocial functioning.

Society's concern about children with extreme conduct problems is justified given the high cost of antisocial behavior to society, including the cost of incarceration of juvenile offenders, the costs associated with vandalism of public property, the cost in suffering of the victims of such children and adolescents, and not least the price paid by the perpetrators of such misery—their blighted futures over the longer term. These "aggressive," antisocial children are at increased risk of being rejected by their peers. They are also likely to develop a veritable litany of problems later in life such as truancy, alcoholism, drug abuse, juvenile delinquency, adult crime and interpersonal problems (see Farrington, 1995; Robins and Rutter, 1990). Their scholastic underachievement and failure have debilitating short-term and long-term consequences—notably (in the latter case) in high rates of unemployment and dependency on state support. Hard-pressed parents (particularly mothers) are quite likely to manifest stress-related disorders such as anxiety states, depression and psychophysiological disorders (Webster-Stratton and Hammond, 1999). Paradoxically, children with less serious difficulties are more likely to receive the scarce resources of therapy than those with the more extreme disorders.

It is vital to interrupt the transgenerational trend of antisocial/aggressive behavior. Research (Herbert, 1987b) indicates that maltreatment and witnessing parental aggression during early childhood, are predictive of children developing conduct problems. Conduct problems, in turn, predict later partner violence, which first emerges during adolescent dating experiences. Rates of partner violence double among young couples who move from dating into cohabiting, and who bear children at a young age, and thus, aggressive behavior becomes highly stable across the life course of the individuals, and is transmitted from generation to generation with families.

The developmental literature provides clear guidelines about the conditions conducive to the acquisition of internalized rule (norm) formation. These include firm moral demands made by parents upon their offspring, the consistent use of sanctions, techniques of punishment that are psychological rather than physical such as threatening to withdraw approval and an intensive use of reasoning and explanations, or inductive methods. Intervention with conduct-disordered youth involves working with both the youth and parents, often in groups, Kernberg and Chazan (1991) describe intensive intervention toward goals such as achieving new understanding, directing attention, developing ownership and self in various modes of interaction. A variety of economic social and family conditions preclude the operation of these factors in the lives of some children. Disharmonious, rejecting home backgrounds, the breakdown of discipline, parental loss, and broken homes are but a few examples of distal life variables that are linked etiologically to conduct disorders (Herbert, 1987b). The role of structural factors (e.g. poverty, poor housing) as causes of crime are not dealt with here but are not to be underestimated. They undermine parent–child relationships.

Of course, there is a sense in which very young children are asocial or antisocial. What happens as the children mature is that they have to learn to avoid certain behaviors and adopt others; that is to say, they must be trained to check certain impulses and to regulate their behavior in terms of certain informal and formal rules of conduct. The conduct disorders represent one of the most intensively studied of all forms of childhood psychopathology, however, there is still a debate about why there is this failure or distortion of socialization, why antisocial trajectories broaden and deepen with development in some children yet taper off in others, and why they are so difficult to deflect once stabilized.

There seems to be a typical developmental progression in which children start to show oppositional and argumentative behavior early in life (e.g. between the ages of three and eight) and then gradually progress into increasingly more severe patterns of conduct problem behavior. Most children who move on to display the more severe type of conduct problems do not change the types of behavior they display, but instead add the more severe conduct problem behaviors. That is to say, most children who show the more severe behaviors continue to show conduct problems from the lower levels of earlier childhood.

Children who begin to show conduct problems prior to adolescence are usually referred to as childhood onset conduct disorders. However, there are a substantial number of young people who begin showing antisocial behavior as they approach adolescence, with no history of oppositional behavior during childhood. They have been referred to as "adolescence-limited" conduct problems to reflect the findings from many longitudinal studies that young people who begin showing conduct problems in adolescence are much less likely to persist in their antisocial behavior in adulthood. Additionally, boys revealing childhood-onset conduct problems behavior are more aggressive and have more neuropsychological deficits than boys with the adolescent-limited pattern. It would seem from these findings that onset in early childhood represents a much more severe pattern of dysfunction, whereas the adolescent-limited pattern may be better considered an exaggeration of normal developmental process. Intervention issues are discussed in Part 3 and Appendix 1.

Educational failure (see Goldstein, 1995). Depression, education failure and school refusal are frequently linked as causes and effects of each other. Mass formal education has created serious problems for the life goals of adolescents, school is a bridge between the world of childhood and the world of adulthood. For children unwilling or unable to learn, school is a place where the battle against society is likely to begin. Failure in a success-orientated world has significant consequences for the well-being of adolescents, not only at school, but in other facets of their lives. There is a strong association between emotional disturbance and underachievement at school—a perennial matter of concern to both teachers and parents. Emotionally disturbed adolescents tend to distract and harass their teachers, and disrupt and anger their more conscientious fellow students.

A sense of failure very often manifests itself in an obstinate facade behind which the student hides. There is a vicious circle of self-fulfilling prophecy at work. Tell teenagers often enough that they are fools, criticize them whatever they do, even if it is commendable within their own capabilities, and in the end they are likely to become extremely demoralized and even give up. Why should they work hard when all their efforts, good or bad, are condemned? Their confidence will be destroyed and once again they may retreat behind a mask of stupidity and "don't care" laziness—signs of what clinically is referred to as "learned helplessness." (See Goldstein, 1995, and Herbert, 1998a, for a discussion of classroom management and some of the broader issues of reluctance or refusal to go to school.)

Young people who do well at school tend to enjoy good health, have average or above-average intelligence and well-developed social skills. They are likely to have a good opinion of themselves, the ability to gauge accurately their effect on others, and to perceive correctly the quality of others' approaches and responses to themselves. Early maturing boys and girls also have many advantages in terms of capability and self-confidence.

Delinquency. Although conduct problems can create misery for everyone concerned with the younger child, the disturbance (referred to as Oppositional Defiance Disorder) can often be contained within the home or classroom—although often at great cost. As children grow older those problems that involve a persistent defiance of authority, together with a refusal or inability to show self-restraint, become more serious in their implications. They extend more and more beyond the confines of the child's life at home and school. The reverberations of the child's misdemeanors may eventually lead them to not only being labeled "conduct-disordered," but also to earning the designation "juvenile delinquent" if he or she infringes the law, is apprehended and found guilty. A sizable number of children with conduct problems become delinquent. Conduct disorder diagnosis is the most "high-profiled" problem of adolescence,

Delinquent activities peak at around 15 years for boys and 14 years for girls and by the mid-twenties most former offenders have gradually become broadly law-abiding members of the community. The number of young people committing detected and adjudicated crimes in the United Kingdom and the United

States has increased markedly. What was once an almost completely male preserve now includes substantial numbers of female offenders. The average age for the first court appearance of juveniles is lower, and there is a marked trend towards more violent offenses. The term "juvenile delinquent" is an administrative or legal term, not a clinical diagnosis (Mishne, 1986).

In the United States, the Office of Juvenile Justice and Delinquency Prevention reports alarming increases in juvenile delinquency and involvement of juveniles in violent crimes, including murder. Further, it is reported that juveniles committed 14 percent of all violent crimes in 1994 and 25 percent of all property crimes in that year. Females were arrested for one of every seven violent crimes in 1994. It is predicted that the rate of juvenile arrests for violent crimes will more than double by 2010 (Snyder, *et al.*, 1996). The problem of juvenile crime is disconcerting as the proportion of crimes committed by juveniles is growing annually. Additionally, youth are experiencing violence in various realms of their lives as reflected by growing rates of abuse and neglect, family disruptions due to divorce and single parenthood, group violence, and street violence. Protecting society from the unlawful actions of society's youth is one charge for helping professionals. However, on the other hand, protecting youth from violence and preventing their participation in violent acts is a challenge confronting social workers and other helping professionals in a wide array of community and agency-based service programs.

A cognitive-behavioral approach to the difficult task of changing delinquent behavior is probably the most promising (see review by Herbert, 1998d). There is little doubt that interventions which usually require multilevel inputs become more challenging the older the child. In the absence of early treatment a large percentage of children with conduct disorders is likely to remain circulating through the revolving door of social services, mental health agencies, and criminal justice systems. Retrospective and prospective studies suggest that most antisocial adults have childhood histories of antisocial behavior (Farrington, 1995; Robins and Rutter, 1990). There is an urgent need for programs which can be distributed widely for purposes of training practitioners who in turn counsel and train parents, who in turn (hopefully) train and socialize their children more effectively.

Drug abuse. The new millennium continues to witness the previous decade's rise in the use of substances by adults and youth. Families of all ages and composition are placed at greater risk of having a member who abuses substances or of being a victim of crime or injury as a result of another's substance abuse.

Use of alcohol and tobacco remains high among youth, and the use of marijuana has been documented to have increased. About 93 percent of youth graduating from high school report having tried alcohol with about 41 percent reporting that they experience binge drinking (Duncan and Petosa, 1994). Smoking, drinking, and illicit drug use have all increased among American youth. As many as 42 percent of high school seniors reported having used illicit drugs during the 1996 academic year with marijuana being the drug most commonly used (Winters, 1998). There is concern that children at pre-teen ages are having greater access to drugs such as cocaine and heroin (Thurman, 1997). Smoking among adults decreased from 40.4 percent of adults to 26 percent between 1964 and 1990. Smoking among high school seniors remained at about 30 percent from 1980 to 1993 (Bonnie and Lynch, 1997).

Actual use of substances by adults is difficult to measure. According to trends identified from two studies involving sample sizes of 4,372 and 17,809 respondents, trends in lifetime usage reporting illicit drug use for adults age 26 and older in 1993 averaged 37.3 percent. There were 88.7 percent reporting drug/alcohol use, and 76.9 percent reporting cigarette use during their lifetime (Substance Abuse and Mental Health Services Administration, 1996).

Due to the availability and increased use and abuse of drugs and alcohol, estimated need for substance abuse treatment in the United States is alarming. According to one estimate of The National Institute on Drug Abuse, which included not only reported frequency of usage but reported problems and symptoms, as many as 3.5 million people were reported to be in need of treatment in 1991 (Epstein and Gfroerer, 1998).

Increased usage of substances, pressure for legalization of marijuana, and continuing lack of information about indicators of causation and treatment success give rise to continuing concern. It is clear that increased substance abuse has links with delinquency, crime, arrests, and a range of conduct problems (Winters, 1998). Concerns of substance abuse during family members' lifetimes are very serious and are long-range concerns for professionals who work with families across the range of assessment, intervention, and long-term evaluation in support of efforts for prevention and innovation in intervention.

The terms "drug abuse" and "drug misuse" refer to the observation that a particular form of drug taking is a harmful (abuse) and/or socially unacceptable way of using that substance (misuse). "Users" are likely to develop "tolerance" for a drug, which means that their body has adapted to the repeated presence of the drug so that higher doses are required to maintain the same effect. The body may react with "withdrawal effects" to the sudden absence of a drug to which it has adapted; they involve severe physical discomfort. When this occurs and leads to a compulsion to continue taking the drug so as to avoid these symptoms, we speak of "physical dependence." The more important and widespread problem of "psychological dependence" refers to an irresistible psychological compulsion to repeat the stimulation, pleasure or comfort provided by the drug's effects.

The key factor in drug taking is opportunity—the availability of drugs and people to tempt and "prompt." Users have generally been exposed to drugs by their peers or by people (not infrequently family members) whose values incline toward nonconformity or even deviance. Rebelliousness, low self-esteem, a poor sense of psychological well-being, depression, and low academic aspirations are among the characteristics commonly found in adolescent drug users. The boredom and hopelessness of unemployment also play their part. Substance abuse presents a similar picture. High-risk drug taking is defined as uncontrolled use, whether or not it is already demonstrably harmful. A person is also taking an unacceptable risk if he or she is a regular user, that is, taking drugs at predictable intervals.

It is most important for professional people and parents to be on the lookout for signs that may lead them to suspect drug use. It isn't easy, because some of the signs are not uncommon in adolescence generally. There is often a gradual change in the adolescent's habits and a general lethargy. Other signs include: aggression; loss of interest in school work, sports, hobbies, and friends; furtive behavior and frequent lying; bouts of drowsiness and sleeplessness; unexplained disappearances of money and belongings from the home.

Heroin addicts usually stop bothering about their appearance, their speech may become halting, and they tend to drop old friends and take up with new ones. Users of heroin may receive unexplained messages or telephone calls, followed by an immediate and unexplained departure. Spots of blood may be noticed on their clothes, and needle marks on the back of the hand and the inside of the elbow. There may also be thickened brownish cords under the skin where veins have solidified as a result of the injections.

There is a tendency for the addict to be hostile to society, and therein lies part of the trouble when it comes to treatment and rehabilitation. A hospital too often epitomizes society in the mind of the addict. More informal methods are therefore required, and in most countries clinics run on "non-institutional" lines within the community are available. Community support groups and networking are services that can be found in most communities.

Multiple substances are experimented with and abused by many. Interestingly, there is no pharmaceutical answer to drug abuse. Despite a lack of agreement about treatment, many substance abusers do recover. Dependence on cocaine is a serious, life-threatening addiction that often involves other drugs and exposure to illnesses, including HIV-AIDS. Research suggests that psychosocial treatment, including behavioral treatment, is relatively effective. Budney and Higgins (1998) report encouraging results from behavioral intervention incorporating psychosocial counseling, behavioral reinforcement utilizing coupons for merchandise in exchange for abstinence from cocaine, and a variety of interventions and follow-up activities for lifestyle management in the community environment.

Community-based and often ex-addict operated clinics are frequently successful in working with addicts. The addict who is desperate for drugs has an uncanny instinct for putting the most subtle and painful pressures on families and doctors alike. These tactics are familiar to ex-addicts who know from their own experiences the kinds of behavioral changes and lifestyle changes to be overcome for recovery to be possible.

Children and families exposed to and utilizing substances are at great risk for continuing abuse with even more substances. Early intervention and prevention of substance experimentation are important in the lives of children and families as we continue the battle against substance abuse and its harmful outcomes.

Sexual Encounters and Sexual Abuse (see Jones and McGraw, 1987)

Seductions/incidents. Many childhood sexual experiences of different kinds come about through sexual contact with adults. Almost all children encounter rather explicit sexual situations between the ages of six and 12. Many minor confrontations that occur seem to pass children by, and leave them practically unscathed. This is where robust and healthy attitudes to sex are so important.

Not all children get to adulthood with only minor sexual experiences to assimilate. And this is really one of the most pressing problems facing parents. How much might one traumatic sexual encounter at an early age affect a child varies from case to case. If a seven-year-old girl is coaxed into some kind of sexual play by an older male relative, what effect will it have on her chances of establishing a happy physical relationship later in her life? If an adolescent boy is seduced by a homosexual older boy or a grown man, is the boy likely to be deflected from normal heterosexual interests himself? There are no ready-made answers to such questions; and, as is the case in many matters dealing with human sexuality, there is little solid evidence to produce.

All the good work put in by parents during a young child's life is not likely to be swept aside by one chance encounter. If the parents have sensitized the child to negative attitudes and fears about sex, such a traumatic event may well serve to trigger a real emotional problem. Children react differently to sexual exploitation from very early in their lives. Each child's coping is different, and every child is to be valued and helped to overcome and resolve fears associated with sexual experiences in their lives.

Tables 6 and 7 provide physical and behavioral warning signs (respectively) of possible child sexual maltreatment, signs that indicate the fears and coping strategies generated by the trauma.

Child sexual assault or victimization is more common than once thought—as many as 20 percent to 30 per cent of girls and slightly less for boys. Young men more than young women are reluctant to report sexual victimization according to one study (Finkelhor, 1979). The perpetrator of child sexual abuse is generally known to the child. Intrafamilial abuse is most commonly perpetrated by fathers; stepfathers are over-represented in the abuse statistics.

Outside the family, abuse is most likely to be committed by people who are trusted to have contact with the child alone, e.g. friends of the family, neighbors, peers, baby-sitters or club leaders. The majority of abusive incidents are perpetrated by men, but women also sexually abuse children. The role of siblings is now being recognized. A majority of children are initially abused between the ages of eight and 12 years although the abuse may continue beyond this age. Fourteen percent of abuse against boys and 6 per cent of abuse against girls is perpetrated by women acting alone. Women are more often involved as co-abusers. Serious problems tend to arise when sexual contacts (initiated, say, by a relative or good friend of the family) continue over a long period of time, and the child, intimidated by terrifying threats or confused by blandishments, is too afraid, emotionally conflicted or guilty, to disclose his/her "secret" to parents or to authorities.

It may seem obvious, indeed trite, to ask why sexual abuse causes problems. But the answers are by no means simple; they are many-sided, and (indeed) some 33 percent, according to David Finkelhor (1979) viewed the abuse as neutral or positive.

Table 6. Physical Warning Signs of Possible Child Sexual Abuse

- Sleeplessness, nightmares, and fear of the dark
- Bruises, scratches, bite marks
- Depression/suicide attempts
- Anorexia nervosa
- Eating disorders or change in eating habits
- Difficulty in walking or sitting
- Pregnancy—particularly with reluctance to name the father
- Recurring urinary tract problems
- Vaginal infections or genital/anal damage
- Venereal disease
- Bed-wetting
- Vague pains and aches
- Itching or soreness

Table 7. Behavioral Warning Signs of Possible Child Sexual Abuse

- Lack of trust in adults
- Fear of a particular individual
- Withdrawal and introversion
- Running away from home
- Girl takes over the mothering role
- Sudden school problems, truanting, and falling grades
- Low self-esteem and low expectations of others
- Stealing
- Drug, alcohol, or solvent abuse
- Display of sexual knowledge beyond the child's years
- Sexual drawing
- Prostitution
- Vulnerability to sexual and emotional exploitation
- Revulsion toward sex
- Fear of school medical examinations

He describes four ways in which, more commonly, sexual abuse can devastate individuals:

1. Traumatic sexualization. Children usually feel frightened, confused, or distressed when they are being sexually abused and may also experience physical pain. Their early experiences of sexual behavior and sexuality are therefore traumatic. The physical and emotional pain involved in sexual abuse means that sex becomes associated with bad feelings which can continue into adulthood and lead to fears and phobias about sex, and a dislike or avoidance of sex, touching, or intimacy. Not all children experience distress at the time they are being abused. Whatever their reaction, when children are sexually abused they are exposed to sexual experiences which are inappropriate or too advanced for their age or level of development. They are also given confusing and incorrect messages about sexual behavior. Survivors grow up confused about their own sexual feelings and normal sexual behavior. Abusers sometimes reward children with attention, affection, presents, or money after the abuse. Children learn from this behavior that sex can be exchanged for rewards. Adolescent and adult survivors may come to believe that having sex is the only way to obtain affection.

2. Stigmatization. Even if the child doesn't understand exactly what is happening, or hasn't been told to keep the abuse secret, s/he still often understands that there is something wrong and shameful about what s/he is experiencing. When sexual abuse is discovered or disclosed other people sometimes react with shock, or blame the victim.

3. Betrayal. When a child is abused, especially by a relative or someone s/he knows and likes, her/his trust in that person is betrayed. The child's trust and vulnerability are manipulated by the abuser. Abusers often build up trusting relationships with a child and may make her/him feel wanted and cared for before the abuse takes place. The child may feel further betrayed by the lack of support and protection from other non-abusing adults, even a parent.

4. Powerlessness. A child experiences an intense sense of powerlessness when s/he is sexually abused. The child's body is touched or invaded against her/his wishes and this may continue again and again. The child repeatedly experiences fear and an inability to control the situation. Many children attempt in their own way to try to control the situation and stop the abuse but their attempts are often useless and meet with failure.

The puzzle, as with other stressors that affect children as they grow up, is the considerable variation in the adult adjustment of individuals who were abused in their early years. Some experience various psychological problems of differing severity, while others appear to be relatively unscathed. Derek Jehu (1992) has attempted to account for the individual differences in outcome following child sexual abuse, and to identify some psychological processes that provide the link between such abuse and the occurrence of psychological problems in adulthood. According to Jehu, people develop "schemas" in response to life experiences. In particular, traumatic experiences early in life, especially those of an ongoing and cumulative nature, are important in the establishment of maladaptive schemas which are persistent.

Schemas are cognitive structures that organize experience and behavior. They contain certain core beliefs about oneself, other people, and the world in which one lives. These beliefs influence one's thoughts, feelings, and actions. More particularly, they interpret and attach meaning to certain relevant events. The very long-term nature of negative self-deprecatory schemas may result from certain cognitive, behavioral or affective processes which create self-fulfilling prophecies. Cognitively, the perception of events is influenced by schemas and this may contribute to their maintenance. Input from these events is selected and interpreted in ways that are consistent with existing schemas, so that input that confirms a schema is likely to be emphasized and exaggerated, while input that is discrepant with a schema tends to be denied, minimized, or rationalized.

Individuals may engage in those forms of behavior that confirm their existing schemas. For instance, victims who believe and expect that they will be unable to protect themselves, may fail to mobilize coping resources to deal with real threats and therefore suffer harm, which confirms their schema that they are unable to protect themselves. Furthermore, such self-defeating behavior may evoke responses from others which confirm the victim's schemas. Thus a victim who does not trust others may act towards them with suspicion, so that in turn they respond to the victim with rejection and hostility, which serve to confirm the victim's lack of trust in people.

Schemas may be maintained for powerful emotional reasons, because to change or relinquish well-established and familiar beliefs can be very threatening and anxiety evoking ("What will it be like to be different?", "Will I get hurt or distressed?", "Will my partner still love me if I'm different?"). Schemas have been likened to an old shoe, too comfortable to throw away. Furthermore individuals often feel hopeless about changing their schemas which they perceive as being inextricably part of themselves ("This is how I have always been," "This is who I am.").

For a more complete discussion on interventions with victims of sexual assault, see Faller (1988), Sgroi (1982), and Stevenson (1999). The first responsibility of families and professionals is to protect children from victimization and thus assure safety and maximum potential for healthy social and emotional development. In situations where sexual abuse and victimization are suspected, a range of professionals including social workers, nurses, doctors, and others can provide intervention.

It is not within the scope of this book to deal adequately with such a disturbing and complex issue. However, it is important to be alert to possible warning "signs." Do seek experienced and expert help as many of these signs in children and adolescents are open to alternative explanations; and are thus vulnerable to misinterpretation as sexual abuse (see Babiker and Herbert, 1998; Herbert, 2000; Spencer and Flin, 1990). See Tables 6 and 7 for a listing of some of the physical and behavioral warning signs of possible sexual abuse.

Summary and Comment

We have attempted in this chapter to sketch in the broad developmental themes that are important for your understanding of childhood and adolescence. A framework of normal development is vital for your assessment of what is not normal, usual, "healthy," or functional in a potential client's behavior. It is particularly difficult to pinpoint the onset of serious problems when childhood and adolescence are notable for the changes that take place, some of them very rapid indeed. So many signs of normal change look like "symptoms" of emotional disturbance. Therefore you need multiple criteria (working guidelines) for arriving at the decision that you are dealing with a problem with serious implications. Proceed cautiously and consult acknowledged experts, colleagues, or supervisors if necessary. This is a ferociously complex area fraught with value judgments, ethical issues, and technical difficulties. You will find a few of the typical problems illustrated in these pages but the topic is so vast that you should supplement your knowledge base from other literature and from your experience from workshops and supervised practice.

The advice is particularly pertinent to the issues of physical, emotional, and sexual abuse. The legal, moral, technical, and social ramifications of these problems go far beyond the scope of this kind of book. What is critical to remember is that most children can cope with traumas if the aftermath is sensitively dealt with by adults, parents, and/or the authorities. What is more damaging in the short and longer term is the abusive situation that goes on and on. As so many emotional, physical, and sexual incidents of an abusive kind occur in the child's home, this is precisely what tends to happen.

CHAPTER 6

Responsiveness in Parents and Children

Family groupings have been traced back to the Pleistocene period, some 500,000 years ago. This durability and universality of the family suggests that as an organization it has significant survival value for the individual and the species. But longevity of this order does not mean that the family is unchanging. It has been, and is, susceptible to social, economic, and historical forces. For example, the large extended family has given way in industrial societies to small nuclear units of parent(s) and offspring. There is an increasing number of single-parent families. In 1994, 26 percent of families with children were headed by a single parent (Kids Count Data Book, 1999). Then again, there are several variations in parental roles to take into account.

Birth parents give the child life, physical appearance, intellectual potential, and certain personality characteristics and special talents. The legal parents carry responsibility for the child's maintenance, safety, and security and make decisions about the child's residence and education. Parenting parents provide the day-to-day love, care, attention, and discipline. For many children the three components of parenting are embodied in one set of parents.

In the case of foster children there will at least be a split between birth parents who are also legal parents and the foster parents undertaking part of the parenting function. In foster care there is quite commonly a three-way split, with birth parents, parenting (foster) parents, and the local authority as legal parent with custodial authority. Adopted children are likely to have two sets of parents: the birth parents and the adoptive parents. The latter combines the legal and parenting roles.

The Egyptians, Romans, and Greeks all sanctioned adoption. In earlier periods, adoption was utilized primarily to serve adult ends—particularly to acquire heirs in order to provide continuity for a family line. Views on adoption have changed markedly over the years. Today's philosophy is unmistakably child-centered. In essence, the value of adoption in modern society is that it safeguards the child by providing a permanent family arrangement. Of course, adoptive parents—like biological parents setting out to rear an infant—are faced with the rather daunting task of transforming helpless, unsocial, and self-centered infants into more or less self-supporting and responsible members of the community.

Parental Responsiveness

With the birth or adoption of the first child the tasks of the parents, the roles they occupy, their orientation toward the future, all change profoundly. This simple step into parenthood provides a severe test for the parents. The inevitable changes in the partners will, in turn, alter their relationship and may place stress upon it until a new equilibrium can be established in their lives. In order to reestablish a degree of equanimity they rely on various coping "mechanisms" (see Chapter 4). There may be reverberations in all of this for the child.

In working with parents the professional will be particularly interested in assessing the parents' responsiveness to their child because so many of the parental functions are dependent to some degree on this attribute. The needs of children who are potentially at risk if not responded to consistently are of two kinds: survival functions such as the need for food, shelter, and physical care; and psychosocial functions, including the child's requirements of love, security, attention, new experiences, acceptance, education, praise, recognition, and belongingness.

If they are to survive, infants and children must also acquire vast amounts of information about the environment they inhabit. The transmission by adults of information of various kinds from one generation to another, as we have seen, is called socialization. One of the main objectives of this training is the preparation of children for their future, one of the major themes of this chapter.

129

Problematic Parenting

The definition of problematic behavior is a difficult one because it is largely a relative judgment, and a social, subjective one at that. It is formulated largely in terms of its consequences for the offspring—his or her well-being. Social workers sometimes aid pediatricians and health professionals in cases where infants fail to thrive, in the absence of any organic (physical) illness. They have to explore the social and emotional context in which the child is nurtured.

According to Browne (in Browne and Herbert, 1997), the following are important aspects to the assessment of high-risk parent–child relationships and determining how safe is the child.

1. Knowledge and attitudes to child rearing. Research suggests that abusing and non-abusing families have different attitudes about child development. For example abusers tend to have unrealistic and distorted expectations about their children's abilities. They may have much higher expectations about their children and this influences discipline and punishment. They may have unrealistic beliefs that babies should be able to sit alone at 12 weeks and take the first step at 40 weeks. More importantly they may expect their infants to be able to recognize wrongdoing at 52 weeks. Not surprisingly a significant proportion of sexual and physical abusive incidents involve fruitless attempts by parents to force a child to behave in a manner that is beyond the child's developmental limitations.

Research also suggests that one of the differences between abusing and non-abusing parents is that the abusing group see child rearing as a simple rather than a complex task. Many show a lack of awareness of their child's abilities and needs.

2. Parental perceptions of child behavior. Abusing parents tend to have more negative conceptions of their children's behavior than non-abusing parents; they perceive their children to be more irritable and demanding. This may be related to the fact that abused children are more likely to have health problems, eating or sleeping (or other behavioral) disturbances. Alternatively, it may be a direct result of unrealistic expectations on the part of the parents.

3. *The quality of parenting.* Parental responsiveness is a major element in assessing the quality of parenting. It is a complex and many-sided phenomenon, but there are at least three different elements which make for what one might assess to be *sensitive* responsiveness: the tendency to react *promptly, consistently,* and *appropriately* to their offspring. A social worker or health visitor would be concerned if parents continually failed to show these reactions in response to their child's hunger, pain, crying or other communications and actions.

The interactions between parents and children (particularly the early ones) are of crucial significance in the child's development. And parenting is not simply a matter of being *reactive;* it is also about being proactive: initiating play, pre-empting accidents and facilitating learning, by imaginative, resourceful care. Personal factors can interfere with these intricate processes. To take an extreme case: a mother suffering from depression may find it difficult to "tune in" to the child in a sufficiently sensitive manner to be able to construct with him/her a mutually beneficial and stimulating sequence of interaction.

It is worth noting that although society delegates its most crucial functions to the family, there is little formal education or training offered to would-be parents; even the informal learning and experience once available to older children caring for younger siblings in large families, or the help from the experienced members of the extended family and from relatives living nearby, may not be available to the relatively small and isolated nuclear family (mother, father, children).

Parent–Child Attachment

The question of sensitive or insensitive responsiveness has been linked in part with the quality of the emotional "bond" or "attachment" that forms between the parent and baby. Obviously, the infant's survival depends upon a loving and long-term commitment by adult caregivers. Attachment of mother and infant has been thought to be the basic component to long-lasting security and sense of self-worth into adulthood. Studying infants in institutions and orphanages from World War II separation, Bowlby (1982) concluded that separation of mother and child resulted in serious physical, mental, and emotional damage to children. Later, recognizing that his sample was somewhat extreme and that his subjects were deprived of contact, love, and nurturance from nearly any source, he softened his conclusions but remained firm in the importance of lasting and consistent relationships in the development and nurturance of a child. The phenomenon of attachment continues to be of interest to researchers and has resulted in extensive study of early infant-caregiver studies and the impact of infant experiences on later development. Gaining security, self-image, and a sense of self are all part of the process of development in response to various sources of nurturance and of relationships. Different responses of children reared in apparently similar ways continue to be of great interest to researchers (Skolnick, 1998).

Understanding the meaning of attachment of the child to early caregivers is a significant consideration for those of us working with children and families to provide services and information that strengthen parenting and child well-being. Bowlby and Ainsworth's assumption that internal patterns of attaching and relating produce a lifelong template that enters into relationships and differences of interacting throughout the lifespan has implications for clinical work with clients of all ages (Bowlby, 1988; Ainsworth, *et al.*, 1978; Pistole, 1999).

This is not the place to review the complex and detailed studies of bonding about which there has been so much controversy; however, there seems to be no reliable evidence that skin-to-skin contact is necessary for the development of mother-love, and, what is more significant, mother-to-infant attachment does not depend on such contact occurring during a sensitive period of short duration after the birth of the baby (see Sluckin, *et al.*, 1983).

We are *not* putting forward the idea that early human contact and relationships are of no consequence. Far from it. All relationships have to have a beginning; close mother–infant contact is decidedly desirable whenever possible. Mothers tend to like it, and lactation is facilitated. Where better to begin than at the very beginning, with the newborn child placed in its mother's arms? Mutual awareness and familiarity have an opportunity to develop. What we are talking about is foundational learning, learning how to relate to a stranger, a baby. It would seem that this learning comes quickly for some but for others more slowly. The range of individual differences is wide.

The period after birth, with its heightened emotional arousal and excited expectation and fulfillment of a new family member, may have tremendous significance for *all* members of the family. Remember that parental bonds and relationships have their own complex, many-sided developmental histories, stretching over many years. Among the factors that can influence the way a mother behaves and relates to her offspring are her age, her cultural and social background, her own experience of being parented, her personality, her previous experience with babies, and her experiences during pregnancy and birth.

Insensitivity to cultural values in clinical and social work practice can lead to much individual suffering if methods used are contrary to cherished cultural and/or religious beliefs. For some ethnic groups, bonding ideas, if applied insensitively by doctors and nurses, may have disturbing repercussions. In many Asian families, for instance, birth is a less personal event than in European families. An Indian baby is thought to be bonded to the family group rather than to the mother in particular. Unless hospital staff are sensitive to ethnic differences in behavior and attitudes after birth, these parents could feel intense conflict over "bonding procedures."

Understandably the hard-pressed social worker cannot afford to be as complacent as the scientist in risking what the statisticians call Type II errors, for example, denying relationships that actually exist because of a cautious attitude to evidence. After all, it has been suggested that separation of the mother and infant for several weeks immediately after birth may not only damage the subsequent mother–child relationship but additionally that such mothers are prone to child abuse. In fact, the evidence for such far-reaching claims is simply not available; these notions do not stand up to painstaking inquiry and investigation.

It is reassuring to realize that there are variations in the way that maternal feelings arise and grow. Mothers generally expect to have positive maternal feelings toward their infants at the time of birth. Indeed, some mothers do report an instant love toward their newborn babies. Others report that they feel nothing. However, you can reassure mothers that they do not need to worry if they feel initially detached from their babies, as this appears to be a fairly common occurrence. Some 40 percent of mothers of first-borns have been found to express an initial indifference to their infants, a state of mind that soon evaporates as they get to know their offspring.

When subjective and objective reports of the development of mother love are scrutinized, it becomes apparent that the growth of maternal attachment is usually a gradual process.

Allaying parents' fears. The practical advice to parents who have had an enforced separation—at whatever time—from their children is: do not spend time worrying needlessly. Adult bonding need not be impaired in the case of those separations in the maternity hospital, unless you talk yourself into a crisis.

Where the separation occurs later in life, children may be upset for a short time, but they will soon recover if parents appear their usual selves and avoid fussing over them in nervous expectation of the worst. We know that a child's separation from its caregiver does not inevitably result in maladjustment. Far from it. Brief separations are fairly common for all children and seem to have little adverse effect. The key issue is to provide good and stable substitute care during the absence or absences (see Sluckin, *et al.*, 1983).

Paternal bonding. Paternal love puts a large question mark over the bonding doctrine, for it implies that a father's love is of a lower order and quality than the mother's. Yet it is not always the female who cares for the baby. This is so even in some animal species: male marmosets, to take just one example, carry the infant at all times except when it is feeding.

Most human fathers develop a strong love for their off-spring, even if they were nowhere near the delivery room when they were born. A study of first-time fathers suggests that they began developing a bond to their newborn by the first three days after the birth and often earlier. They tended to develop a feeling of preoccupation, absorption, and interest. There are no clear indications that the early contact by the father with the newborn facilitates this paternal bonding. Nevertheless, the opportunity for father and infant to get to know one another early is important, especially as contemporary western society is witnessing a massive increase in the number of single-parent families; and in some, it is the father who is the caregiver.

Fostering and adoption.   If maternal bonding theories were correct, it would hardly be possible for foster or adoptive parents to form warm attachments to their charges, whom they may not have seen as babies at all. It could be said that it is possible to look after children satisfactorily without ever becoming attached to them, but how many adoptive or foster parents would say that they felt no bond with their child? Tragic "tug of love" cases have occurred because foster parents have grown so fond of the children in their care that it becomes unbearably hurtful to hand them back to their biological parents.

Not only is there no "blood bond" between adoptive mother and the child, but she has missed out vital weeks, months, and sometimes years of exposure to the youngster. Not surprisingly, there is nothing to suggest that adoptive parents are in any way inferior in their familial or parental roles than biological parents. A painstaking study of children who had been in care throughout their early years followed them upon their leaving care. One group of children was adopted, another returned to their biological families. It was found that the latter did less well than the adopted children, both in the initial stages of settling in and in their subsequent progress. The reason lay primarily in the attitudes of the two sets of parents: the adoptive group "worked" harder at being parents, possibly for the very reason that the child was not their genetic offspring but a child chosen by them.

The attitude of some people to adoption in the 18th and early 19th centuries was very different from the one shared by most of us today. We gather from George Eliot's novel *Silas Marner* (1929) that on religious grounds it was believed that "to adopt a child, because children of your own had been denied you, was to try and choose your lot in spite of Providence: the adopted child ... would never turn out well, and would be a curse to those who had wilfully and rebelliously sought what it was clear that, for some high reason, they were better without." Adoption was only permissible and likely to succeed if it came about by chance, not intent. George Eliot, in her usual insightful manner, made the point that the "blood bond" is less important than the bonds forged by long-term tenderness and affection. And she has been shown to be correct.

Researchers provide evidence that adoption is notable for its high "success rate" both in absolute terms, and relative to other forms of substitute care. Like other parents, adopters will have their share of difficult children and will try to make sense of them. A commonly held belief which can be very worrying to adoptive parents is the notion that infants who are deprived of maternal care and love are affected adversely in their ability to form bonds of affection and also in their ability to develop a repertoire of socially appropriate attitudes and behavior.

An attitude of therapeutic pessimism was created in the minds of many social workers when considering problems in older children who were adopted, or the breakdown of fostering arrangements as a result of their belief in a link between their experience of early maternal separation/deprivation and the development of lasting difficulties in personal relationships and social/emotional functioning. An intolerable burden of anxiety about the child's future was also placed on parents who adopt older youngsters. But what is the evidence for such misgivings? It all began with studies of babies and young children in Dickensian-like institutions. The plight of these infants was linked theoretically to what happens to animals separated from their mothers.

Current concern about children who for whatever reason cannot be cared for by biological parent(s) calls for establishing a permanent family for each child. The situation of children in out-of-home care covers a broad range from the infant who is placed for adoption upon birth, to the abused two-year-old, to the 14-year-old who may have experienced several foster families and unsuccessful adoptive placements. Children placed in foster or adoptive families at older ages bring with them their histories of life experiences. Many will seek renewed relationships with biological relatives in their adult years, others will not. For about 90 percent of children in adoptive families, the new family becomes a permanent family for the child. For others, the adoptive family, not unlike some biological families, dissolves and the child may again return to the custody of legal authorities. Barth and Berry (1988) and McDonald, *et al.* (1996) provide extensive reporting of research studies on fostered and adoptive care respectively.

Responsiveness in Children

Examples of chicks or ducklings following a person have been seen by many people in nature films. Although normally attached to their birth mother, such infants can become attached with ease to an "adoptive" parent or (in the laboratory) to a moving inanimate object. Konrad Lorenz (1973) found that during a restricted period just after hatching goslings instinctively follow the first large moving thing they see. These young creatures not only tend to follow this moving object but they come to prefer it to all others, and after a time will follow no others.

This type of early learning is referred to as imprinting. The fascinating question that arises from studies of imprinting is whether human attachments, preferences, or other behaviors are acquired during restricted periods of development on an imprinting-like basis. The most influential writings have been those of John Bowlby. His early opinion was that the child's strong attachment to its mother was necessary for normal, healthy development. Bowlby (1982) argued that the period in the infant's life when a major new relationship, for example, to the mother, was being formed was a vital one for determining the nature of that relationship.

At that time he thought the deprivation of maternal affection, or protracted maternal separation, was liable to result in maladjustment, which could show itself in a variety of ways, including delinquency. He was suggesting then that not only the presence of adverse influences such as a harsh rejecting mother but the absence of crucial stimulation disturbs, possibly irreversibly, the child's ability to make relationships with people. Fortunately more recent, painstaking reviews on the effect of maternal deprivation and other types of early experiences indicate the more optimistic conclusion that early experience if distressing can be remedied; dysfunctional responses can be reversed (see Bowlby, 1982; Rutter, 1972). Such early experience is no more than a link, albeit an important one, in the chain of development. Development is influential but shapes behavior less and less powerfully as age increases. What is probably crucial is that for some children some adverse aspects of their early learning are continually repeated and reinforced and long-term harmful effects appear (White, 1991). We must not forget the likelihood that later problems and deviance may be the result of later adverse life experiences, for example, exposure to delinquent peers, and not only early learning experiences. Development is an ongoing process. This is not to deny the vital importance of the comforting presence of a loving parent or parent substitute especially before the age of about five years in facilitating the child's healthy psychological development. An example of this truism is provided by the studies of Mary Ainsworth and her colleagues. They (Ainsworth, *et al.*, 1978) have examined the relationship between the infant's response to separation and reunion and the behavior of both mother and child in the home environment.

Each individual infant can be assessed for the quality of attachment to the parent. The final assessment of infant to parents attachment can be described using four broad categories of the infant's response to the presence and absence of the mother (adapted from Ainsworth, *et al.*, 1978; source, Browne and Saqi, 1987).

1. Anxious/avoidant infants (Insecurely Attached Type I) show high levels of play behavior throughout and tend not to seek interaction with the parent or stranger. They do not become distressed at being left alone with the stranger. On reunion with their parent, they frequently resist any physical contact or interaction.

2. Independent infants (Securely Attached Type I) demonstrate a strong initiative to interact with their parent and to a lesser extent, the stranger. They do not especially seek physical contact with their parent and are rarely distressed on separation. They greet their parent on return by smiling and reaching.

3. *Dependent infants* (Securely Attached Type II) actively seek physical contact and interaction with their parent. They are usually distressed and often cry when left alone with the stranger. On their parent's return, they reach out and maintain physical contact, sometimes by resisting the parent's release. Generally they exhibit a desire for interaction with the parent in preference to the stranger.

4. *Anxious/resistant or ambivalent infants* (Insecurely Attached Type II) show low levels of play behavior throughout and sometimes cry prior to separation. They demonstrate an obvious wariness of the stranger and intense distress at separation. They are also more prone to crying when left alone with the stranger. They are ambivalent and frequently mix contact-seeking behaviors with active resistance to contact or interaction. This is especially evident on the parent's return: on reunion, these infants continue to be distressed as usually the parent fails to comfort them.

Ainsworth's findings suggest that maternal sensitivity is most influential in affecting the child's reactions. In the homes of the securely attached infants, sensitive mothering was exhibited to the infant's behavior, while insecurely attached, anxious and avoidant infants were found to have their interactive behavior rejected by the mothers. It was suggested that the enhanced exploratory behaviors shown by these infants were an attempt to block attachment behaviors that had been rejected in the past. A disharmonious and often ambivalent mother–infant relationship was evident in the home environments of the insecurely attached anxious and resistant infants. The resistant and ambivalent behaviors shown were seen as a result of inconsistent parenting.

There can be too much of a good thing, a point when mothering becomes smothering. And, of course, the same applies to fathering. There can also be too little parental input. Parental nurturance is undoubtedly a vital ingredient in the child's and

139

adolescent's healthy development, but as with everything moderation is the watchword.

Parental Patterns

Parental Overprotection

Overprotective parents frequently alternate between dominating their offspring and submitting to them. There are two types of parental overprotection. The dominating form of overprotection may lead to excessively dependent, passive, and submissive behavior on the part of the child. It is thought that if youngsters are discouraged from acting independently, exploring, and experimenting they will likely acquire timid, awkward, and generally apprehensive behaviors.

Parental Dominance/Restriction

Children whose parents are authoritarian, give the child no voice, and use physical punishment as a means of discipline tend to be more dependent and, eventually, rebellious adolescent offspring. Restrictive, authoritarian parents attempt to shape, control, and assess the behavior and attitudes of the child according to a set standard of conduct, usually an absolute standard, often motivated by theological considerations. Obedience is valued as a virtue, and punitive measures are used to curb self-will when the child's or teenager's actions or beliefs conflict with what parents think is correct conduct. They believe in bullying—as opposed to educating—their offspring into such values as respect for authority, respect for work, and respect for the preservation of traditional order. Verbal give-and-take is discouraged because the child should accept unquestioningly the parent's word for what is right.

The children of domineering parents often lack self-reliance and the ability to cope realistically with their problems; later they may fail or prove slow to accept adult responsibilities. They are apt to be submissive and obedient and to withdraw from the situations they find difficult. They also tend to be the sort of boys and girls who become many of the adults who have never left home, psychologically, and in many cases, physically as well.

Parental Rejection

There is a group of parents whose concern for their children is minimal and whose attitudes are casual, laissez-faire, lax, or even indifferent. For some, rejection means callous and indifferent neglect or positive hostility from the parents; but it may also be emotional and subtle. Children come to believe that they are worthless, that their very existence makes their parents unhappy. The term "emotional abuse" has been added to the concept of "physical abuse" and is defined in terms of the neglect of all or some of the basic needs of children. A list of the physical injuries that may indicate that a child has been the victim of non-accidental, abusive acts is given on p. 51.

Emotional abuse is less tangible and even more difficult to diagnose. It is defined in terms of the neglect of all or some of the basic needs of children. There follows a list (Table 8) suggested by the distinguished pediatrician and analyst, Donald Winnicott (1958).

Table 8. Basic Needs of Children

- Physical care and protection.
- Affection and approval.
- Stimulation and teaching.
- Discipline and controls that are consistent and appropriate to the child's age and development.
- Opportunity and encouragement to acquire gradual autonomy, that is, for the child to take gradual control over his or her own life.

Emotional abuse or maltreatment leaves internal scars including feelings of guilt, rage, insecurity, helplessness, anger, inferiority, and inadequacy among other feelings. Nevertheless, despite its damage and lifelong potential damage, emotional abuse is not easily seen nor readily diagnosed. In an effort to bring greater attention to emotional abuse, O'Hagan (1993) proposes that psychological abuse has the potential to damage creativity, mental processes, and intellectual and moral development of the child. The seriousness of this definition extends the meaning of emotional abuse beyond emotional response and affective responses.

The concept of emotional abuse is in danger of being over-inclusive and far too vague. It is therefore an advantage to have rather more tangible indicators to pinpoint the presence of emotional abuse. In particular there are four types of damaging parental behavior.

Indicator 1   entails punishment of positive "operant" behavior such as smiling, mobility, manipulation.

Indicator 2   is behavior that results in discouragement of parent–infant bonding, for example, pushing children away every time they seek proximity, comfort, and affection.

Indicator 3   involves the punishment of self-esteem as when parents endlessly criticize their child.

Indicator 4   is parental behavior leading to punishing those interpersonal skills (for example, friendliness) that are foundational for adequate social presence and performance in environments outside the family, such as schools, peer groups, and so on.

One might say that emotional abuse consists of behavior that seriously undermines the development of the child's competence.

A rejecting or abusive parent tends not only to ignore the offspring's need for nurturance but also to punish manifestation of that need. One would expect, therefore, that more severe forms of rejection would lead the youngster to suppress such behavior. Parents who provide little attention and care, but do not actually punish dependent behavior, are likely to intensify their offspring's needs for attention and care. The more a youngster is "pushed away" physically or emotionally, the more he or she clings.

Parental Permissiveness

Permissive parents attempt to behave in a non-punitive, accepting, and affirmative manner toward their offspring's impulses, desires, and actions; consult with them about policy decisions and give explanations for family rules. Such parents allow young people to regulate their own activities as much as possible, avoid the excessive exercise of control, and do not encourage them to obey absolute-defined standards.

Prevention

Can parents preempt the development of antisocial attitudes and behavior? Life is too unpredictable and people too mysterious and complex in their makeup to justify our saying yes in an unqualified manner. Child-care practices are subject to fashions, not to say fads. It has been generally assumed that it matters a great deal how the infant is handled, and that unless it is reared "correctly," its future could be blighted. The plain fact is that, despite much study, there is little hard evidence concerning the relationship between specific early child-rearing practices and subsequent personality development. Thus, we do not really know how early breast feeding and bottle feeding (at one time matters of solemn prescriptive concern) compare as regards their psychological consequences, or whether indeed, they make any difference. Likewise, we cannot be sure whether on-demand feeding is, or is not, better than feeding at fixed intervals, and we do not know whether early or late weaning makes a difference to the child's personality development.

Broader matters of parenting style are significant. The evidence, according to Diana Baumrind (1971), is that those parents she describes as "authoritative" tend to raise children who have high self-esteem and who cope confidently with life. These parents tend to direct their children's activities in a rational manner determined by the issues involved in particular disciplinary situations. They encourage verbal give-and-take and share with the child their reasoning behind their policy. They value both the child's self-expression and his or her respect for authority, work and the like. Baumrind points to a

143

synthesis and balancing of strongly opposing forces of tradition and innovation, divergence and convergence, accommodation and assimilation, cooperation and independent expression, tolerance, and principled intractability.

In the example of a secure, facilitative mother (for example), she appreciates *both* independent self-will and disciplined conformity. Therefore, she exerts firm control at those points where she and her child diverge in viewpoint. But she does not hem the child in with restrictions. She recognizes her own special rights as an adult, but also the child's individual interests and special ways. She affirms the child's present qualities, but also sets standards for future conduct. She uses reason as well as power to achieve her objectives. Her decisions are not based solely on the consensus of the group or the individual child's desires, but she also does not regard herself as infallible or divinely inspired. This approach to parenting has been categorized as "democratic". Many persons other than parents have an influence on children's personality and behavior. But parents can encourage a strong "immune system" in their offspring—protection against some of the stresses and snares of growing up. Such a system would depend, in part, upon:

- strong ties of affection and respect between themselves and their children;
- firm social and moral demands being made on their offspring;
- the consistent use of sanctions;
- techniques of punishment that are psychological rather than physical such as threats to withdraw approval;
- an intensive use of reasoning and explanations; and
- responsibility given to children and adolescents.

These generalizations are guidelines that you, in turn, can interpret to meet the particular values and circumstances of your clients.

Guideline 1: **Foster bonds of respect and affection.**
Such bonds tend to make all teaching endeavors much easier; the more affection there is as a foundation for disciplinary

tactics, the more notice the child will take of what he or she is being told.

Guideline 2: **Make firm social and moral demands (set limits).** This means attempting to establish and convey a reasonably coherent idea of the aims and objectives that lie behind the training and supervision of young people. Children whose parents set firm limits for them grow up with more self-esteem and confidence than those who are allowed to get away with behaving in any way they like. Supervision does not mean intrusive surveillance, but it does mean knowing where children and teenagers are, who their friends are, and so on. It is important to give the youngster a reasonable amount of freedom of choice within those limits.

Children who get their own way all the time interpret such laissez-faire permissiveness as indifference. They feel nothing they do is important enough for their parents to bother about.

Guideline 3: **Prepare children for life by developing family routines.**
Most routines are useful shortcuts to living. For example, routines help a child to master and carry out automatically such daily tasks as feeding, washing, dressing, going to bed, and helping him or her to achieve more with less effort.

Habit is taught by repetition of routine. A child feels secure if the main events of his or her day are as regular and familiar as the sunrise. If going to bed, eating, and washing always happen in more or less the same way, the child accepts them with little or no fuss. The morning ritual of preparation is a potent factor in getting a child off to school. The bedtime ritual is a particularly powerful habit; a regular routine of supper, bath, and then a story before bed make the child's world seem well-ordered, safe, and comfortable. It is not trivializing to set up these routines. Psychologists and social workers who visit chaotic homes know how disturbing the lack of routine is to young children and how unhelpful to older ones who enter the relatively orderly life demanded at school.

Guideline 4: **Teach children the family rules.**

Everyone needs some self-discipline or rules of conduct in order to adjust his or her needs and desires to those of others. Children need the affection and approval of people around them; being self-centred and egotistical will not win this approval.

The ultimate aim is to give children the ability to discipline themselves, to compromise between what they want and what society demands of them. Once they can do this, their dealings with other people will be easier.

Guideline 5: **Choose rules carefully.**

Parents are in trouble if they proliferate the "don'ts"—make demands for the sake of the demands, rules for the sake of rules. Any limit set should be for the child's or adolescent's safety, well-being, and mature, emotional, and social development. It is crucial to ensure that children know exactly what the rules and constraints are, and what is expected of them. Rules are most effective when they are relatively uncomplicated, fair, understandable, and applied fairly and consistently so that the youngster knows what will happen if they are broken.

No one can advise parents about which rules to insist upon. Every family has different values, different interpretations of what is right and wrong. Their standards of behavior will accord with those of their community or religion, as well as with their own values, lifestyles, and personalities.

Guideline 6: **Be consistent.**

When teaching your child to distinguish between appropriate and inappropriate actions, it is important to be consistent. It is confusing if he or she is punished for his or her behavior today and gets away with the same thing tomorrow merely because your reasoning or mood has changed. Parents are indignant if asked whether they ever break a promise to their child. Of course not! It would undermine the child's trust and devalue the currency of their words. Yet they may be quite unaware of idle threats they make and of the impact of such threats.

Guideline 7: **Be persistent**.
Parents often stand out against rebellious, non-compliant behavior for some time, only to give in eventually. The child will soon infer that the meaning of their parents' word is ambiguous and that if he or she makes a nuisance, the parent will give way.

Guideline 8: **Give explanations/reasons.**
Parents might well say, "I wouldn't automatically obey a regulation myself unless I thought there was a good reason for it." So why not try to explain to children, and more particularly adolescents, why we have to have rules in a complicated world, and what would happen if everyone went their own way? Children are more likely to internalize standards if they are justified in terms of their intrinsic value, rather than in terms of the punishment and odium that follow from their violation. They do need to know! When small, they cannot comprehend, unaided, the reasons for training. Later on, when in a position to understand explanations, they may be sidetracked; worse still, there may be no possible meaning to the demands made upon them, because what is being asked is unreasonable.

Guideline 9: **Tell children what they should do, not only what they can't do.**
Explain clearly to children what is required of them. Emphasize the positive, not only the negative. Notice the child in good behavior, not only naughty behavior. By attending to positive actions parents make them more likely to occur.

Guideline 10 **Giving young people responsibility gives them the opportunity to practice and to be responsible.**

Guideline 11: **Encourage parents to listen carefully to what their child says.**
When children are expected to be seen and not heard, their parents suppress undesirable behavior without paying attention to the needs and messages that lie behind it. Children's communications are often in code. As professionals or as parents we need to be empathic and to look at what they are

saying with an ear tuned to the hidden messages. Those children who show-off in front of strangers may really be communicating their uncertainty, even their shyness.

For parents, and professional people who work with children, it is vital to be able to communicate understanding. Haim Ginott (1969) is concerned that the two-way nature of good communication between adults should also form the basis of conversations with children. A dialogue with a young child requires respect and skill. He advises parents to listen carefully to what children say. Messages should preserve the child's and parents' self-respect; statements of understanding should precede statements of advice or instruction. Ginott says that in this way parents provide a mirror to their children's personality; they learn about their emotional likeness (as they get to know their physical likeness) by having their feelings reflected back to them.

The child who comes home saying, "I hate school," learns that it is not everything about school that she dislikes when her mother says, "It's been a bad day today, hasn't it; you have physical education on Monday—are you still feeling a bit embarrassed getting changed in front of the others?" Or when Tom says, "My teacher made me stay in today," parents would do well to resist the temptation to answer: "Now what have you done?" or "I suppose you deserved it," both of which would have inflamed his feelings. Instead, they might acknowledge them by saying: "You must have felt awful ... would you like to tell me what happened?"

Summary and Comment

The themes of parental responsiveness, including parent–child attachment and parental styles, are explored in this chapter. The effects of parenting variations and of physical and emotional abuse are described. Guidelines for doing preventive work with families may help facilitate pro-social behaviors and protect against antisocial behavior in children.

There is a discussion of fostering and adoption and of some of the unnecessary fears that adoptive parents have about the latter. Fortunately, it is possible to allay many of the anxieties parents have about separations and substitute care.

Responsiveness in children is another theme dealt with. The concepts of bonding and attachment are described; and there is some reassuring evidence that adverse early experiences are amenable to intervention. Despite the potential of early experiences to have lifelong impact, certainly early experiences do not lead inevitably to psychological disturbance in maturity. There is no simple remedy for poor parenting or child maltreatment. Treatment can be lengthy and costly and may be introduced long after the critical episodes have taken their toll. Prevention is effective in reducing the incidence and severity of maltreatment and in improving not only parenting skills, but also, parent–child relationships throughout much of their lives together. Prevention in the lives of individuals, in families, in communities, and in society can bring about not only changes in relationships but changes in the value placed on families and children, the very core of all of our communities and cultural groupings.

CHAPTER 7

Loss and Change Experienced by Children and Families

Psychologists have shown an increasing interest in the themes of change, loss, and gain that present in any major period of transition during our lifetime. We looked at adolescence in Chapter 5 and the task that teenagers face in mastering massive changes in their lives. It is truly a stage of transition. They lose one identity, that of child, and don another, that of adult. Here is what it feels like according to one 15-year-old:

Lately I've been in a daze, and I can't think straight. Maybe because some of my brain cells are dying and I'm just about 16. My whole world is changing. Before I used to have a regular routine and all I was concerned with was school. But now I'm thinking of my future.

The point about this, whether it is an adolescent change or some other life crisis—such as divorce, the break-up of a family, or the constituting of a new one—is that new behaviors, different responses to changing circumstances, are required.

Stages of Transition

This is where your understanding of typical reactions to major transitional events will help you to guide your clients in their efforts to cope with the difficult changes in their lives. Here are the stages that tend to occur following disruptive life experience.

Immobilization. The individual has a sense of being overwhelmed, being unable to make plans, to understand or to reason. A kind of paralysis sets in.

Minimization. The person may cope with this state of "deep freeze" by minimizing the changes. The sorrow and pain caused by a girl's bereavement due to the separation of her mother and father are minimized in her awareness. The youngster may try to trivialize the changes brought about by his new stepmother's entry into the home ("I don't know why everyone makes such a fuss over nothing"). Some children and adults will deny that a change has occurred.

Depression. Depression is a common reaction for adolescents in response to transition and loss, particularly the physical changes of puberty. Middle life and old age represent a dramatic transition in the lives of adult men and women. Don't be surprised if there is an upsurge in feelings of misery and inner turmoil for any of these groups. Misery gives way in some vulnerable individuals to more disturbing feelings of depression. Depression can be a statement of helplessness or powerlessness over events being out of, or beyond, control. Some depressed clients entertain ideas about committing suicide.

Letting go. This is the stage of accepting reality for what it is, of figuratively "letting go" of the past, which means for the toddler the dependency of infancy, for the adolescent the safety of childhood, of total parental nurturance, of childlike irresponsibility.

Testing. The "letting go" provides a bridge to the testing phase, in which the individual may begin testing him- or herself vis-à-vis the new circumstances and trying out new behaviors, skills, and even new lifestyles, to the chagrin sometimes of family and friends. At this time there can be quite a lot of anger and irritability expressed.

Search for meaning. Following this stage of activity and self-testing, there is a more gradual movement toward a search for meaning and understanding of how things are different and why this is so.

Internalization. Eventually these new meanings are internalized, taken into the "psyche" and behavioral repertoire of the individual.

151

Transitions, it is important to remember, involve considerable stress. They are most distressing if they are unpredictable, involuntary, unfamiliar, and of high intensity and magnitude and if the rate and degree of changes are excessive. Professionals can help parents and parents can help their sons and daughters by warning them of the likely changes or interpreting them, thus making them more predictable and manageable. Of course, being able to talk about personal and intimate matters to clients will depend upon a relationship of trust and good communication; in the case of parents, fostered in earlier years; in the case of professionals, nurtured over several sessions.

Childhood Bereavement

Childhood security may be shattered temporarily by the death of a loved parent or relative. The trauma can be lessened for the child through sensitive caring and explanations (see Herbert, 1996a, 1996b). The quality of the relationships as evidenced in the continuity and reassurance of loving care matters more than the disruption of bonds as such. Where ill-effects do occur, they are more likely if the mother dies when the child is very young; the father's death is more likely to have adverse effects if it occurs when the child is older.

Children are remarkable in the way in which they seem to accept the sad facts of life and get on with living. A simple, straightforward explanation of the death of a grandparent is usually sufficient, particularly if given in a calm manner.

Long-term problems are less associated with the death of a parent despite the finality of the break in an emotional attachment than it is with divorce where attachment may still be retained.

Parental Bereavement

Not all children are born and not all survive birth. Parents who experience the loss of a child prior to birth either through miscarriage or fetal death (death after the 20th week of gestation) experience psychological and emotional pain and loss. In occurrences of miscarriage in early pregnancy, the couple may experience loss and grief. The couple may progress through the stages of loss defined by Kubler-Ross (1969) in a relatively short period. For many, the anticipation of future and successful pregnancy lessens the pain. The stages of denial, anger, bargaining, depression, and acceptance in the grieving process are perhaps more difficult for the woman, whose body must readjust. Psychologically, she may have welcomed and recognized the reality of early pregnancy more deeply than the father. Unfortunately, social and cultural practices do not prepare her for the inability of most family and friends to understand her feelings of loss nor to be sympathetic to her loss, as rarely is the grief of a miscarriage felt deeply by others.

In situations of fetal death or stillbirth, socially or culturally prescribed customs are even more lacking. Some couples will want to see the infant, perhaps hold it, and may desire photographs. There may be a funeral and burial involving close family and friends where the ritual of saying goodbye brings closure and comfort at this time of loss. For some couples this difficult time of loss and grief is facilitated through the support they receive through this open process of recognizing the death of their infant. For others, the fetus may be disposed of at the hospital, and the couple may grieve in the absence of any healing ritual. In either situation, the loss is very painful. For the young couple experiencing perhaps death and pregnancy for the first time, depression and lasting inability to cope with the loss may require professional help. There is increasing recognition of the need for mothers to recognize the dead infant as a person and to grieve the loss (Germain, 1991). Recognizing the baby as a person and making the death public tend to aid the healing process for the mother and father.

When a child or teenager dies due to illness or an unexpected accident, the family experiences serious and deep loss and grief over the death of their loved one whose life was not lived to a mature end. Frequently, the process of loss is prolonged and painful. The family may seek counseling, experience severe depression, make public statements about their loved one, and always find a vacuum in their lives. For some, the stress of the experience of such severe loss may even result in separation and/or divorce. Loss of a child is extremely stressful to family members and is an experience that holds lasting pain. In these situations, helping the family come to some acceptance of the loss and to find ways to celebrate the life and memory of their child is important for all the members.

Divorce or Separation

If all divorces, all broken homes, led to serious psychological difficulties, society would indeed have an appalling problem. According to the U.S. Bureau of the Census (1993), about four out of 10 first marriages end in divorce. In other words, it is likely that young children are involved in the precipitating events and aftermath of a divorce. Most children do not want their parents to separate, and they may feel that their father and mother have not taken their interests into account. A marital separation may result in children's re-appraising their own relationships with their parents and, indeed, questioning the nature of all social relationships. For younger and middle-school age children in particular, there is the painful realization that some family relationships may not last forever. Responses of children to divorce and separation reflect coping abilities associated with their age and stage of psychosocial development.

Young children often exhibit regressive responses reflective of feelings of loss and abandonment. Pre-school children usually appear to be very sad and frightened when their parents separate, and they become very clinging and demanding. Bedtime fears and a refusal to be left alone, even for a few minutes, are not uncommon. Children attending school or nursery may become very anxious about going there and may protest strongly when left. Vivid fantasies about abandonment, death of parents, and harm are encountered. Such children often express aggression toward other children. Such fears are likely to be most acute if contact has been lost with a parent. If, however, relationships between parents and child can remain intact and supportive, these fears are lessened.

With somewhat older children, grief and sadness remain a prominent feature but anger becomes more marked. This is usually directed at the parents, especially the one with whom the child is living—which more often than not means the mother. Regardless of the actual events leading to the breakdown, she is likely to be blamed by the child for everything that has happened. The absent father is quite likely to be idealized, regardless of realities, while the mother is held responsible for driving him away. Children, especially in the age group seven to eight, may express very strong yearnings for their father.

Preadolescent children tend to demonstrate less of their inner hurt and distress, which is not to say that it does not exist. Covering-up is common, and they seek distractions in play and other activities. It may be difficult to get through to such children; they are loath to talk about what they are feeling because of the pain it causes them. Underneath this apparent detachment is often anger; again, they may align themselves very strongly with one parent and even refuse to see the other.

Children of all ages react powerfully to divorce. Adolescents sometimes show overt depression; they appear to "opt out" of family life and withdraw into other relationships outside the home. Worries about their own relationships, sex, and marriage may surface. Adolescents may have been exposed to family disputes for much of their lives, yet feel abandoned or rejected as a result of divorce in their teen years. According to Bogolub (1995), older children may be able to separate themselves from their parents' difficulties. On the other hand, older children may react with anger and self-damaging behaviors. Delinquency is associated with the break-up of homes where there has been a great deal of parental disharmony; the association is not with the disruption of the home, as such. The loss of a parent through a marital separation is much more likely to cause long-term problems than a loss through death (see Herbert, 1996b). A life-skills and behavioral counseling program for groups of divorced and separating parents, devised by Edelstein and Herbert (2000), is described in Appendix 3.

Even though all children react to divorce and break-up of their families, the resiliency of children and the ability to cope in situations of loss is immense. This is not to say that there will not be lasting memories or regret associated with the loss, but children move on in stages of their development. There are immediate reactions to parental separation. Usually they are seen in an acute form for a matter of months and then begin to subside. Studies of children's reaction to divorce vary but tend to find children to be resilient in response to family break-up. Wallerstein and Blakeslee (1989) reported that lasting emotional damage occurs for children of divorce as they fail to be adequately nurtured emotionally and carry their experience of unstable relationships into their adult lives. Amato and Keith (1991) found only minimal differences between children from divorced families as compared to children from families who remained together. Divorce has become common and is an event that impacts on children. Issues of custody, care giving, nurturance, presence of a consistent and loving parent, communication with the absent parent, and membership in extended families of both biological parents are all variables that intervene in the childhood of our children. Bogolub (1995) provides an extensive review of the literature and raises many concerns about the change in the standard of living experienced by women and children in situations of divorce.

Divorced and single-parent mothers are confronted not only with financial losses but constant care-giving demands alongside employment and career tracks as they are most likely to be the custodial parent. Many worries may deplete the last emotional resources of the mother left alone. Young children need special attention and care but she may have to seek employment. Finding substitute caregivers can be expensive. Housing, too, is a common and costly problem. Children from broken homes may fare better than youngsters from unhappy, unbroken homes. There is no room for complacency. Such relatively reassuring information is not repeated in the area of delinquency.

In situations of divorce, decreased financial resources are experienced by children from all social classes. It has been reported that children from upper-income families may experience the greatest drop in available resources and lifestyle (Furstenberg and Cherlin, 1991). In situations of children from low-income families, they will likely experience poverty, particularly in situations where their mothers lack employable skills.

About half of America's children spend some time in single-parent households, generally with their mothers who are either divorced or never married. In situations of divorce, child support is generally awarded; however, the failure of fathers to pay support has resulted in child support enforcement and interstate enforcement of collection of overdue payments (Children's Defence Fund, 1996). The seriousness of support for children is a major issue that can necessitate change in their residence, lifestyle, school achievement, and educational opportunities.

From the professional's point of view, if called in to work with a family, it is vital to appreciate how an atmosphere of strife and turmoil in the home, prior to separation, is one of the most corrosive influences. This quarreling is something that children describe as very damaging—especially episodes of hostility between mother and father.

Of the factors that are significant to a benign outcome for children—after all the misery of a divorce—three are of the utmost significance:

- communication about separation;
- continued good relationship with at least one parent; and
- satisfaction with custody and access arrangements.

Children who consider themselves most damaged are:

- those whose parents are not able talk to them about divorce (apart from blaming their ex-spouse);
- those who do not get on well with at least one parent after separation;
- those who are dissatisfied with custody and access arrangements, whatever these happen to be.

Most children would like two happily married parents, but most would prefer to live with a single parent rather than two unhappily married ones. It is a natural wish on the part of workers to keep parents and children together, but there are times when "heroic" work to maintain an intact family is counter to the best interests of all concerned. Unhappily married couples may be unable to remain together, or may have found other partners, and may be at risk for verbal abuse, domestic violence, and child abuse as frustrations end up being acted out. Domestic violence, or the risk thereof, is often an issue in cases of divorce mediation but, even though extremely dangerous, may be treated as a side issue in the mediation counseling as couples move toward divorce (Greatbatch and Dingwall, 1999). In working out reasonably healthy arrangements for divorced couples and their children, it is important for all families to manage custody arrangements wherein mother and father can continue parenting their children. Hopefully, it will be the parents' choice to be nearby and available to their absent children during their child's development to young adulthood. Nonresident parents, often due to their own work and perhaps new family commitments, travel expenses, and things like schedule challenges, are likely to make fewer in-person contacts over time with their absent children (Stewart, 1999). So often, workers know the trajectory of child development, transitions in family lives, and length of time that development and parenting extend over. Yet, it is indeed difficult to help the separating family plan for perhaps the next 15 years of shared parenting. In these situations, it is imperative that genuine regard for healthy relationships and child development be shared by separating parents, or at least that the information about the trajectory of development be part of the mediation and counseling experience.

Reconstituted Families

Reconstituted families, in which one or both partners have been married before and are combining two families into one, are a very common phenomenon. In about one out of every three marriages, one or both parents have been married before. The difficulties of being a stepchild are legendary, so are the problems of being a stepparent of such families. Research studies have confirmed these "legends." There is an increased risk of psychological problems in persons whose parents remarry, especially where it is the parent of the same sex as the child who finds a new spouse.

There are, of course, many instances of stepparents who have brought great happiness and solace to the children in their new lives. The friction, jealousy, and ambivalence which are a common feature of stepchild/stepparent relationships can be overcome with empathetic handling—trying to see things from the child's point of view. For example, if the stepchild lets herself go, and calls her stepfather "daddy" and shows him affection, might she not lose the love of her real father because of her disloyalty?

The stepparent herself (or himself) is not immune from conflict. To what extent should the stepmother try to be a "mother" when X still has a mother? Should a stepfather be permitted to discipline the child?

More devastating than the fear and jealousy aroused by remarriage may be the fear of abandonment felt by a child whose parents allow a succession of romantic attachments to take priority over their relationship with their child.

The family plan (illustrated earlier) will assist you to compare the current life tasks and life events of the various members of the "reshuffled pack"—the reconstituted family. Assess whether these individual needs and problems clash, thus adversely affecting the new family's ability to get on with life.

Single-Parent Families

The number of such households is on the increase and the lone mothers and fathers tend to have a difficult time of it. The problems tend to be the same whether parents are on their own involuntarily or from choice, because of death, divorce, separation, or through being unmarried.

You are likely to meet the assumption that children from one-parent families will have more problems than children from two-parent families, but there is little hard evidence to confirm this fear. It is our belief that children from one-parent homes are no more likely to become delinquents, drop-outs, vandals, or drug addicts than those from more "conventional" families. Such problems are related to social and economic conditions and to adverse parental attitudes and behaviors. It is not then a matter of being brought up by a single parent per se that puts children at a disadvantage, but the poverty and caretaking demand that are only too often associated with single status.

The worries that single parents may consult you about are the following:

Disciplinary problems. "Can I manage a teenage boy alone?"
Understanding. Father: "I'm not sure I have the understanding and sensitivity of a woman, for bringing up a girl."
Interests. Mother: "I can't really work up the enthusiasm and knowledge for fishing—his great love."
Sex education. Father: "How do I explain to her the facts and practical matters to do with her periods?"
Gender identity. Mother: "Will he grow up effeminate without a father to identify with?"

None of these anticipated difficulties are necessarily real problems, nor, if they are perceived by the parent as such, insuperable.

Support. The main need of a lone parent is support and then good accurate information about children and their development in special circumstances.

The man or woman alone will need financial, practical, and personal help. They need support over their feelings. Looking over your family life map can highlight the tasks and events that arouse the strongest emotional reactions in them. Review with your client their support system. Problems arise when the parents cling to their children to make up for losing their partners, requiring them to grow up prematurely and creating a kind of emotional claustrophobia. Or they may try to support their children by overcompensating for what they are missing—waiting on them hand and foot, letting them do what they like.

Substitute care. Any working mother comes to see how inadequate the facilities for full-time day care are in most areas. As we saw in Chapter 6, the need to make reliable and stable arrangements for substitute care for young children while the single parent is at work can make all the difference between a reasonable standard of living for the family and a miserable insecure existence. The choice is usually between babysitters, day-care centers, and cooperative grandparents.

If you are asked for advice about child care bear the following points in mind:

- A reliable sitter can provide stable and good-quality care.
- Choose someone who is looking after only two or three children, thus providing a family atmosphere and a personal relationship with the child.
- Interview the sitter and preferably observe her at work in her home setting.

Summary and Comment

Feelings about loss are generally associated with death, desertion, or tragedy and experienced as painful and dreaded episodes that are unwanted but inevitable in the course of life. Despite the dread and unhappiness experienced in association with loss, individuals typically are able to cope, heal, and move on to new and different stages and experiences in their lives. The healing process of coping, accepting, and entering new and different stages of life represent transitions and changes that are common to the human life experience.

This chapter about transition and change provides information about responses to change and transition, even in situations of pain and loss. Strengths exhibited by clients as they struggle to cope with major changes are reflective of their will to overcome the pain of the transition. Such strengths are evident even in difficult situations where their will to survive becomes crucial in their voyage to overcome pain and loss.

Various stages of transitional events and typical reactions are discussed in considering the experiences of change and loss. Gaining an understanding of typical reactions to major transitional events will help you to support your clients in their attempts to cope with difficult changes and trauma in their lives. The theme of change is the charge of many of the helping professions dealing, as they do, with experiences of loss, bereavement and effects of separation and divorce. These issues are discussed in some detail. The chapter endeavors to explore some of the myths surrounding substitute care, single parenthood, and reconstituted families. Common worries that single parents often experience are discussed. Some of the difficulties of rearing children alone and of step-parenting are explored. As a social worker or other helping professional, you will likely encounter some or all of these concerns in your work with families and children. This chapter describes the kinds of support and the range of systems that will be useful to your clients as they endeavor to cope with difficult situations that arise in their lives. Gaining an understanding of transitional events in the lives of your client and the characteristic reactions generated will help you to intervene in crisis situations and work with families through their process of transition, coping, and moving on with daily living.

PART III
You as Helper

The most important instrument in your work with parents and children is yourself. It is essential, therefore, to spend some time preparing yourself before you start work. There are several questions you need to ask yourself.

- **Why am I involved in this?** You may be involved in work with parents and children for a variety of reasons. We have all been children and adolescents, and many of us are parents. So we have our own experiences and prejudices; we will be immersed in family matters at both the personal and the professional levels. Whatever your reason for being involved, examine your personal motives and underlying assumptions. The area of child care is value laden; certain kinds of problems are particularly sensitive and even threatening to us. The issue of trying to help people change involves important personal, moral, and ethical considerations.

- **Do I have the right to intervene?** Behavior therapists (like others who set out to change people) are accused of controlling behavior. Such allegations imply that clients exist in a vacuum of free will before entering an intervention. Behavioral workers (for example) talk, on the one hand, of liberating clients from some of the unwanted controlling forces in their lives, but assume, on the other hand, a freedom of choice when it comes to accepting an intervention. They tend to say, as do other therapists, that if a client requires help and requests it, then help should be provided. The difficulty with this comforting principle is that people can be coerced in ways subtle and unsubtle, tangible and intangible, to "seek" help. Some clients, for example, children, are not in a position to ask for help or powerful enough to reject the offer of help. These matters should be thought through very carefully. Advocacy on behalf of the child will be an important part of your work. Indeed, advocacy on behalf of hard-pressed, demoralized mothers will be another.

- **What is my support system?** Working in a team provides an ideal support system. It is important to have people around you to back you up, share ideas, stimulate, and challenge you. You may require supervision from an experienced practitioner if you are learning to use a specialized approach like family therapy or behavior modification. If these caveats sound rather daunting then remember the positives: your potential to help individuals and families in distress and the support you can give to and gain from your colleagues. This support may be "moral"—when a colleague feels that he or she has failed with a client; it may be "technical"—a word of advice or a different and perhaps more objective perspective on the case. Commitment, knowledge, and ethical practices are important therapeutic ingredients and enhance the effectiveness of the intervention. You need to believe in what you are doing. Confidence is anti-therapeutic only when it becomes dogmatic certainty or impedes the professional's willingness to evaluate his or her work and change direction when a strategy is not working.

CHAPTER 8

Intervention: Preliminaries, Planning, and Implementation

Preliminaries

No one profession has all the skills with which to remedy the range of problems we have been looking at in Parts 1 and 2. Social workers are likely to be heavily engaged, often because of their statutory responsibilities. Members of primary care teams—GPs, nurses, and health visitors—are also in the front line. At times several professionals may be engaged in a family's life and problems, so it may be good practice to identify a key worker who coordinates and monitors a complex situation which otherwise might become confused because everyone thinks someone else is doing X, Y, or Z.

Cultural Factors

Ethnocentricity in direct social work practice can lead to embarrassment and worse if ideologies and methods are in conflict with deeply held cultural and/or religious beliefs. Let us take two examples, one from Asia and another from Africa, to illustrate how the bonding doctrine—an issue we dealt with in Chapter 7—if applied insensitively by doctors and nurses, can have disturbing repercussions. We should note that, in some Asian communities, mothers are considered unclean for the first three days after birth and close physical contact with the baby is avoided. The infant is handled by a close relative of the mother or father, depending on local custom. Some immigrant parents could feel intense conflict over "bonding procedures." Then again women from certain parts of Ghana are said to "lie between life and death" when in labor. The period of confinement is regarded as an anxious time because it is widely believed that a newborn baby may in fact be a spirit child and not a human child at all. If it is a spirit child, it will return to the spirits before a week is out. Thus for the first seven days (in some areas, three days for a boy or four for a girl) mother and child are confined to the room in which the birth took place. The parents are not allowed to mourn its loss but should show signs of joy at being rid of such an unwelcome guest. It is possible to see the "adaptive" element in such cultural beliefs; they may help parents to come to terms with death, especially in areas where there are high infant mortality rates. This is speculative; what is more certain is that when it comes to making decisions about arrangements for birth, possible bereavement, and early child care, the primary consideration should be the well-being of parents and child and a sensitivity to their personal and cultural values.

What Resources Are Available?

Parents and members of the community are important resources. Other sources of support are the:

- social worker;
- general practitioner;
- school counselor;
- educational or clinical psychologist;
- teacher;
- psychiatrist;
- child and family guidance (psychiatric clinic);
- probation officer;
- youth/community worker;
- priest/vicar/minister;
- marriage guidance counselor;
- psychotherapist; and
- police.

It is useful for workers to attend as many workshops and courses on family work as possible in order to learn and test new techniques and strategies. One advantage of working in a team is that members can pool and share their learning.

Communicating With Clients

The language you will encounter in your work could range from adult speech through teenage slang to baby talk. There is a great deal of power in language, and most parents and young people are not familiar with technical terminology. So don't put them at a disadvantage. At the same time guard against the embarrassingly artificial tone of voice and speech styles some people adopt with children (and the very elderly). Collect your own examples and metaphors that aid clients in obtaining a vivid idea or mental picture of an important concept.

The following are examples of this:

- I (MH) tell my clients to imagine that their child has an L plate on his or her back to remind them to be patient and tolerant when the child makes a mistake or forgets a lesson. They are, after all, learners about life.
- I (MH) remind them of the time they learned to ride a bike and first managed to gain balance. They continued to have a wobble and occasionally fell off. When we imagine a child has mastered a new skill (for example, not wetting his or her bed), there is still likely to be a failure or two—representing the "wobble" at the top of the learning curve.

Reviewing Goals

You would be wise to carry out a careful review of goals that have been negotiated and agreed with your clients. As a reminder:

- Goals are the changes to be sought. The goal tells you how the "target behavior" (the focus of therapeutic attention) is to be changed: whether the aim is to increase, decrease, maintain, develop, or expand the target behaviors.
- Prior to designing a program, a goal should be translated into a set of behavioral objectives. A behavioral objective specifies:
  - the desired behavior;
  - the situation in which it should occur; and
  - the criteria for deciding whether the behavioral goal has been reached.

Here is an example:

Target behavior = teasing brother.

Goal = play with brother without teasing him.

Behavioral objective = play with brother without teasing him, in the absence of mother.

Monitoring Change

Not all interventions lend themselves to the measurement of behavioral change per se. The goals, particularly if the intervention involves a counseling approach, may require an evaluation of a rather more subjective kind. On the Childwise Parent Skills Training Program (Herbert and Wookey, 1998) we have been attempting to develop methods that encompass the subtle complexities of clients' thoughts and feelings without sacrificing the requirement of rigorous monitoring of their progress.

At every session it is our practice to invite people to indicate on (for example) a –5 to +5 scale (see Figure 6) how they feel they are progressing toward the agreed goals. What we may perceive as "progress" is not always felt to be so by the client. Sometimes our own feelings of pessimism are contradicted by the client's reporting a renewed feeling of confidence and of being able to cope.

Parental involvement. The extent to which parents (or others) will be involved in the specification of behavioral objectives, observing, recording, and implementing, an intervention plan will vary. The setting and participants affect ways in which difficulties most often present themselves. A program may involve work in the consulting room, classroom or institution, the parental home, or even on the neighborhood street, and include the use of specific techniques by a professional, a significant adult, or the child.

Figure 6. An example of goal-setting and evaluation by the client

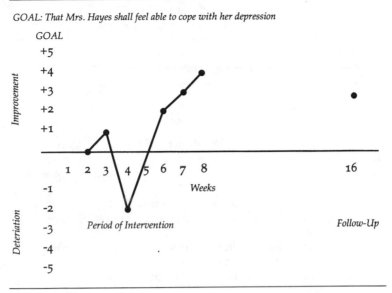

GOAL: *That Mrs. Hayes shall feel able to cope with her depression*

(From Sutton, 2000, with permission.)

Planning the Intervention

We have arrived at Stages 3 and 4 of the ASPIRE procedure which deals with planning and implementing the program. The flow chart below is a general guide only to the intervention and some of the points or procedures you need to bear in mind (see Gambrill, 1977; Hudson and McDonald, 1986).

Flow Chart 2. From Planning To Implementation

PLANNING	PHASE I
Step 1.	Consider informal and/or direct solutions.
Step 2.	Identify client's strengths.
Step 3.	Consider the wishes of those around the client.
Step 4a.	Begin with problems where success is likely.
Step 4b.	Select relevant areas of change.
Step 5.	Choose your intervention.
Step 6.	Monitor your client's progress.

IMPLEMENTATION	PHASE II
Step 7.	Implement the intervention.
Step 8.	Review your intervention.
Step 9.	Gradually fade out the program.

FOLLOW-UP	PHASE III
Step 10.	Conduct a follow-up exercise.

PHASE I: PLANNING

Step 1: **Consider informal and/or direct solutions.**
Before going further with a formal intervention, consider whether informal and/or direct approaches are worth trying. These may include:

- having medical or physical examinations—for example, a hearing defect may result in a child being viewed as disobedient and difficult;
- changing a child's bedtime routine may make him or her more likely to stay in bed and go to sleep;
- separating two children who disrupt classroom activities may stop their interaction;
- giving children responsibility may encourage them to behave more responsibly;
- making direct requests to change may be effective—for example, telling a child firmly that his teasing is causing upset to his sister and that he must stop.

Step 2: **Take an inventory of your client's strengths or positive actions.**
It is important to identify or develop new behaviors/attitudes that are positive and familiar behaviors/attitudes of the client.

Step 3: **Consider the wishes of those in the client's environment.**
This is particularly important if they are suffering as a result of the behavior and have a potential part to play in a program.

Step 4a: **Begin with those problems that have a high probability of being successfully changed.**
With success, the incentive to take on more difficult or complex behaviors will be enhanced.
Step 4b: **Select areas of change that are relevant to the individual.**

170

If changed, the client's new actions are likely to be encouraged and maintained.

Step 5: **Select your intervention approach (and specific methods).**
The choice is wide and confusing. Some of the options are listed in Chapters 9 to 12. Whatever method you use, it is desirable to monitor your client's progress.

Step 6: **Monitor ("track") your client's progress (or lack of it).**
Choose a method of measuring or assessing the behavior that reliably estimates the extent of the problem, which can be used conveniently, and which does not involve redundant information. Although there are various sophisticated procedures for assessing behavior, for most programs straightforward and simple methods are adequate.

The three main methods of assessing behavior are by rating the difficulties (see Figure 3b, page 36), recording how often the behavior occurs (known as frequency counting or event recording and illustrated in graphical form in Figure 7).

Figure 7.   A graphical record of progress in treatment

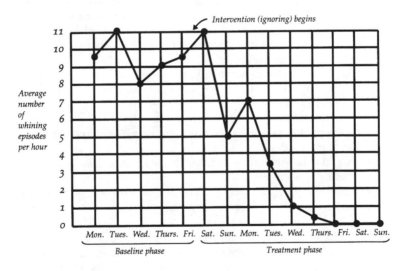

PHASE II: IMPLEMENTATION

Step 7: **Implement the intervention.**
Begin your intervention. Keep a close watch on what happens in the early stages to ensure that the program is being followed correctly and any unforeseen problems that arise are dealt with quickly. This may mean contact by visiting or phoning the parents every two or three days in the first week or so.

Data collection begun in the baseline period continues throughout the intervention period.

Step 8: **Review your intervention.**
In the light of the data collected relating to the target behavior(s), or any other objective information, it may be necessary to modify or change the intervention in some way. In the case of behavioral work the program is *flexible* and if the chosen target behavior is not changing after a reasonable period of time (e.g. two weeks—although there is no set time), review all aspects of the work.

One of the features of behavioral work is that it is "an approach" rather than a technique. This means that if your intervention is not working, examine most carefully the behavior of all participants and the program, and change (if necessary) some features of the intervention. If you have the "story" about the "why's" of the case right (see Chapters 11 to 12) any difficulties are likely to be traced to the application of the approach rather than the approach *per se*.

Ask the following questions:

- Are there powerful competing reinforcers or interfering factors in the client's environment operating against the program? Can these be modified?
- Are the reinforcers well chosen and effective?
- Is the parent working effectively and being reinforced for his or her participation?
- Are the behavioral objectives realistic? Are they within the client's repertoire?
- Have you proceeded too quickly? Is it necessary to go back to an earlier stage in the intervention plan?

Step 9: **Phase out and terminate treatment.**
Do this with care: the durability of any improvements may depend upon it. The decision to terminate treatment should be made jointly with your client. The time for the program to end depends upon the goals established at the beginning of treatment. New or elaborated

goals may emerge during the intervention. Try to ensure natural, intermittent reinforcement in the child's different settings. A guideline is to teach only those behaviors that will continue to be rewarded after training, provided they are adaptive in the sense of contributing to the child's effectiveness and well-being and that of the community.

PHASE III: FOLLOW-UP
Contact your client(s) to check on the maintenance over time ("temporal generalization") of the improvements they made.

Step 10: **Conduct a follow-up exercise.**
You may find the following questions useful in a semi-structured interview:

- When did the program end? ... How long did it take? ...
- How would you describe the situation with X now?
- What were your original "target" behaviors?
- Have any of these behaviors reoccurred (frequency)?
- How badly (intensity)?
- When, where, and how often?
- How would you describe your relationship with X now?
- Do you still worry about X?
- Do you now feel more in "control" than you did before?
- Do you spend more time playing and talking with X?
- Do you find it easier to praise X than you did before?
- Has the amount of physical contact between X and yourself changed more/less?
- Has your relationship with your other children changed?
- Have X's relationships with his/her brothers and sisters changed?
- Has X's father changed in his attitude to X?
- Has X's behavior toward his/her father changed?
- Do you feel that your relationship with your husband has changed?
- Do you think the program worked/failed?
- Who or what made it work/fail?
- How would you describe your relationship with the therapist?

An Illustration of an Intervention

We left Avril's family in Chapter 4; we decided to initiate an intervention. Her mother now takes up the story.

From the beginning of the psychologist's visits my feelings were mixed! First of all there was a feeling of relief. Something was at last being done. Something concrete. I was going to be helped. For a short while I felt euphoric ... but I was defensive as well because I knew that I must accept a certain responsibility for the way Avril was. I did not want to do that. I had had enough of failure. But I recognized I would have to face up to the truth if I went ahead with a management program. It was quite a struggle at times and my pride took quite a battering. I was very pleased that all the work in the program was going to take place in the home. It seemed natural and logical that it should.

There were problems in initiating the program as Avril's mother says:

At the beginning of Dr H's intervention, however, I was unable to cooperate effectively. I was desperately unhappy and depressed with no clear understanding of how I came to be so. Each day I moved through a suffocating fog of failure, frustration, and guilt. Myself I saw as an unattractive and undesirable individual. I felt that my intellect had atrophied. My daily round of housework and child rearing held no rewards, but left me bored and exhausted. Against this background a natural shyness had developed into a real fear of going out and talking to people. The fear of rejection was greater than the fact of loneliness. My home had become a prison. Because of these feelings, Dr H decided to work on two levels: with the family on Avril's management program and with myself—a total lack of social and personal confidence with its resulting social isolation for the child as well as myself; the accumulating anger from failing to cope with her. The angry feelings gradually eased as Avril's program progressed and I learned to express the resentment I felt when she misbehaved, but in a more controlled manner, by giving appropriate commands. We discussed my parents' way of bringing me up and how it had influenced my attitudes. The hardest problem to deal with was the self-doubt and isolation. Being depressed for several years and feeling inadequate had eroded my self-confidence and produced a profound dislike for myself. It was necessary to change that before I could look up and outwards.

Dr H asked me to role-play as a means of learning new ways of coping with my fears and suspicions of people. I started by writing a self-portrait. Dr H took each point and changed it to some extent. Where I was serious, introverted, careful, I was to be rather more spon-

174

*taneous and impulsive, even a little frivolous without "overdoing" it.
I was to think and act like an attractive woman; in fact we created a different "persona" and role to my usual ones, but not too far out to make
the task impossible. We went over it in great detail like a script.*

*The next step was not easy. What I had to do was go out and live
my role daily. It was certainly very difficult at first. I felt like a second-
rate actor with severe stage fright. But the remarkable thing was how
it gradually became easier, and when the results were good I felt elated.
I discovered casual conversations with local mothers in the park and
shopping soon unearthed common interests. I gradually developed new
friendships with women in similar circumstances to myself, all with
children for Avril and Stella to play with. For the first time since
Avril's birth we were making regular visits outside the immediate
family. Social skills are like any other; the more practice you get the
better you become. As my confidence grew with each success so Avril
also relaxed and she began to look forward to these visits eagerly.*

*Throughout this period, during which there were regularly held dis-
cussions about my own situation and problems, we also worked with
Mrs—(a social worker) on Avril's problems.*

Selection of Goals for Treatment

Treatment objectives were negotiated between the therapists
and the parents. The first goal was to increase adaptive behaviors in certain specified situations, as identified by the parents,
with the main aim of creating opportunities for Avril to win
positive reinforcement for socially appropriate behavior. There
were four specified situations, one of which was putting away
her toys. The second goal was to reduce the frequency of five
target behaviors specified during assessment: (1) non-compliance; (2) aggression; (3) whining; (4) commanding; and (5)
tantrums. All were carefully defined.

It should be noted that the introduction of the positive side
of the program (rewards) was not a smooth one. There arose a
series of disputations between mother or father and Avril about
incentives. It was evident that we had planned a reward system
that contained several loopholes as far as a perceptive and
resourceful entrepreneur like Avril was concerned. As so often
happens in behavior programs, we had to think again. A

detailed plan was worked out with regard to the behaviors that the parents wished to encourage. A more careful contract was designed, one which specified precisely how the parents were to respond. The parents and therapist spent much time going over precisely what both parents were going to say when they issued commands to her. What came through very forcibly was that both parents tended to indulge in an internal debate when action was required (for example, the removal of Avril from the room, the technique called "time-out"). They would silently argue with themselves, "Should I?" or "Shouldn't I?" before they gave Avril a command. They were often reluctant to carry through a threatened sanction, feeling "sorry" for her or guilty afterward. My ploy in cases like this is to ask the parents if they would break a promise to give their child a treat. The inevitable denial and explanation of the importance that a child should trust one's words invites a discussion about breaking promises about punishment and the consequent debasement of the currency of words and trust.

Precise cues were suggested to the mother so that she might avoid these agonizing dilemmas and so she could act at the right time in a decisive manner. Authoritative commands, it was hoped, would nip Avril's target behaviors in the bud and prevent their unpleasant repercussions. On the consequential side, it was suggested that when she tried her delaying strategies, at the point of implementing time-out, she was to be picked up, with no eye-contact and no verbal communication, and placed in the hall (for three minutes), thus eliminating the attention she was gaining from her diversions. The response to this detailed plan was encouraging and the frequency of some of the target behavior began to diminish.

A critical point came at about the sixth week of the program. Mrs Hayes became very despondent about the program, feeling that Avril's target behavior of aggression was not responding to her efforts. But despite the protestations, hostility, and resentment that she expressed to the therapist, she persevered. Reinforcement in the form of encouragement and praise is as important to the mediators of change in the child as to the problem child herself. After all, they are being asked to change "addictive" or reinforced habits and are in a learning situation too.

The frequency of the target behaviors decreased gradually. The record showed that from baseline frequency, non-compliance had reduced by 54 percent, aggression had fallen by 68 percent, tantrums by 95 percent, commanding by 94 percent, and whining by 100 percent. Whining responded most swiftly to systematic ignoring (see Figure 7).

By the end of the program there was an average occurrence for both non-compliance and aggression of less than one per day. As Avril's positive behaviors increased, there were more opportunities for the parents to "enjoy" her which in themselves stimulated a high degree of mutual social reinforcement.

Termination

This phase came at the end of 12 weeks of treatment. Mrs Hayes faded out the token reinforcement program but retained the use of positive social reinforcement (on an intermittent schedule—that is, an occasional basis—consistent with real life) and the occasional use of time-out as a back-up to her now generally effective verbal control. The goals that were selected for treatment were achieved to the satisfaction of both parents. This expression of satisfaction, which was confirmed by the monitoring of Avril's behaviors, constituted the main criteria for terminating the case. As a by-product of the program, Avril now gave the appearance of being a far happier child to the therapist, her parents, and their relatives. Mrs Hayes no longer looked the harassed woman of the not-too-distant past. She now had a lightness in the presentation of her personality.

Follow-Up

A series of checks by telephone and visits indicated that Avril maintained her improvement for 12 months (our standard follow-up period). Mrs Hayes felt that she had successfully reintroduced the program for short periods as and when it was necessary. She experienced a setback when she let her criteria slip and began to take the line of least resistance. A booster program was contemplated, but within a week of going back to recording, Mrs Hayes found that she had the situation in hand, and the need for an intervention disappeared.

Summary and Comment

This chapter outlined the 10 steps common to many interventions. There is no one way (or set order) for doing these things—preliminaries, planning, and initiation—but they may prove helpful to those who wish to work in accordance with a systematic plan. The importance of the key worker is stressed; as is the need for sensitivity to cultural nuances illustrated with examples from Asian and African attitudes to birth and death. Resources that are likely to be of help to you and your client are listed.

The chapter contains a case illustration that provides the reader with an insight into what it feels like to be involved in an intervention—in the mother's own words. Many of the details of therapy—the selection of goals, their monitoring, the program itself, and its termination—are provided.

CHAPTER 9

The "How" Question: Helping People to Change

This chapter on how to help clients—the question of approaches—is written with several professions (but most particularly social work) in mind. One of the main difficulties for those who work with families is to find a reasonably clear, signposted path through the "jungle" of claims and counterclaims, contradictions and ambiguities, concerning the best way of going about things. Which approach do I use, and when? There is a bewildering array of choices including: family therapy, behavior modification, counseling, various brands of psychotherapy, cognitive therapy, skills training, and many others. The literature is not always helpful or easy to understand and incorporate in practice.

Is it best to be eclectic or is eclecticism somewhat disreputable in psychological circles? If it is, it shouldn't be; psychology has been forced to abandon general (i.e. all-encompassing) theories of human action in favor of more modest, middle-range theories dealing with different aspects of psychological functioning (for example, learning, cognition, personality). Even these theories tend to be fragmented and contentious. So why should practitioners eschew an informal eclecticism? The trouble is that eclecticism so often degenerates into a fragmented, unsystematic approach—a choice of what is fashionable, seems easy, or "feels comfortable," as opposed to what is theoretically coherent and empirically supported (see Schaffer, 1990).

The task of helping a family can be a dauntingly broad one, encompassing (for the social worker) concerns ranging from poor housing and the need for day care for a worker, to marriage guidance and "systematic desensitization" for a phobic child. The practitioner's role might consist of being a resource-mobilizer, helper, friend, adviser, teacher, therapist, or counselor, and possessor of expert know-how of strategies for social action. Such diversification calls for a remarkably flexible response on the part of the practitioner. The scope of the analysis and level of intervention can also range widely, from the large grouping (the neighborhood or community) through the small group (the family), the couple (parents or partners) to the particular individual (child or adult).

This is not only a book about social work as such, but there is room to underline the importance in any intervention of mobilizing human resources—activating or reactivating helpers, friends, and social networks. There is evidence that a network of supportive persons and the quality and intimacy of the support provided can mitigate the effects of stress. The generalist practitioner in the social work profession has a range of interventive techniques and a broad understanding of working with individuals, families, and communities at the various interfaces of personal and social systems. The generalist social worker carries out practice processes, or intervention processes, across various system levels. At this level, the generalist is very helpful in resource delivery, social policy development and analysis, development of various delivery structures, and in intervening in various human and social problems. Understandably, the generalist social worker is not expert in all practices or with all problems; instead, this professional is skilled in the processes of applying practice knowledge and skills in various human and social systems, including various networks that facilitate bringing resources and support systems together. The skilled generalist can extend resources far beyond the interventive skills of a single professional helper by the brokering and linkage processes involved in mobilizing help and resources for various problems and at various levels of social and human systems (Mattaini, 1998).

Mobilizing Human Resources

A professional can assist his or her clients by putting them in touch with people, clubs, specialized self-help groups, and other resources. Surveys have shown that one important way in which people cope with their problems is to turn to family and friends rather than to professionals for help and they, in turn, act as a buffer against some of the harmful effects of stress. As social networks, ties, and contacts promote psychological well-being, it is important for the professional to identify their presence or absence for the client. Ascertain the frequency and intimacy (the meaningfulness/emotional intimacy) of this support for your clients using the rating scale in Table 9. Intimate or close relationships of the type provided by primary groups (those people with whom one has face-to-face interaction and a sense of commitment) are the most significant sources of support. The supportiveness of relationships is reflected by the availability of:

- emotional support (the expression of liking, respect, etc.);
- aid (material assistance, services, guidance, advice);
- social companionship;
- affirmation (the expression of agreement); and
- social regulation (appropriate roles support such as mothering, fathering, partnership—husband/wife/companion, etc.).

Different kinds of support are helpful for different life crises. And the particular persons and circumstances involved in a potentially disruptive life event determine what is likely to be most effective. The support of peers and encouragement at work are positively related to well-being.

Table 9. Sources of Support and Intimacy

	Frequency					Meaningfulness (importance)				
	Never	Hardly ever	Quite often	Often	Always (regularly)	None	A little	Quite a lot	A lot	Of great significance
A partner	0	1	2	3	4	0	1	2	3	4
Parents	0	1	2	3	4	0	1	2	3	4
Other relatives	0	1	2	3	4	0	1	2	3	4
Children	0	1	2	3	4	0	1	2	3	4
Friends	0	1	2	3	4	0	1	2	3	4
Neighbors	0	1	2	3	4	0	1	2	3	4
Colleagues/ workmates	0	1	2	3	4	0	1	2	3	4
Other parents	0	1	2	3	4	0	1	2	3	4
Acquaintances	0	1	2	3	4	0	1	2	3	4
	How often can you expect help and support from:					How meaningful/significant is the help and support you get from:				

Marital Work

There has been a lot of research into the adjustments required of married and co-habiting couples, into the conflicts, manipulations, and changes that take place in the course of a marital relationship or some other form of intimate partnership. The emphasis on conflict and manipulation is somewhat misleading. The evident fact is that in many ongoing marriages there is great deal of interaction which is playful, complementary, and joyous, as well as much that is hostile. The fact that most marriages survive, and are judged to be happy, indicates that the majority of adjustments are fairly satisfying.

A process of bargaining may underlie some of the similarities in marriages of long duration. It is one of the great platitudes—part of popular wisdom—that marriage is a matter of give-and-take. We saw, in Chapter 4, that people initiate and prolong relationships of intimacy as long as those relationships are reasonably satisfactory with regard to what are called their "rewards" and "costs." In marital interactions the social exchange model helps us to assess (in part) what is going wrong with a partnership. For example, immature individuals are not always able to manage the give-and-take of friendship. What is called "exchange theory" gives us pointers to why this should be so; it also provides one method of improving people's social attractiveness and their relationships. In this theoretical model, social interactions and relationships are compared to economic bargains or the exchange of gifts. All activities carried out by one individual, to the benefit of another, are termed "rewards," while detrimental activities—hostility and anxiety—are seen as "costs."

A notable feature of a partnership that is "working" is the balance in the relationship that exists between the partners, often called "status symmetry." It concerns the mutual respect and lack of dominance and exploitation that characterize intimate and lasting relationships. In friendly or loving relationships there is an overall balance in the influence of each of the participants.

It is useful to draw up a balance sheet. On the debit side, the term "cost" is applied to deterrents that may be incurred in contacts with another person—such as criticism, neglect, hostility, anxiety, embarrassment, and the like. For attraction to another individual to occur (or to be maintained) the reward–cost outcome must be above the "comparison level," a standard against which satisfaction is judged.

In this model marital discord is dealt with by redistributing (with the help of a contract) prevailing rates of reinforcement (satisfaction) and punishment (dissatisfaction) within the relationship. Individuals are encouraged—following discussion, negotiation, and (hopefully) compromise—to maximize satisfaction while minimizing the dissatisfaction provoked by the couple. This is where contracts can be very useful, not only for marital work but for family relationships that are tense and unhappy (Sheldon, 1980). An example of a marital work contract is given in Figure 8.

At times of crisis brought about by the loss and disorganization that follow the break-up of a home, there is a double jeopardy for many children: the "loss" of the leaving parent and the "emotional loss" of the remaining parent, insulated often in grief and in shock (see Edelstein and Herbert, 2000; and Appendix 3, Separation and Divorce: Helping Parents and Children Cope with the Aftermath).

Family Therapy

There are many variants: the Milan Systemic Approach (Tomm, 1984), the McMaster Family Model (Epstein, *et al.*, 1983); de Shazer's Brief Family Therapy (de Shazer, 1985); Problem-solving therapy, (Haley, 1987); Social Network Therapy (Speck and Atneave, 1974), to name but a few. Not surprisingly, there are significant differences when it comes to defining the activity of treatment covered by the rubric "family therapy". What unites most family therapists as they engage in their divergent treatment strategies is a perspective which requires that children's problems be understood as the consequence of the pattern of recursive behavioral sequences that occur in dysfunctional family systems. As Jordan and Franklin (1995: 199) put it in an orchestral metaphor:

> *...understanding individual family members without understanding the whole family system would be like trying to understand a concert by listening to the instruments one by one. All the instruments syn-*

Figure 8.   A sample contract

CONTRACT between James and Nell Small

We: (he) and   (she) have decided together to improve our relationship, and with that in view we have jointly agreed to do our level best to put into practice the following rules and to monitor progress. In doing this our goal is (i) to make changes in our behaviors and attitudes, and (ii) to become more aware of our own (and our partner's) point of view. We will make the following changes:

He

1. Be more ready to say sorry,
2. Control my irritability and temper.
3. Show more interest in my wife's appearance.
4. Sit down for a chat for at least half-an-hour when I get home from work.
5. Refrain from making fun of her friends and church activities.
6. Help with jobs around the house.

She

1. Stop interfering when he corrects the child.
2. Be more relaxed about things.
3. Show more interest in my husband's work.
4. Be more ready to forgive and forget.
5. Be willing to make physical contact (e.g., not to pull away when he holds my hand, puts his arm around me).
6. Remember to check that there is gas in the car.

We do not guarantee 100% success at first, but we are committed to trying to make things work. In the case of rules being broken we agree to sit down and go over the particular disappointing incident *calmly*.

We also agree to keep a record of progress.

Signed _____ (He)

_____ (She)

---

chronised together with their own unique chords, rhythms, and arrangements is what makes the music. Similarly, the way families synchronise together as a group accounts for the functional and dysfunctional behaviour patterns of their members.

This perspective, influenced by a General Systems or Cybernetic paradigm is an attempt to understand living organisms in a holistic way, but it was many years later, in the 1950s that practitioners such as Jackson (1957) applied it to work with families. The systems approach as it translates to family work embraces the concept of reciprocal/circular causation in which each action can be considered as the consequence of the action preceding it and the cause of the action following it. No single element in the sequence controls the operation of the sequence as a whole because it is itself governed by the operation of the other elements in the system. Thus any individual in a family system is affected by the activities of other members of the family, activities which his or her actions or decisions (in turn) determine. An individual's behavior is both stimulus and response.

Family therapists, whatever their methods and theoretical underpinnings, tend to believe that behavior problems in children are symptomatic (or, indeed, artifacts) of dysfunctional family life; the goal of treatment is therefore the improvement of family functioning. Family therapists help families to move from entrenched habits—individual behaviors and interpersonal interactions—which preclude them from finding solutions to the problems of life that confront them. The members are encouraged by a variety of therapeutic strategies and homework tasks to feel and act differently in order to understand the alliances, conflicts, and attachments that operate within the family unit. Clients are encouraged to look at themselves from a fresh perspective and to seek alternative solutions to their dilemmas. For the purposes of this book, we draw from several approaches, particularly the structural approach to family treatment. From this approach we consider systems, subsystems, boundaries, and rules that influence family members in their efforts to find balance in their relationships with others in the family.

In order to understand the family pattern across the generations (the extended family) and the alliances, conflicts, and attachments within the family unit, clients are encouraged to look at themselves from a fresh perspective and to try alternative solutions to their dilemmas. The structural approach to producing family change is associated with (among others) the name Salvador Minuchin (1974) and the Philadelphia Child Guidance Clinic. The focus of attention is very much on the developmental tasks faced by the family and its members at various stages of its (and their) life span. Day-to-day patterns of relationship—communication and interaction—between members are inferred from highly charged or repetitive sequences observed and analyzed in the therapy room. You can see from all of this that the therapeutic task is defined in far broader terms than the individual—be it parent or child. The child—brought to the clinic as the "patient" or "client" by the parents—would be viewed as one part of a complete network of personal and family relationships.

Family therapists see the total network of family transactions as greater than the sum of its parts, hence their rejection of the parents' labeling of a problem as "my son's/daughter's problem" as simplistic. The family system is viewed as the total functioning of three subsystems (spouses, parents and children, children alone)—all contained within a defined boundary and, in turn, operating within a social-cultural context.

The family changes continuously. For example, as children grow into adolescents they bring new elements into the family system. The peer group gains more influence. The youngster learns that friends' families work by different standards and rules. The teenage culture introduces its values with regard to sex, religion, politics, and drugs. Parents, too, are changing in resonse to life events, stresses, and parenting demands in a changing world as described in Chapter 3.

Assessment and Intervention

Empirical assessment models have been derived from research on the classification and assessment of family functioning and clinical work with families. Examples are: the Olson Circumplex Family Model (Olson, 1986); the McMaster Family Model (Epstein, *et al.*, 1983), and the Beavers Systems Models (Beavers and Hampson, 1990). Jordan and Franklin (1995) provide a useful review of methods and critical issues in this area of assessment. A most important person not to be left out of the assessment is the referrer (Palazzoli, *et al.*, 1978)—the one who has identified the problem as needing a solution. The major concepts for an assessment and formulation in family therapy are listed by Dare (1985) as follows:

1) Seeing the family as having an overall structure.
2) Understanding the symptom as having a potential function.
3) Understanding the location of the family on the life cycle.
4) Understanding the intergenerational structure of the family.
5) Making an overall formulation linking the preceding four features.
6) Linking the formulation to appropriate interventions.

There are family therapists who neglect to assess the influence of wider social systems (e.g. school, neighborhood, socio-cultural network). Their concentration on therapy with nuclear families within clinical settings tends to impose a form of "tunnel vision" of family life and difficulties. Such therapists, have allowed their vision of assessment in family work to become myopic. The family replaces the person/patient as the locus of pathology. The social context is played down as a source of influence. It is an article of faith that the outward and visible signs of the families' problems, as manifested to a group of observers/commentators behind a one-way screen, represent reliably, what is going wrong. A common criticism of family therapy has to do with the nature of evidence: what it should be; where it should come from; what is its status? How representative of a family's repertoire the samples of interaction (sometimes distorted by observer effects) seen in the clinic are likely to be, is a crucial issue.

Treacher and Carpenter (1984) question whether neglect of the wider social content of families—when they are being assessed—can be justified at a theoretical level. They maintain that it is often best effected by an intervention at another system level. For example, a worker who is attempting to produce change in the family which is experiencing many problems may be better advised to assist in the formation of a housing action group, designed to influence the housing department, than to concentrate on a more limited goal of defining boundaries between the members of a family who are crowded into a small, damp and decaying flat.

Family therapy and individual counseling/psychological therapy tend to be polarized by some theorists—unnecessarily, in the author's opinion. The skills of working individually with members of a family are often indispensable to the systems approach—especially when the therapeutic task is to help a child or adolescent to learn social skills, to overcome a phobia or to cope with an attention deficit. The either/or dichotomy of symptom reduction vs systemic reorganization simply does not apply to some casework, where either or both approaches might be called for.

Assessment. Typically, an assessment by a family therapist (see Lask, 1980) might concern itself with whether there is:

1) too great a distance between members of the family leading potentially to emotional isolation and physical deprivation;
2) excessive closeness between members of the family leading potentially to over-identification and loss of individuality;
3) an inability to work through conflicts, solve problems, or make decisions;
4) an inability on the part of parents to form a coalition and to work together, with detrimental effect on the marriage and/or the children;
5) an alliance across the generations disrupting family life as when a grandparent interferes with the mother's child-rearing decisions;
6) poor communication between members; and
7) a failure to respond appropriately to each other's feeling.

Some of the ways in which a child may contribute (wittingly or unwittingly) to a family's inability to cope with conflict have been described by Lask (1980):

1. *Parent–child coalition*, where one parent attacks the other, using one of the children as an ally.
2. *Triangulation*, where both parents attempt to induce a child to take *their* side.
3. *Go-between*, where a child is used to transmit messages and feelings.
4. *Whipping-boy*, where one parent, instead of making a direct attack on the other, uses their child as a whipping-boy.
5. *Child as weapon*, where one parent attacks the other using the child as a weapon.

6. *Sibling transfer*, where the children agree to divert the parents from arguing.

Intervention Techniques

Piercy *et al.* (1986) identified 54 techniques useful in family therapy and provided a much broader discussion of these numerous techniques. We identify only a few intervention techniques particularly useful in our discussion of intervening in the family.

- *Enactment* is the direct illustration by the clients (as opposed to mere description) of the problems that exist between them. Clients are encouraged, where appropriate, to talk directly to one another rather than to (or through) the therapist.
- *Boundary clarification*. The creation of clarification of boundaries between family members is a feature of structural work. A mother who babies her teenager may hear with surprise her daughter's response to the question "How old do you think you mother treats you as—three or 13?"
- *Changing space*. Asking clients in the therapy room to move about can intensify an interaction or underline an interpretation being made about a relationship. For example, if a husband and wife never confront one another directly but always use their child as a mediator or channel of communication, the therapist blocks that manoeuvre (called triangulation) by moving the child from between the parents. Here she may comment, "Let's move Sally from the middle so you can work it out together."
- *Re-framing* is an important method in fulfilling the objective of helping clients in a covert—less directed—manner. It is an alteration in the emotional or conceptual viewpoint in relation to which a situation is experienced. That experience is placed in another "frame" which fits the facts of the situation as well (or more plausibly), thereby transforming its entire meaning. Giving people different "stories" to tell themselves about themselves or about events—stories that are less self-defeating or destructive—is also a feature of behavioral work.

There are many models of family therapy in use throughout the maze of service organizations and broad array of practitioners. The effectiveness of various family therapies, as compared with other models, is a complex issue and one that continues to be of interest to researchers. Effectiveness and efficiency of various modalities of working with families is of concern to managed care and case management organizations in this day of cost containment and high demand for service. Effectiveness of various family therapies and related concerns are discussed in reviews by Herbert (1998b) and Reimers and Treacher (1995).

Improving Relationships Within the Family

All social interaction involves mutual influence because of human interdependence and the key role of cooperation in human societies. This influence is most potent when it has its source within a happy and cohesive family. Indeed the presence of family cohesion has a marked effect on the psychological well-being of family members. Factors indicating a degree of cohesion are:

- Members spend a fair amount of time in shared activity.
- Withdrawal, avoidance, and segregated (separate) activities are rare.
- Interactions that are warm are common, and interactions that are hostile are infrequent among members.
- There is full and accurate communication between members of the family.
- Valuations of other members of the family are generally favorable; critical judgments are rare.
- Individuals tend to perceive other members as having favorable views of them.
- Members are visibly affectionate.
- Members show high levels of satisfaction and morale, and are optimistic about the future stability of the family group.

When these features are absent, the family members who are particularly at risk are those already vulnerable for other reasons: the young, the elderly, those coping with stress such as hospitalization, alcohol dependence, or caring for a large number of children. The list above indicates areas on which you might focus in order to encourage more cohesive activities and attitudes. Contracting—mentioned already and discussed more fully later in this chapter—could facilitate such an objective.

Behavioral Approaches

Behavioral therapy represents a theory (indeed a philosophy) of treatment and behavior change rooted in broad, empirically based theories of learned human behavior, but today it draws upon principles from several branches of experimental psychology such as social and developmental psychology and cognitive science. It differs from earlier therapeutic traditions in finding its origins in controlled laboratory experiments on learning processes conducted on animals and humans (e.g. Pavlov, 1927; Skinner, 1953) rather than clinical casework (e.g. Freud, 1946). Traditional psychotherapy is not a natural science, even though the value of various of its methods and theories has been empirically validated (see Lee and Herbert, 1970). On the other hand it is the proud claim (which has gone unchallenged) that behavior therapy enjoys a scientific status which stands in sharp contrast to alternative therapies, notably psychoanalytic psychotherapy.

At its simplest level there are certain basic learning tasks that are commonly encountered in child therapy: (1) the acquisition (learning) of a desired response in which the individual is deficient (e.g. compliance, self-esteem, self-control, bladder and bowel control, fluent speech, social or academic skills); and (2) the reduction or elimination (unlearning) of an unwanted response in the child's repertoire (e.g. self-deprecatory self-talk, aggression, temper tantrums, stealing, facial tics, phobic anxiety, compulsive eating) or the exchange of one response for another (e.g. self-assertion in place of tearful withdrawal). Each of these tasks (and potential ameliorative methods) may be served by one or a combination of the four major types of learning: *operant* and *classical* conditioning; *observational* and *cognitive learning*. Although contemporary behavioral therapies continue to draw on their original stimulus—response theories in the application of operant and classical conditioning methods, as Kazdin in his 1978 history observes, the behavior approach has grown and diversified a long way from the monolithic enterprise it was in the late 1950s and early 1960s.

The Behavioral Therapies (Herbert, 1987a; 2001)

The use of the plural "behavioral therapies" indicates the distance traveled in theoretical sophistication and range of application, in the four decades since operant and classical conditioning principles of learning were first applied systematically to the clinical problems of children and adolescents. The names of the various therapies which, to varying degrees, are rooted in behaviorism represent milestones on a journey of ever-increasing conceptual elaboration and theoretical inclusiveness: applied behavior analysis, behavior modification, behavior therapy, cognitive-behavior therapy, behavioral psychotherapy, behavioral casework, behavioral family therapy and functional family therapy (see Herbert, 1994, 2001). The central theoretical assumption of behavioral work is that much abnormal behavior and cognition in children is on a continuum with normal (non-problematic) behavior and thought. These phenomena do not differ, by and large, from their normal counterparts in their development, their persistence, and the way in which they can be modified. The laws of learning that apply to the acquisition and changing of normal functioning (e.g. socially approved) behavior and attitudes, are assumed to be relevant to the understanding of dysfunctional actions and cognitions. Of course, there is much more to learning and learning to behave dysfunctionally than is conveyed by influences from the environment. For example, there may be a learned behavioral, cognitive or affective overlay to problems which have an organic basis—conditions such as epilepsy or an adverse constitutional (temperamental) predisposition—and which are therefore accessible to some alleviation by behavioral methods.

Behavioral work starts from a clear objective of producing planned, goal-directed change. Behavior therapy based on the one-to-one (dyadic) or behavioral family therapy (systemic) model tends to take place in the clinic. Behavioral training based on the triadic or behavioral consultation model (using significant caregivers or teachers as mediators of change) generally takes place in the home, or is geared to the home. It may be located in a school or, when it involves group work, in a community center. Although the distinction between treatment and training is at times indistinct, the treatment model is most appropriate to the emotional disorders of childhood (e.g. fears and phobias) and the training model to the longer-term problems (e.g. antisocial behavior and pervasive developmental disorders).

A Social Learning Approach to Family Violence

Concern about aggression and violence in society, both outside and within the family, has reached such a pitch that a note of despair, and sometimes hysteria, is now common in the media.

As a general principle, we can confidently claim that the maintenance of aggressive behavior is largely dependent on its consequences (and this might include "letting off steam" by a frustrated parent) and tends to be repeated, whereas those that are unrewarded or punished are generally discarded.

Coercive families. In what have been called coercive families the cues or messages are frequently negative ones, with the "sound and fury" of criticism, nagging, crying, shouting, hitting and so on. Communication between members may not be so much aversive as impoverished or practically non-existent. Sitting down to negotiate a contract with members of the family facilitates communications and introduces them to an important means of resolving interpersonal conflicts and tension of the kind that arise in the family—discussion, negotiation, compromise.

It is all very well to negotiate a contract, but what goes into it? We have to remember that coercive family systems which permit behavioral control by the use of pain are quite likely to produce children who exhibit frequent aggressive actions. Negative reinforcement is most likely to operate in certain closed social systems where the child must learn to cope with aversive stimuli such as incessant criticism. In such a family a boy will find that his violent actions (e.g. hitting) terminate much of the aversive stimulation—teasing, bullying, and so on—from his brothers and sisters; in addition, as many as a third of his coercive behaviors are quite likely to receive a positive payoff, such as, getting his own way.

In planning your contract or some other intervention (see Appendix 2) you must remember that people rarely show aggression in blind, indiscriminate ways. Rather aggressive (or more extremely violent) actions tend to occur at certain times, in certain settings, toward certain individuals (as objects), and in response to certain forms of provocation.

Assess these in terms of contemporary (i.e. current) circumstances which *instigate aggression* (viz. physical or verbal assaults, deprivation, frustration, conflict, exposure to aggressive models; and *maintain aggression* (viz. direct, vicarious, and self-reinforcement). Your choice of approach might include the following:

- *Reduce stimuli which set the stage (so called "discriminative stimuli") for aggressive behavior.* The absence of a supervising adult may be the signal for a child to threaten or hit another in order to take away his or her toy. This would be a rewarding consequence for the dominant child. Better organized supervision in the playground or home would be one response to this situation.
- *Reduce the exposure to aggressive models.* If a child is mixing with a bully who is providing an example of aggressive behavior it is advisable to detach him or her from this relationship as soon as possible. If parents are modeling (sometimes unwittingly) hostile attitudes and aggressive actions, your target for intervention is as much their behavioral repertoire as that of their offspring.
- *Reduce aversive stimula.* It is crucial to attempt to change the circumstances in which a client's aggressive behavior stems from frustrating, depriving, or provocative experiences instigated by other people or life circumstances. This is easier said than done, but a resourceful profes-

sional is often able to mitigate some of the contributory aversive "triggers."

- *Provide models of non-aggressive behavior.* If possible, bring children into contact with children who do not adopt aggressive actions to cope with life. You might be able to demonstrate non-aggressive problem solving by means of role-play or by video demonstrations of similar-aged children using such strategies.
- *Develop relevant social skills.* There are countless social graces and nuances that make social life easy and pleasurable for all concerned. However, there are many people—children and adults—who lack some of the crucial skills required to cope with life and to solve problems in a constructive and adaptive manner. Aggression may become part of their repertoire for "righting" perceived wrongs and for getting their own way. Social skills can to an extent, be taught. Such issues are dealt with in Chapter 12.
- *Apply (if appropriate) methods of desensitization, relaxation, and communication training.*
- *Discussion, if it is honest and defused of rhetoric, can be a potent antidote to misunderstanding and resentment.* In families where parents smack or beat their children for their "naughty" behavior, and often as a means of releasing their tensions, there are several things you can discuss with them (assuming that you are assured of the essential safety of the child):
- Ensure that the parents' *expectations* of the child are appropriate for his or her age and ability.
- Ascertain that their *attributions,* their theories of causation of their child's behavior (e.g. "There's a demon inside him"; "It's her bad blood"; "She does it because she hates me") are not wildly distorted.
- Check whether there are sufficient *positive interactions* (e.g. play, outings, conversation) and rewards and encouragement.

- Teach the client *cognitive self-control strategies* (e.g. self-talk).

Cognitive Behavioral Approaches (e.g. King, *et al.*, 1999)

The critical role of cognitive processes in childhood learning (see Bruner, 1975) has led to a reappraisal by many behavior therapists (some reluctantly) of the significance of "private events," regarding the cognitive mediation of problem behavior. Thus, we arrive in the 1980s and 1990s at propositions underpinning what came to be known as cognitive-behavioral therapy— namely that thoughts, feelings and behavior are causally related, and that phenomena such as schemata, attributions, opinions and self-statements require investigation in order to understand children's psychological difficulties (Kendall and Gosch, 1994). Cognitive-behavioral therapy (CBT) focuses on goal setting and self-directive behavior by the child, also divergent thinking as a means to inventive solutions to personal difficulties. The techniques used have their roots in cognitive therapy (e.g. socratic questioning, persuasion, challenging, debate, hypothesizing, cognitive restructuring, verbal self-instruction and internal dialogues). Others are drawn from behavior therapy (e.g. operant procedures, desensitization, exposure training, social-skills training, role-play, behavior rehearsal, modeling, relaxation, exercises, redefinition, self-monitoring). The methods share a common assumption: that children, and indeed their parents, can be taught to eliminate some of their maladaptive behaviors by challenging their irrational beliefs and faulty logic, by getting them to instruct themselves in certain ways or to associate wanted behavior with positive self-statements and unwanted ones with negative self-statements. To help adolescents (and indeed, parents, at times) we examine and dissect some of the faulty reasoning underlying the self-talk: the exaggeration ("No one loves me ... there's no hope!"), the need to be all-competent, to show no weakness, to be acknowledged and loved all the time, to be forever right. Counseling on such illogicalities, the prompting and practicing of new self-talk ("I can manage ... I'm a good parent"; "Think first, act afterward ... keep cool") may bring some relief.

A number of procedures are available for the purposes of controlling impulsive actions; they include self-management by the client of hostile feelings, together with his or her observations of the circumstances in which they occurred and their consequences. You might provide the client with positive self-statements for dealing with anger:

- *Preparing for provocation.*
  This is going to upset me, but I know how to deal with it.
  What is it that I have to do?
  I can work out a plan to handle this.
  I can manage the situation. I know how to regulate my anger.
  If find myself getting upset, I'll know what to do.
  There won't be any need for an argument.
  Try not to take this too seriously.
  This could be a testing situation, but I believe in myself.
  Time for a few deep breaths of relaxation. Feel comfortable, relaxed, at ease.
  Easy does it. Remember to keep your sense of humor.

- *Reacting during the confrontation.*
  Stay calm. Just continue to relax. As long as I keep my cool, I'm in control.
  Just roll with the punches; don't get bent out of shape.
  Think of what you want to get out of this.
  You don't need to prove yourself.
  There is no point in getting mad.
  Don't make more out of this than you have to.
  I'm not going to let him get to me.
  Look for the positives. Don't assume the worst or jump to conclusions.
  It's really a shame that she has to act like this.
  For someone to be that irritable, he must be awfully unhappy.
  If I start to get mad, I'll just be banging my head against the wall. So I might as well just relax.
  There is no need to doubt myself. What he says doesn't matter.
  I'm on top of this situation and it's under control.

- *Coping with arousal.*
  My muscles are starting to feel tight. Time to relax and slow down.
  Getting upset won't help.
  It's just not worth it to get so angry.
  I'll let him make a fool of himself.
  I have a right to be annoyed, but let's keep the lid on.
  Time to take a deep breath.
  Let's take the issue point by point.
  My anger is a signal of what I need to do. Time to instruct myself.
  I'm not going to get pushed around, but I'm not going haywire either.
  Try to reason it out. Treat each other with respect.
  Let's try a cooperative approach. Maybe we are both right.
  Negatives lead to more negatives. Work constructively.
  She'd like me to get really angry. Well, I'm going to disappoint her.
  I can't expect people to act the way I want them to.
  (From Novaco, 1975, with permission.)

All the methods described above attend to the "A" term (antecedent events) in the ABC equation. The following ones are more to do with the "C" term (consequent events or outcomes). Procedures based on selective reinforcement (making aggression unrewarding or costly) can reduce aggressive behavior. Some childish aggression (e.g. temper tantrums) may be ignored (if that is not a dangerous option) when attention has been positively reinforcing. It can be ignored when an incompatible pattern is desirable, pro-social conduct is rewarded and thus encouraged; it may be penalized by methods such as response-cost and time-out.

Contracts

Contracts draw on various ideas and concepts for their ratio-nale. Two theories—exchange theory (which comes from social psychology) and contingency (reinforcement) theory—are most prominent, and give rise to six key concepts.

- communication;
- negotiation (bargaining);
- compromise;
- reciprocity;
- expectations (rules); and
- reinforcement.

Social psychology tells us that groups which exist for any length of time (and we can think of the family group as a par-ticular example) have a definite communication structure. For example, there tends to be consistency in the number of com-munications individuals receive, and in the number and content of communications they initiate. There is a positive cor-relation between the frequency of communication ("in" and "out") and the status of the individual in the group. One can imagine that a powerless member of the family is allowed or able to say very little for herself.

It is important to point out to clients that the responses of one individual are the cues for the responses of the other, which in turn become cues for the responses of the first. Shout (or whisper) and the other person is likely to shout (or whisper) back. Cues are by definition "carriers" of information; and transmission of information is the essence of communication. So what kind of messages do people give each other—not only in what they say (verbal cues) but in what they do or the way in which they say things (non-verbal cues)?

Reciprocal contractual agreements are not unnatural to most people: they exist in families and other groupings, whether explicit or implicit. Many of the problems that arise are due to the arrangements not being reciprocal or explicit enough. Contracts (whether written down or agreed verbally) have the effect of structuring reciprocal exchanges. They specify who is to do what, for whom and under what circumstances; reinforcement contingencies (to take one example) can be made explicit between individuals who wish behavior to change (e.g. parents, teachers, nurses) and those whose behavior is to be changed (children, students, clients).

At a time of crisis when marital partners or teenagers and their parents (or indeed brothers and sisters) are at loggerheads, angry and resentful, contracts provide an opportunity for a family to take stock and to break through vicious circles of retribution and unreason.

Contingency agreements are contracts drawn up between two or more people in which a set of mutual expectations is written down detailing reciprocal benefits and the "costs" or penalties for transgressions. The main assumptions underlying the use of formal verbal agreements or the stronger written form of contracts, are as follows:

- The publicly endorsed, unambiguous, and specific commitment to a future course of action will prove more binding, a better guarantee of compliance, than more casual "promises" or ephemeral statements of intention (think of those turned-over new leaves at the New Year).
- To obtain such results the parties concerned must not feel they have been unduly coerced into their contractual arrangements.

Applications.
The following elements of contracting are important for the clients:

- Be very specific in spelling out the desired actions.
- Pay attention to the details of the privileges and conditions for both parties; they should be (a) important as opposed to trivial, (b) functional (if manifested more frequently they will increase the chances of the parties' obtaining from their environment the natural kinds of rewards which most people desire and enjoy).
- If parents wish their youngster (or adults their partner) to desist from certain actions and activities, encourage them

to express these in terms of positive change. For example, if they would like X to stop being so critical and negative they should specify the change they wish to bring about by inviting X to accentuate the positive, pleasant, or praiseworthy. This would then have to be spelled out in terms of specific examples of behavior—words and deeds. Reciprocal requirements can be asked of parents or partner.

- Get parents (or partner) to write down five items of behavior they wish their son, daughter, or spouse would do more often.
- Don't let the parties be vague, for example, "I wish he'd be more helpful." Be concrete and specific, "I wish he'd help me set and clear the table."
- Parents may want their son to complete his homework and attend school regularly. He, on the other hand, desires more free time with his friends or more pocket money. A husband may wish his wife would be more attentive; she might like him to be sociable, and so on. Encourage discussion, negotiation, and compromise.

See the example contract in Figure 9.

Helping Your Client as an Individual

There are different levels at which you can help your client, ranging from the general (emotional support, information, advice, etc.) to the specific and technical (for example, behavior therapy). To be in a position to give effective help to your client presupposes:

- communication skills;
- a good relationship;
- mutual trust and understanding; and
- "therapeutic" conversational skills.

Communication training. Communication training is one of the more promising of the new behavioral methods that have developed from social skills therapy and assertion training. It is

Figure 9. Contract

CONTRACT between Mr. and Mrs. S—and Anne S—

Mother and father would like Anne to:

1. Let them know about her movements when she goes out at night; Anne will let them know about her movements when she goes out at night by:
     telling them were she is and with whom;
     letting them know when she'll be home.
2. Be less moody; she won't sulk for hours on end when reprimanded or thwarted.
3. Be more ready to say sorry; i.e., she will apologize when she's been in the wrong.
4. Show more concern about her school work (e.g., homework); i.e., she will put in at least an hour per night.
5. Stop being so rude to her father; i.e., walking out when he gives her advice.

Anne would like her father and mother to:

1. Stop criticizing her friends all the time; i.e., stop calling them names and saying they're no good, unless they are making a particular, constructive comment.
2. Admit when they are in the wrong; i.e., they will apologize when they have been in the wrong in their confrontations with her.
3. Give her more pocket money (a sum agreed) and review the amount every six months in the light of the rising expense and changing nature of her commitments.

All agree:

1. That the terms of the contract will not be changed except by mutual discussion and agreement.
2. That disputes will be settled by the witness (grandmother), whom all accept to be objective and fair-minded.
3. That successful execution of the contract for a month will be rewarded by a family treat (first month: an outing to a fancy (named) restaurant).
4. That failure to carry out individual terms of the contract will result in a fine on each occasion: an amount of X for Anne; and Y for Mr. and Mrs. S—respectively. The money is to go in a "penalty box" (kept by the grandmother), the proceeds of which will go to a charity of her choice.

Signed Anne ....

Mr. S— ....

Mrs. S— ....

Grandmother (witness) ....

(From Herbert, 1987, with permission)

valuable for training professional students in the vital skills of being clear and comprehensible in their work. At the same time it provides them with a method applicable to many of their clients-to-be, notably offenders (see Herbert, 1998c). The method concentrates on the following:

- A series of exercises that puts the complete skills of communication into their component parts and teaches each of these in a carefully graded sequence to small groups of clients (or trainee social workers).
- Use of the principles of modeling, shaping, behavioral rehearsal, and positive reinforcement (see Chapter 11).
- The "teacher" seeks directly to impart communication skills, to identify blocks in communication, and to overcome these by training clients (students) in more effective methods of interaction.

The good relationship factor. Among the most frequent complaints by parents of the professionals who provide them with services are lack of concern, care, and warmth: in other words, the absence of a supportive relationship. This is a particularly sad state of affairs as it is widely held that among the most important qualities associated with "healing" properties are the therapist's understanding, respect, acceptance, genuineness, empathy, and non-possessive warmth. These attributes are stressed in the counseling (client-centered) literature and their effect is related to aspects of the client's well-being or self-esteem.

Whether a trained professional has a monopoly of these qualities (or some unique deployment of them) is thrown into doubt, surely even for those who give most weight to the relationship factor in therapy, by the absence of significant differences in the results of professional as opposed to non- or paraprofessional helpers. The consistency of positive findings supports the potential value of non-professional assistance. This is good news for those social workers who believe in utilizing community resources (parents and other non-professionals) in the helping endeavor.

Therapeutic conversational/communications. The art of talking (therapeutic conversation or communications) is highly valued in the difficult task of encouraging change in the understanding and actions of adult and young clients. Helping people to discover insights into their mental processes and behavior is a well-known feature of therapies.

Psychotherapy. The word "psychotherapy" means literally "the treatment of problems of the mind." The term also implies that treatment is carried out by psychological methods rather than by the use of physical measures such as drugs. Clients do a lot of talking about their lives, their present and past, their personal relationships. Psychotherapists, to a greater or lesser extent, also talk, offering interpretations, reflecting back to the clients their feelings, and providing reassurance. Some analyze transference feelings, that is to say the client's feelings that have their origins in past experiences and relationships but are now displaced onto the person of the therapist. It is difficult to define psychotherapy in any tidy fashion because so many different theories of personality and viewpoints about the nature of mental problems determine the approach of the particular therapist. One clinician may be a psychoanalytic psychotherapist but even then he or she could be trained in the Freudian, Jungian, or some other school. Another may be influenced by the Rogerian ideas of client-centered therapy. Typical problems dealt with by psychotherapies include:

- an avoidance of situations/people/objects one should not have to avoid;
- a sense of emotional turmoil (anger, fear, anxiety, dread, guilt, depression, disgust);
- a feeling of helplessness, of not being fully in control of one's life;
- a feeling of unhappiness, distress, misery; vague feelings that life is not being lived as meaningfully, effectively, or joyfully as it should be;
- a feeling of having lost control;
- a loss of ability to make decisions;
- a loss of the ability to make choices;

- a loss of the feeling of being real, vital, committed to or enthusiastic about life;
- a sense of conflict, apathy, aimlessness;
- a sense of alienation (with self and/or society); and
- a sense of being compelled to do things against one's will.

These problems also lend themselves to an expert behavioral approach. It is crucial in behavioral assessment and treatment to reformulate these complaints in operational terms, that is, in overt terms of what the client says and does, and in a manner that lends itself to quantifying of the problem. Such problems are also the "bread and butter" of counselors.

An Illustration

A problem in which short-term psychotherapy utilized insight and "ventilation" (the release/expression of suppressed emotion) is the case of Jason, who acted in an extremely rebellious, disobedient, and aggressive manner his parents could not cope with. When his innermost thoughts and feelings were tapped by analyzing projective material (his stories and paintings) and by observing his repetitive games with the "family group" of dolls, it became apparent that he believed his parents had stopped loving him when his brother was born. He had been the only child for five years and had little understanding that love can be shared rather than monopolized. He had the idea that his mother and father got angry with him and punished him, not because he was being difficult and negativistic, but simply because their feeling toward him had changed and they no longer loved him. His intense jealousy of the baby was not apparent on the surface. His overzealous attention to the infant—as it appeared—covered feelings of hatred and envy. Not realizing this, the parents were not able to cope with the situation. In this case the function of the treatment as it was seen by the therapist was not only to release and interpret the child's feelings, and to educate him about the inclusiveness of love rather than its exclusiveness, but also to help the mother to understand and tolerate the source of her child's anxieties and aggressions.

If the child is very young, conventional methods of psychotherapy as used with adults are not very suitable. The child is not always able to put anxieties into words. He or she is not always interested in exploring past life or attitudes. Play is a familiar

205

mode of expression for the child and it is deployed by some child psychotherapists as a part-equivalent of "talking-therapy".

Play. Whatever the theoretical framework of a particular clinic, it is fairly common practice for children to be made to feel at ease in a playroom in which they can paint, construct things on a sand tray with miniatures, act out dramas with dolls and puppets, be aggressive with guns and choppers, and in fact, give expression to a wide range of feelings and fantasies. The skilled therapist may detect recurrent themes in the child's play, preoccupations which point to conflicts or areas of tension in the family, at school, or in some aspect of the child's life which are blocking development. In its simplest form, play therapy is a modifying or reshaping of attitudes and feelings. But the therapist cannot simply sit down with the child and explain the self-defeating nature of his or her attitudes toward self and the environment. The child must come to see for him- or herself and to feel within that what he or she is doing is self-defeating and unnecessary. This is not usually achieved overnight. The child's attitudes need to be analyzed carefully and on a broad front and not with a superficial, facile, and "pat" formula. Genna, who had a dread of going to school (school phobia) appeared to be afraid of a harsh teacher and a bully in the school. A careful analysis of her personality and home and school background revealed that the problem was more a fear of leaving home rather than going to school. The mother, an anxious woman, whose mothering style was overprotective, was having marital problems, and the child overheard her saying to her husband that his infidelity was "killing" her. The child was afraid that her mother might die when she was not at home to keep an eye on things. There were other issues to this case and a good deal of time was required to right matters and get the child back to school.

Virginia Mae Axline (1947), in her book *Play Therapy*, describes the non-directive form of play therapy. Her approach is based upon the fact that play is the child's natural medium of self-expression. An opportunity is given to the child to "play out" feelings and problems just as, in certain types of adult therapy, an adult "talks out" his or her difficulties. Non-directive therapy with children is based upon the assumption that the individual has a growth impulse that makes mature behavior more satisfying than immature behavior. The basic principles which guide therapy are as follows. The therapist:

- endeavors to develop a warm, friendly relationship with the child;
- accepts the child exactly as he or she is;
- establishes a feeling of permissiveness in the relationship so that the child feels entirely free to express his or her feelings;
- is alert to recognize the feelings expressed by children and to reflect those feelings back to them in such a manner that they gain insight into their behavior;
- maintains a deep respect for the child's ability to solve his or her own problems if given an opportunity to do so. The responsibility for making choices and for instituting change is the child's;
- does not attempt to hurry therapy along. It is a gradual process;
- does not attempt to direct the child's actions or conversation in any manner. The child leads the way and the therapist follows; and
- establishes only those limitations to the child's behavior that are necessary to anchor the therapy to the world of reality and to make the child aware of his or her responsibility in the relationship.

Play therapy is an avenue to understanding children's coping and responses to crisis and may involve dolls, art, puppets, stories, and toys. Case examples of play therapy with children in crisis due to abuse, violence, foster care, divorce, illness, and other problems are available in the literature (Webb, 1991).

Talking to and Guiding Young People

Haim Ginnott (1969) is concerned that the two-way nature of good communication between adults should also form the basis of conversations with young people. A dialogue with a child or teenager requires respect and skill. Ginnott advises adults to listen carefully to what young people say. Messages should preserve their own and the youngster's self-respect.

There is a myth around that says that adolescents are beyond help. They may not be easy to help, indeed there may be an initial reaction of prickly disdain, but teenagers who experience problems can be helped by sharing knowledge and hard-won experience. When they face really tough decisions, most are open to sensitively and sensibly proffered guidance. People are most susceptible to help during periods of rapid change, and adolescence is such a period of flux. Parents are especially receptive to advice at times of crises. Yet high on their list of complaints about professionals are failures of communication. These failures involve:

- insufficient information;
- inaccurate information;
- an overload of information at any one time; and
- information that is difficult to comprehend because of technical jargon or poor presentation.

Providing Information

This then is another way of helping your client by providing the factual data, or know-how about how to get access to information. That information should help them to make informed choices and decisions. You may know people who can offer objective, matter-of-fact information or guidance to your client because of their special expertise. Within therapy, the therapist may influence the client by providing information or interpretations; by changing clients' attitudes, values, behaviors, and perceptions; by teaching problem solving and social skills; by altering the client's pattern of interests, attitudes, and understanding.

Counseling

Counseling has, as its main aim, the production of constructive behavioral and personality change. Such change emerges from a relationship of trust, one which emerges from confidential conversations between the professionally trained counselor and the client (Egan, 1986).

Carl Rogers has played a major part in developing the client-centered, non-directive approach to counseling or therapy. In the Rogerian "client-centered" approach, the goal of the intervention is to work in such a facilitative, non-intrusive manner as to remove the incongruence the individual has developed between experiencing the inner self and the self he or she presents to the outside world. In this way it is hoped to increase positive self-regard and self-direction.

Rogers's (1951) client-centered therapy comes from an academic background in counseling and is less influenced by psychoanalytic thinking than most others in the so-called humanist-existential (or ego psychology) strand of psychological work.

Framework for Counseling

- Verbal exchange is the means of influence.
- The basic assumptions about the nature of man and woman are not pessimistic (fatalistic?) like Freud's.
- Rogers has a clear notion of the wholeness of the self. The person is essentially good, rational, realistic, social, forward looking.
- He or she may need help with their basic impulse to grow. For Rogers this means positive growth with outcomes of self-actualization and socialization."

The counselor should feel warm and positive toward clients, accept the experience that they are experiencing (empathy), and evince "unconditional positive regard."

The therapeutic process is akin to good education or socialization and is seen as a freeing of the "growth capacities" of the individual, which permits him or her to acquire "more mature" ways of acting and reacting, which are less fraught with anxiety or conflict. Rogers is talking about a learning process, within a humanistic rather than behaviorist context. The attributes of the counsellor that facilitate such learning are thought to be:

- Genuineness and authenticity: the conveying of "realness" to clients.
- Non-possessive warmth: the attitude of friendly concern and caring.
- Accurate empathy: the capacity to see things from the clients' point of view, to "feel with" them, so that they feel they are understood.

Counseling from a client-centered perspective involves the painstaking exploration of problems. There is an attempt to clarify conflicting issues and discover alternative ways of describing them and/or of dealing with them. Counseling helps people to help themselves. This helping method (like the problem-solving approach but unlike some of the other methods) emphasizes the "self-help" element, the need to call on the inner resources of the person who is in difficulties. To this end, the counselor provides a supportive relationship that enables the individual to search for his or her own answers.

Non-directive counseling and therapy are based upon the assumption that the individual has, within, not only the ability to solve his or her own problems satisfactorily, but also a growth impulse that makes adult behavior more satisfying than childish behavior. This assumption puts the non-directive approach well toward the "consumer" model of service delivery described in Chapter 1.

Counseling in a Crisis

In your work with children and their parents you will be called upon to disentangle what look like insuperably knotty problems. The tempo of your work is relatively unhurried; after all, these difficulties have been around a long time. They require a painstaking assessment and a lot of thought. But emergencies come along—acute crises—and your task is to respond quickly to alleviate the immediate impact of disruptive stressful events. There are many potential crises in family life that may include:

- child diagnosed as mentally/physically handicapped;
- separation/divorce;
- loss of a member of the family (bereavement);

- an attempted suicide in the family;
- physical illness or injury;
- mental illness (e.g. schizophrenia, depression) of a member of the family;
- the discovery of sexual abuse of a child/adolescent in the family;
- police involvement (a child's delinquent act) or a court appearance;
- drug abuse discovered;
- anorexia nervosa diagnosed;
- youngster runs away from home;
- truancy; and
- family violence.

The Impact of Children with Special Needs

Children who are disabled (intellectually and/or physically) or chronically ill are more likely to have behavioral and emotional problems than healthy children, a fact that puts an additional strain on parents struggling to cope with the disability/illness in its own right. Hilton Davis (1993) points out how each disability/disease presents specific problems to the children and family. When children are hurt, ill or disabled, they need physical and personal attention, and this has consequences for all members of the family. At a relatively trivial level, one of the parents has to stop cooking, reading or watching television to see to the child, to cuddle him/her or kiss a bruise better. If the child is sick, parents become worried, arrangements have to be made to look after her/him while one parent takes the other children to school, or they have to make time to go the doctor. Time may be lost from work, and the other children lose attention. Such consequences are a routine part of family life but, in chronic disease, they become a way of life. Anxiety may be the norm, outside commitments may be impossible and child-care duties are increased, including appointments with professionals and even periods away from home for hospital admissions.

Davis (1993) describes how parents are profoundly affected by illness in their children, with as many as 33 percent of parents of children with cancer, even in remission, having such severe depression and anxiety that they require professional

211

help. In a study conducted by Davis with one of his students, 31 percent of mothers of children with diabetes were found to have stress levels that would have benefited from a professional mental health intervention. Communication and relationship problems are reflected in increased marital distress, sometimes in divorce. There is evidence of increased disturbance in siblings. At times, particular events, or their accumulation, reach crisis proportions.

It is noted that the deprivation of "special needs children" have received great attention, legislation and funding directed to assuring that the extensive, difficult, and often costly needs of children are met—either in biological or adoptive family settings or in substitute care such as foster homes, group homes, and other institutional settings. In the United States, the Adoption Assistance and Child Welfare Act of 1980 (P. L. 96-272) defined special needs children and provided subsidies to increase the availability of care. Special needs children include older adoptees or those above four years of age, children with emotional or behavioral problems, sibling groups available for adoption or adopted, developmental disability or medical condition, and racial minority children. Adoption subsidies, special subsidies for care in situations of disabilities or medical conditions requiring specialized treatment, care, and/or equipment, and subsidized care of children lingering in foster status versus permanent homes are available to help meet the needs of these children (Petr, 1998).

There is no substitute in an emergency for common sense. All the crises described above have attracted a specialist literature. Literature on the care and nurturance of children in families is particularly broad and organized around concepts that range from healthy pregnancies, parenting two-year-olds, entering children in school, getting ready for adolescence, to parenting the older adolescent. Other literature abounds in adoption, caring for terminally ill children or children with chronic illnesses such as childhood diabetes, to meeting the needs of children with physical and/or mental disabilities that range from mild to extremely disabling. In this volume, our purpose is not to review this vast bank of literature, but only to mention it as a resource. Certainly, not all family crises or clinical disorders revolve around the care and development of children. Nevertheless, children with special needs and critical care demands or crises of loss and bereavement present immediate demands for families and may require immediate but thoughtful and calm intervention. For the professional who must help a family through various life crises, a few general, common-sense responses include:

- Remember that during a crisis most people (because their defenses are down) are receptive to the right sort of help.
- Do not perceive yourself in this set of circumstances as a long-term therapist or a specialist in an area such as bereavement counseling although such a role, or person, may become necessary if the client doesn't seem to be regaining his or her equilibrium.
- You are not there to identify or resolve all of the stresses and complications brought about by the crisis.
- Being aware of the stages of a crisis allows you to assess whether the client is "stuck" at a particular point in what theoreticians call the "crisis work," thus hindering the mastering of the emergency and delaying its final resolution. Although active crisis states vary in duration, the actual condition of intense disequilibrium is limited usually to between four and six weeks. Stages in crises of different kinds will vary, but here is one example. Colin Parkes (1972) has charted the course of grief following bereavement. It encompasses pangs of grief and pining for the lost one, also a process of searching and yearning for the departed person that may look quite irrational to the observer. Parkes also described the anger that may flare up and the feelings of guilt that may give way to apathy and depression. Stages of loss are defined as well by Kubler-Ross (1969) in her extensive work on death and dying.
- Simply identifying for a person in crisis what is happening, or for concerned relatives explaining the normality of such events, provides untold relief and a sense of security. The unknown, especially the apparently irrational, bizarre happenings (to oneself or others) in times of crisis, add to the burden of the trauma itself. Reassurance is one

of the most potent therapeutic remedies available to the emergency counselor.

• Understanding is the other remedy: providing the client with a non-judgmental, sensitive ear and voice—listening and responding to his or her anguish. This is not the time to be coldly logical, expertly clever, or coldly objective.

Summary and Comment

We have examined several approaches—group and individual—used in the helping process. Change is the key word in all of this, be it facilitated by contracts, direct advice, counseling, or psychotherapy. Therapies are many and varied. Many social workers, psychologists, and psychotherapists call themselves "eclectic," drawing what they regard as the best or most valid from the various systems of therapy. Eclectism implies a broad knowledge and skill base grounded in theory and intervention methodology and not a collection of ungrounded helping efforts.

Some theorists assert that the technical claims of the diverse schools of therapy have never been adequately vindicated. Some comparative studies show little difference in the outcomes of diverse approaches even though a particular therapy, by itself, can be shown to have significant effects when compared to the absence of treatment. Such an assertion that there are insignificant differences between therapeutic approaches with regard to outcome would be hotly disputed by behavioral therapists. Nevertheless, it is just such an assumption that leads Jerome Frank (1973), author of *Persuasion and Healing*, to argue that the effective factors are the same for all therapies and they can be identified with the common components of all types of influence and healing—warmth, respect, kindness, hope, understanding, and the provision of explanations. Various therapeutic approaches defend their knowledge and intervention base and compare outcomes with other methodologies.

If it is agreed that psychotherapy is to a significant extent carried out within the framework of a "good" human relationship, questions must be put and hopefully answered about the nature of the psychotherapists' contribution over and beyond the offering of a helpful human relationship.

This chapter touched upon conflicts and special needs evidenced by families. Mobilizing resources, working with families, providing family therapy, and assessing problems are all related to interventive methodology and results expected. The chapter conveys the fact that the broad scope of problems experienced in families requires a range of interventions and/or information in securing resources and finding other avenues of help when the problem presented is outside your range of expertise. Not only is immediate intervention required in critical situations, but also, there are specific preventive and long-term change-oriented methods to consider. This chapter discussed a variety of needs and interventions within the context of family treatment. Other approaches like group work and behavioral methods are addressed in the following chapter.

CHAPTER 10

More Methods and Techniques

The methods and client systems described in this chapter include a range of ways to work with children and parents. At the level of individual clients, there is much individual work that can be done such as that described by Herbert (1987a). The methods and client systems described in this chapter include a range described in the case example of the Hayes family. Avril, the child, became a unit for intervention designed to change her behaviors that were distracting and disruptive for the family as well as dysfunctional for her. Mrs Hayes, the major caretaker and the parent involved most in Avril's treatment plan, became an identified client as well. Mr and Mrs Hayes, a marital subsystem in the family, entered into intervention more as Avril's parents than as a couple exploring their own relationship. Conjoint marital treatment in this family may have been quite helpful. It is noted that conjoint family treatment, involving two or more family members, may be productive just as individual sessions with family members are often helpful. Conjoint sessions are often helpful in assessment, in situations of communication difficulties among certain members. In the case of the Hayes family, Avril's parents, together with the therapist, were able to formulate a plan for managing her behavioral problems. A word of caution: family problems reach all family members and excluding one or more family members from family treatment will likely distort the presenting problem and may well prevent common problems from being identified and resolved (Janzen and Harris, 1997).

Group Work

At the broader level of groups, the Hayes family could have joined other couples and children in groups of families with similar problems, similar intervention needs, or simply similar learning needs. As Avril's behavior and her relationship with her mother improved, their involvement in parent–child activities, including child-care-center functions, brought them into a group setting with other parents and children involved in similar activities. In this social and educational setting, they became involved in other relationships and participated in the educational setting, essentially a large group setting.

Some of the advantages of working with children and families in groups include functions such as: (1) experiential processes provide benefits of participating in a group where members learn about how others experience similar problems and often gain support for sharing, communicating, and responding to others; (2) dynamic forces of group processes, particularly in instances of treatment groups, allow the members to enter a group from a social role or from the context of the social self; however, through involvement and interaction as trust builds more of the inner self is shared as greater risk taking occurs; (3) social functions in groups offer support, feedback, and support social behaviors such as communication skills; (4) didactic groups provide an arena for learning, information, and discussion (Garvin, 1997; Shulman, 1999).

Children and families alike belong to many groups throughout their lives and, as social beings, generally gain comfort from simple interactions with others. Many adults feel that they have failed miserably as parents, and that their child is uniquely difficult to understand and manage. Sharing experiences with other parents can be comforting, indeed reassuring. The opportunity to express feelings of apprehension, resentment, and anger in a group setting can be beneficial if handled sensitively by the group leader. Group methods of training parents may be combined with individual intervention; a marital relationship might be the subject of intervention at the same time as a program for a child's behavior problems or learning disorder is being implemented.

Discussion Groups

Comprehensive reviews of social group work that involves working with a variety of clients and problem areas in the context of groups such as therapeutic groups, task groups, and discussion groups are available in the literature (Garvin, 1997;

Johnson and Johnson, 1987; Shulman, 1999). For the beginning practitioner working with families and individuals in need of information, feedback, and social contact, involving clients in discussion groups is an appropriate means of extending services that can be economical and beneficial. Discussion groups are common and economic forums for sharing information and learning experiences, and engaging in mutual problem solving. Parent training groups involve all three of these purposes.

You need to plan and organize your group carefully if it is to be effective and not degenerate into a pleasant, but essentially unproductive, "talk shop." There are several basic procedures for discussion groups. Johnson and Johnson's book *Joining Together* (1987) makes the following suggestions which we have paraphrased (giving examples from our work with parent groups; see Appendix 2).

- **Define terms and concepts.**

A group requires a shared language in order to hold a fruitful discussion. Study new terms; try to find agreement on complex, contentious, or ambiguous words, for example, words like discipline, "problem child," punishment, trust, spoiled, bribery, reinforcement, time-out. Give examples wherever possible to illustrate a word or concept's meaning.

- **Negotiate and/or establish goals.**

Clarify the objectives for every session (themes might cover child development, what to do when a child cries, discipline, sex education, adolescent risk taking). Handouts that prepare discussions for a topic, or summarize the previous meeting, are appreciated. Break down major topics into sub-topics. Spread your time over sub-topics in order of importance so that items of significance are not lost. Allow time to review homework tasks if they are part of the agenda, such as, keeping records or a diary for discussion.

- **Encourage free and fair discussion.**

Encourage individuals in the free expression of ideas, feelings, attitudes, openness, reactions, information, and analysis. Do not allow the scapegoating or "bullying" of any one member. Ground rules for the group may be useful here.

- **Integrate the material.**

Relate current themes to past topics; make connections between issues. Fragmentary impressions from several discussion sessions are unlikely to add significantly to a parent's understanding of children and confidence in his or her parenting skills. In parents' groups (see Appendix 1) it is important to try out practical ideas such as time-out by means of role-play or homework tasks. This leads to an important point:

- **Encourage the application of the discussion material.**

Ask group members to attempt to identify the implications of the material for their own lives, the activities they engage in, and their relationships with other people. Encourage them to apply the positive things they have learned and report back to the group the "feedback" they received from this try-out.

- **Evaluate the quality of the discussion.**

Ask group members to take a critical look at their performance as a group and as individuals contributing to a group.

The Role of Course Organizer

Your coordinating or leadership role is absolutely vital if the group is to work. Here are a few more tips.

Set up the room so that all members can see and hear properly. They should be comfortable and should sit facing each other. An approximate circle is ideal. With a family group session, it is illuminating sometimes to ask the group to arrange the room themselves to their own preferences. Stimulating material such as films, case examples, television programs, and magazines or newspaper articles can be used to initiate discussion. The discussion will "spark" if you negotiate clear themes and objectives. You can lead a group through a complete topic in a logical sequence by presenting new points to the group when necessary. It is important to "hold back" those individuals (say a father) who try to dominate the discussion. Have agreed rules for the sessions. Provide opportunities for quiet or timid members to speak; attempt to draw them out. You should ensure that everyone has the right (if they wish) to talk. Ask clarifying questions, and sum up discussion at regular intervals as well as at the conclusion.

According to Johnson and Johnson (1987), a group intervention will be effective if it meets the following criteria:

- The group *climate* should be warm, accepting, and non-threatening—vital if people are to engage in controversy, expose their vulnerability, show their ignorance, take risks with touchy subjects.
- Learning should be conceived as a *cooperative* enterprise—impossible if the participants "come over" as hostile, competitive, ridiculing, arrogant, or judgmental.
- *Learning* should be accepted as the primary purpose of the group—a desideratum that requires painstaking and imaginative preparation of the material and sensitive but firm management of the group.
- Every member of the group should *participate* in discussion—a function, again, of a skillful, facilitative group leader.
- Such leadership functions might usefully be shared for certain themes and/or sessions.
- Group sessions don't have to be endlessly solemn or heavy-going. They should be stimulating and thus *pleasurable*, and (at times) sheer fun.
- *Evaluation* should be viewed as an integral part of the group's activities. Group skills can be improved by constructive, critical evaluation.
- Members should *attend regularly* and come prepared—and the importance of mutual responsibility for the well-being of the group may be underlined by drawing up contracts with participants.

Individual Helping

There are several ways in which you can support a client through a difficult time on a one-to-one basis. Sometimes you may be able to do something directly on your client's behalf—

for example, acting as a mediator in a quarrel, or as an "advocate" in their pursuit of assistance from an impenetrable agency. You may be able to change the external circumstances (perhaps by improving other people's attitudes or by mitigating the aggravating circumstances) which are the cause of your client's difficulties.

If you cannot change the circumstances, you may have to rely on modifying the client's perception of or reaction to the situation. Other methods are described in the following pages. These approaches are not mutually exclusive; they overlap in practice and, indeed converge in the behavioral approach.

Persuasion. Persuasion rests on practical knowledge or practice wisdom. It offers reasons why the client should change his or her beliefs and/or behavior. This does not eschew the arts of persuasion. Subject to ethical constraints and the process of negotiating goals with clients, it is an important component of therapy to voice clear opinions based upon valid information and knowledge of the developmental literature and of hard-gained practice, wisdom, and experience.

Providing instruction. Teaching entails skills of "doing." The client may not be able to act without instruction, training, and monitoring. Because some actions (e.g. child-training techniques) are so ingrained in parents' repertoires, it is not usually good enough to simply advise parents to change. Demonstration, rehearsals, instructions, and practice may be required in order to provide clients with the equipment for change.

Providing explanations. You may be able to offer explanatory "stories" (cognitive restructuring), which help clients to reorder their beliefs about the nature of their problems. Attempting to change a person's beliefs, desires, and actions is a commonplace activity in ordinary life. The therapist is particularly interested in providing helpful explanations ("stories") for changing existing belief systems which he or she considers to generate distressing, self-defeating actions on the part of the client. Insight, then, is not rejected as a facilitative therapeutic agent.

Giving advice. Guidance is most likely to be effective if it is requested. Advice offered (you might remind parents) in a hectoring or self-righteous tone of voice, with a long-suffering or patronizing expression, or by an ill-chosen turn of phrase, can sound like a command. Offer your opinion in a cool, concerned but measured way about what you consider the best course of action, in the light of what you know of the situation. Remarks indicating understanding, such as "It's a real dilemma you face, isn't it?", should (when appropriate) precede advice or opinions. You might also ask: "What do you see as your options/alternatives?" This approach helps to defuse anger, resentment, and irrationality from stressful situations, so that reason can be allowed to function. Always distinguish between factual information and your personal opinion in what you convey to clients. It is a time to be warmly reassuring, solid, and safe; the imparting of information and advice on child development and childhood problems would be seen as an important part of our work. This might be done on a one-to-one casework basis or in a group setting.

Settling Differences

The organizers of an Open University (1982) course entitled Parents and Teenagers have suggested a step-by-step approach to settling differences of opinion between parents and adolescents. Here is a parent (Mrs Brown) working through a potentially fraught situation. She hates motorcycles but her son, Mike, wants to buy one. She asks herself, "Why must he have a motorcycle?" Here is a list of answers.

- There is no public transport worth speaking of.
- He can't afford a car.
- He says his friends go on outings, and without transport he is excluded.
- He claims to be "grown-up" and therefore "responsible" and free to make choices.
- Why should he not have a motorcycle?
- He may have an accident ... get hurt ... get killed. Motorcycles are associated with rough types.

Step 1. **Working out feelings and attitudes about the situation.**
(i)   *I feel .... (e.g. resentful).*
(ii)   *When he .... (e.g. keeps pestering me for a motorcycle).*
(iii) *Because .... (e.g. he knows it upsets me).*

Step 2. **Deciding whether the particular situation is worth bothering about.**
Reasons for: High risk.
Reasons against: There'll be an awful row if I give a final no.

Step 3. **Making an approach.**
(i)   Expressing one's own feelings in an unprovocative manner.
(ii)   Listening carefully to the reply; clarifying one's understanding of the other's position.

Step 4. **Working out a practical agreement/compromise.**
You might provide the parents with the following guidelines:
  • They should work out what is at stake. Deciding whether or not to take (or sanction) a risk depends on:
  • How likely they believe the feared outcome might be.
  • How important/damaging the possible outcome is.
  • How much they/their teenager has to lose.

Remind them to:

  • bear in mind that risk taking is an important feature of adolescent development;
  • ensure that they and their teenager are well informed (e.g. that a potential motorcycle rider has a good machine and is well trained for driving and roadcraft);
  • discuss risk taking with their son or daughter; try to agree what he or she can do to make the experimenting relatively safe; think about what they can do to make it so;
  • try reaching a compromise or give way on one lesser risk so as to obtain their teenager's agreement to forego another one.

Modeling

Bandura's (1976) concept of vicarious conditioning, learning by observation, is central to the child's rapid acquisition of much complex and novel behavior, and also its modification. As he explains, virtually all learning phenomena resulting from direct experience can occur on a vicarious basis of the other person's behavior and its consequences for them. Thus, for example, one can acquire intricate response patterns merely by observing the performance of appropriate models; emotional responses can be conditioned observationally by witnessing the affective reactions of others undergoing painful or pleasurable experiences; fearful and avoidance behavior can be extinguished. Watching and imitating the behavior of exemplary models, is considered by social learning theorists to be the cornerstone of learning for socialization. Modeling has been used to reduce "normal" fears such as the dark, animals and spiders as well as more serious symptoms of anxiety disorder (King *et al.*, 1998). Children are encouraged to observe other children (or adults) approaching and coping with the feared object, or engaging in taught anxiety-reducing strategies. A therapeutic variation of imitation and modeling is role play.

Role-Play

Role-play is an activity we have all indulged in at different stages of our lives, beginning as children playing doctors, mothers and fathers. Role-play is also an educational technique that brings a specific skill and its consequences into focus. It is a vital tool for experiential learning as it allows the participants to play themselves in different or worrying situations, such as adolescents preparing for job interviews; or to play the part of another person in a known situation, such as reversing roles so that parent becomes child, child pretends to be parent. Role-players do not have to be good actors. They put themselves into a situation that is spelled out and "acted out" on the basis of certain assumptions that have been carefully discussed.

By using role-play as an educational technique, insights can be obtained—emotions, reactions, thoughts, behaviors, attitudes, and values can be explored. At the end of the role-play, participants can reflect on the experience, and gain greater understanding of the role-played situations. Role-play can be used as a vehicle for discussion; it can increase communication skills and self-esteem; it illustrates novel situations and ways of dealing with them; and it allows participants to see how others feel in a particular situation. Here are some guidelines:

- When using role-play, have clear and well-defined objectives.
- Ask participants to volunteer for the various roles.
- Use props to identify participants in their roles if this is felt to be helpful.
- Encourage participants to identify with the role they are playing. If they are playing an unknown character, ask them to respond in the way they think that person would. If they are playing themselves in an unknown situation, ask them to respond as honestly as possible to that situation.
- You should stage-manage and direct the role-play. Remind participants to come out of role at the end of the session.
- Debrief the participants. Debriefing is the period when reflection and evaluation occurs. Ensure there is sufficient time for this. As themselves, the players discuss what they learned from the experience—encourage general discussion about the relevance of the situation to their lives.

Teenagers and their parents can be helped to resolve conflict by the use of role-play. The method is used to teach clients basic skills, to help them become more effective in their interactions, and to help them to become more confident when extremely anxious (for example, through enacting scenes such as using the telephone, going to an interview with an employer, or dealing with provocation).

Overcoming fear. Methods found most effective in helping young people to overcome fears include:

- helping to develop skills by which they can cope with the feared object or situation;
- taking them by degrees into active contact and participation with the feared object or situation; and

- giving them an opportunity gradually to become acquainted with the feared object or situation under circumstances that at the same time give them the opportunity either to inspect or to ignore it.

Exposure Training

Behavioral methods have provided the cornerstone of treatment for phobias. The aims of treatment are fourfold:

- to reduce levels of both general and situational anxiety;
- to relieve disturbing physiological symptoms;
- to reduce avoidance behavior; and
- to prevent interference in daily living.

The fearful youngster may be exposed to the phobic object or situation in fantasy, in pictures, or in real life. Exposure may be graded by means of an initially easy but then increasingly difficult series of situations. This gradual mastery of fear-provoking events is also referred to as systematic desensitization.

Self-Control Training

Self-control procedures are designed to give the client a more effective means of manipulating the eliciting, reinforcing, and discriminative stimuli which affect behavior. The worker's role is first to carefully examine the antecedents and consequences of a piece of behavior over which the client wishes to have more control and then to suggest ways in which these events may be altered. They may be altered by either physical or cognitive changes in order that the client may achieve a greater degree of control over the behavior.

An example

Sue was heavily overweight and was anxious to control her eating behavior. She was asked to carefully record everything she ate or drank and the time at which it was consumed over a two-week period. From this data it became evident that her overeating was restricted to certain types of food and occurred during only the latter part of the day. Further investigation revealed that the sorts of food Sue ate to excess were candy, cakes, and cookies that she usually bought at a local store on her way home from work. She never overate in company, only when alone.

A self-control program was designed in order to help her resist the temptation to overeat. She was instructed to take a different route home so as to avoid the store she usually called at; if she was to be alone in the flat, she was to change immediately from her day clothes into a housecoat to help discourage her from going out to the store later in the evening. Her roommates agreed to help by not bringing any forbidden cakes or candy into the flat when Sue was around and they also made an effort to ensure that she was not left alone in the evenings. Sue was allowed to reward herself for sticking to her diet by having a favorite cake or candy at the end of each "successful" week. When tempted to cheat she was told to visualize an unpleasant and humiliating scene where a group of boys made rude and teasing remarks about her size—a hazard which she would do anything to avoid.

Stress Management

Reginald Beech (1985) in his book *Staying Together*, made the point that life stresses are the enemy of personal relationships. It is possible to reduce the impact of stress on our lives, so his list might be useful to your client. I have paraphrased the items you might wish to put to them:

- Keep a running check on stresses in your life. Even the apparently trivial ones, when they accumulate, can become an excessive burden.
- Positive self-talk helps us to keep the stresses and strains in our lives in more reasonable proportion. (We dealt earlier with this technique.)
- Don't try too hard to solve all your problems and expect to erase them altogether. This is usually a vain hope. Concentrate, instead, on reducing stress. Even a small reduction in each stress can lead to a big difference in our ability to cope.
- Don't try to be all things to all people all the time. Ration yourself by taking a sensible view of your commitments, never forgetting to leave time for yourself and for some privacy.
- Don't be at the mercy of your environment. You really can

227

rearrange your world—if the will is there—to fit in with what you would like to happen.

- Learn to say "No." You don't have to say "Yes" to the unreasonable or all of the reasonable tasks that are foisted on you. Examine your needs and priorities in what is being dished out and feel free to refuse sometimes.
- Cut down on the "have to"s. Question what you tend to take for granted; don't just go ahead and do it because you have always done so.
- Don't set out to win everything. When it really doesn't matter then take a philosophical, relaxed approach. Many so-called confrontations aren't worth the effort.
- Delegate. It doesn't always have to be your job. Spread the load more.
- Slow down. Don't set impossibly tiring or tedious schedules for yourself. Introduce rest pauses, moments of reflection, and pleasure into your day.
- Get some balance into your day. Find time for leisure, hobbies, social life, family life, yourself, and your work/studies.
- Curb aggression. Try to plan your way through problems. You'll end up by feeling better.
- Learn to relax. Practice makes perfect. (Relaxation training tapes are available on cassettes and are an important part of a professional's equipment these days. See Ollendick and Cerny 1981 for a training script.)
- Concentrate on staying calm. In an emergency take a deep breath rapidly but quietly; clasp your hands and press them hard against each other. If sitting, brace your leg muscles, pull in your stomach muscles, clench your jaw, and hold the muscular tension for five seconds. Now exhale slowly, feel the tension go out of you, saying the word "relax" to yourself. If you happen to be standing, take a deep breath, clasp your hands behind you, pressing them hard together; force your knees back to create leg muscle tension, pull in your stomach muscles, and clench your jaws. Maintain the tension for five seconds, then let it go slowly, exhaling and saying the word "relax" to yourself. Don't exaggerate the muscular tension but make

sure you can feel it. Fix your gaze on something so that you appear to be preoccupied or deep in thought for a few moments, so as to conceal the stress you are controlling. Repeat the exercise if necessary.

Summary and Comment

The methods and techniques described in this chapter represent only a small selection of those available. It is vital that you do not rely on techniques like items in a cookbook recipe. They should come out of a clearly formulated theory of human behavior, a careful assessment, and a coherent conceptual framework for producing change.

The chapter presents the various advantages of working in groups and increases understanding of the organization and implementation of group work. Individual helping methods such as persuasion, instruction, the provision of explanations or insight, giving advice, settling differences, role-play, stress management, and self-control training are described

Engaging clients in group treatment is both an efficient and effective method. This method is efficient for the agency as valuable staff time can be spent with several clients or with family members together. Group intervention is effective as not only are clients helped by the clinician or group leader but the group experience allows group members to experience the sharing and healing process together. For some, knowing that they are not alone in their experience of personal and/or family troubles is an important part of recovery.

Additional methods such as role-play, modeling, self-control, and stress management are a few examples of the wide range of modalities available. Social workers, counselors, psychologists, and other helping professionals are encouraged to gain expertise in several methods of intervention as clients experience different problems and benefit differently from treatment approaches.

CHAPTER 11

Child Management and Behavioral Methods

Behavioral methods are very much concerned with contingencies, which is a technical way of referring to rules. Before we look at specific applications let us consider the perennial issue of discipline in child rearing, an issue that is concerned with rules and routines.

Rules and Routines

Why should children learn to follow rules and routines? Is it reactionary, indeed Victorian, to insist on obedience and conformity to rules as part of child rearing? The answer is a resounding "No!" Setting limits is crucial, but the limits should not be defined too narrowly. As with all things in child development, there is a balance—a golden mean.

This is where you can help parents to work out their priorities and how to achieve them. Failure is costly for parents. Disobedience and defiance are common problems, and their consequences are frustrating, irksome, even exhausting and debilitating for parents. When they persist they can sometimes prove dangerous, particularly, in homes at risk of child abuse. There are other potentially serious consequences. Obedience is critical, if the complex processes of socialization are to work. Parents have the task of turning helpless, unsocial, and self-centered infants into sociable children and eventually into reasonable and responsible members of the community.

Among the reasons for enforcing certain rules are:

- the need for safety—the child has to learn to avoid dangers;
- harmony within the family—a disobedient "brat" sets the scene for an unhappy home and disharmony between the parents; and

- the social life of the family—"spoiled," noisy, aggressive, destructive children are not welcome in other people's homes and contribute to the social isolation of their parents.

Parents achieve compliance partly through example because their children love them, seek their approval, and want to be as much like them as possible. It is also achieved by consciously steering the child in the way he or she should go. A firm but loving framework of discipline helps children to develop their own guidelines and controls symbolized by what we call "conscience," so that they can look ahead to the consequences of their actions and "discipline" themselves.

You will find that most parents find discipline one of the most difficult parts of their job; so be forewarned and forearmed. They are quite likely to ask you not only awkward questions, but also for specific advice. It does not help matters to find yourself in an area, not of scientific facts, but of value judgments. Guidelines, rather than "formula" prescriptions, will be among the more useful aids you can provide them with. Better still, you might help them to work out their strategies for themselves, by teaching them how to solve problems.

Preparing the Child for Life

A list of guidelines has been provided in Chapter 6. Here are some additional points to note in connection with Guidelines 3 and 4, the two which require broadly compliant responses from children.

The point was made there that most routines are useful shortcuts to living. Those routines, carried out on "auto-pilot," help a child to undertake daily tasks around the clock with minimum effort or fuss—once the habits are learned. In unhappy homes with a disobedient child you can predict fairly safely that one or more of the following situations will be sheer purgatory for parents, especially in single-parent families:

- getting the child up in the morning;
- washing self, getting dressed;
- eating (breakfast, and later in the day, other meals);
- getting the child off to playgroup or school;

- obeying requests/instructions during the course of the day (e.g. "Put your toys away"; "Don't keep switching the television on and off"; "Stop teasing your sister"; "Put that chocolate back on the shelf"; "Don't go out on the road");
- defiance of house rules (e.g. breaking rules about playing with matches, about not switching on the TV before the children's programs begin, about sitting at the table until the meal is finished, or about not taking food out of the refrigerator without permission);
- interrupting (by pestering) mother when she is in the bathroom, on the telephone, cooking a meal, etc.;
- disrupting shopping trips by incessant "I wants," pulling items off the shelves, tantrums, and so on;
- quarreling, fighting incessantly with brothers and/or sisters, teasing, and so on; and
- not going to bed when asked and/or staying there for the night.

You may be asked to suggest practical strategies for managing these situations. The following sections of this chapter should prove helpful.

The compliance that underpins the learning of rules, routines, and good manners can be facilitated by working with parents on the following themes: ensuring that rules are clear and reasonable; that obedience or disobedience is sanctioned consistently; and that the requests and commands that give effect to rules are precise and comprehensible. If there are difficulties with the latter, model how (i.e. demonstrate and check on the client's performance) to make effective requests and commands.

Alan Hudson (1987) recommends the following steps:

- Use the child's name.
- Give a specific direction.
- Include a mention of time (e.g. "right now" or "when you have finished the chapter").
- Say "please."
- Get all the words together in the form of a statement, not

a question. Do not say: "Sandy, will you get dressed for mommy?" Do say: "Sandy, I would like you to get dressed now, please".

- Make the request standing close to the child; with a small child get down close to the height of the little one.
- Use a pleasant but firm tone of voice (no pleading, cajoling, wheedling!).
- Try to be looking at the child. It may be helpful to say: "Sandy, look at me now, please" and then give the desired command.
- If the child obeys or disobeys—ignores/refuses—follow the behavior with clear and predictable consequences:
- Obedience is followed by positive consequences (e.g. praise).
- Disobedience is followed by negative consequences (e.g. loss of privileges, time-out). Discourage parents from smacking or shouting.
- In the case of special circumstances (shopping, visiting) or places (church, restaurants), help parents to pre-empt problems by working out a scenario:
  (a) Explain to the child what is going to happen.
  (b) Promise a treat/privilege if the child behaves well (specify).
  (c) Engage the child in pro-social behaviors that compete with the unwanted behaviors (e.g. helping mom to pack the shopping bag rather than taking items off the shelves at the check-out counter).
  (c) Use response-cost as a penalty for transgressions as discussed later in this chapter.
- Do not keep repeating the request. Follow non-compliant actions with a penalty.

Behavioral methods. The preceding discussion of rules and requests has been a necessary exercise in setting the stage for a discussion of behavioral methods, many of which are potent in correcting the extremes of non-compliance. Of course, parents need some principles and practical techniques for encouraging and maintaining, not only compliant, but also other pro-social behaviors.

Here are some of the main methods couched in a form that can be presented directly to parents for use with their children. Some of the methods are illustrated by means of brief vignettes drawn from case material.

Strengthening New Patterns of Behavior

Principle 1: **Operant learning**

Those methods of intervention, based on operant conditioning, attempt to influence or control the outcome of certain behaviors through the use of positive reinforcement, such as, pleasurable consequences. Voluntary actions ("operants") that are followed by favorable outcomes for the individual are likely to be repeated.

A social worker using operant methods can analyze a family system and find out how the various members reinforce undesired behavior in some members and intentionally or unintentionally ignore or punish desired behavior. It is then possible to make beneficial alterations in such distressed systems by planning with the family systematically to rearrange the consequences of behavior so that all (or certain) members of the family receive social reinforcement for desired behaviors.

Instructions to parents. In order to improve or increase your child's performance of certain actions, arrange matters so that an immediate reward follows the correct performance of the desired behavior. You might indicate your intentions by saying, for example, "When you have put your toys away, then you can go out." When the child has learned a behavior it is no longer necessary to give rewards regularly. Remember that words of praise and encouragement at such a stage can be very reinforcing.

Principle 2: **Modeling**

To teach a client new patterns of behaviors, give him or her the opportunity to observe a person performing the desired actions. Social workers and others in the helping professions are very important as models in shaping behavior.

Modeling is used effectively in at least three situations:
- to acquire new or alternative patterns of behavior from the model which the client has never manifested before (e.g. social skills, self-control);
- to increase or decrease responses already in the client's repertoire through the demonstration by high prestige models of appropriate behavior (e.g. the disinhibition of a shy, withdrawn client's social interactions, or the inhibition of learned fears—e.g. avoidance of gym—or the suppression of impulsive antisocial behavior which gets in the way of social relationships); and
- to increase behaviors which the observing client has already learned and for which there are no existing inhibitions or constraints.

Three variations of modeling—*filmed modeling, live modeling,* and *participant modeling*—tend to be used in clinical practice. Alan Hudson (1987) describes nine steps in the therapeutic use of modeling:

- Provide instructions to the learner (say the parent) about the relevant aspects of modeled behavior to attend to.
- Ask the learner to repeat those relevant aspects to be attended to.
- Model the behavior.
- Ask the learner to report on relevant aspects of the behavior attended to.
- Reinforce the learner for reporting.
- Repeat the modeling, reporting—reinforcing if necessary.
- Ask the learner to imitate modeled behavior.
- Reinforce the learner for imitating the modeled behavior, correcting as necessary.
- Repeat imitation and reinforcement until the behavior is displayed with 100 percent accuracy.

An adult example

Jenny was a quiet, shy woman in her late twenties who found it difficult to cope with her bright, forceful four-year-old daughter and was also experiencing feelings of frustration and anger about her unsatis-

235

factory marital relationship, feelings which she had not dared to communicate openly to her husband. Assessment revealed that Jenny had almost no self-confidence and a very poor self-image, mainly due to past unhappy life experiences. Jenny was well aware of the reason for her self-deprecation and self-doubt but this insight did not seem to affect her behavior. At the Center we began an informed program involving role-playing situations in which she felt unable to assert herself. By modeling appropriate reactions and using relaxation to allay her anxiety we were able to teach her to be more assertive—behavior that reduced her feelings of helplessness and frustration and gave her confidence to make a realistic appraisal of her marriage and exert more control over her life.

Eliminating/Reducing
Inappropriate Behavior

Principle 3: **Satiation**
To get a child to desist from acting in a particular way, allow and encourage him or her to continue performing the desired act until he or she tires of it. Of course this would not be appropriate if the act was dangerous or seriously antisocial.

Principle 4: **Extinction of inappropriate actions**
To stop a child from acting in a particular way, arrange conditions so that he or she receives no rewards following the undesired acts.

Instruction to parents. Ignore minor misdemeanors such as whining, pestering, tantrums. If a child grabs toys or other goodies from his or her small brother, try to ensure the grabbing has no rewarding outcome. Return the toy to its owner. Combine training the older child that grabbing is unproductive with teaching the little one to share. Encourage them to take turns.

Withhold reinforcements such as approval, attention, and the like, which have previously and inappropriately followed undesirable behavior. Remember: your child may "work hard" to regain the lost reinforcement and thus may get "worse" before getting "better." If the problem behavior has been continuously reinforced in the past then extinction should be relatively swift; after all, it is much easier for the youngster to recognize that he or she has lost reinforcers than it is for the child on intermittent reinforcement. In the latter case, extinction tends to be slow.

Planned ignoring of behaviors includes the following:

- As soon as the misbehavior begins, turn away or walk away from your child.
- Say nothing and try not to show any expression at all.
- Resist getting into any debate, argument, or discussion with your child while he or she is misbehaving.
- If you think he or she deserves an explanation for whatever is upsetting him or her, then say "When you have calmed down we will talk about it."

Example of planned ignoring

Suzy is a nine-year-old girl with cerebral palsy, the only child of rather anxious and overprotective parents. They were very concerned at her difficult behavior during mealtimes when, although perfectly able to feed herself, she would refuse to eat unless fed, would throw food and utensils on the floor, and often refused food entirely. Assessment revealed that at school lunches the child showed none of these behaviors. Nor were they displayed at home when she ate informally in front of the television in the evening. Her problem behavior was specific to family lunch at weekends and holidays, the only occasions when the whole family sat down together at the table. It appeared that this setting was providing Suzy with an audience to which she gladly reacted.

In order to combat this, her parents were instructed to ignore any "naughty" behavior and only to speak to Suzy when she was eating properly. They were not to feed her or coax her, and any food refused was to be removed without comment. Between meals snacks were forbidden and the dining room table was rearranged so that Suzy's parents were not directly looking at her. In order to help them ignore her, which they found very difficult at first, they were told to talk to each other, and thus take their minds off Suzy. Within three weekends Suzy was eating normally and has continued to do so. Her parents also used behavioral principles in encouraging self-help skills and have themselves become less overprotective.

Principle 5: **Time-out from positive reinforcement**
The well-known "time-out" procedure is intended to reduce the frequency of an undesirable behavior by ensuring that it is followed by a reduction in the opportunity to acquire reinforcement or rewards. In practice one can distinguish three forms of time-out:

- activity time-out, where a child is simply barred from joining in an enjoyable activity but still allowed to observe it, for example, having misbehaved, he or she is made to sit out of a game;
- room time-out, where the child is removed from an enjoyable activity, not allowed to observe this, but not totally isolated—for example, standing outside a classroom having misbehaved; and
- seclusion time-out, where he or she is socially isolated in a situation from which voluntary escape is impossible.

Time-out sometimes leads to tantrums or rebellious behaviors such as crying, screaming, and physical assaults, particularly if the child has to be taken by force to a quiet room. With older, physically resistive children the method may simply not be feasible. So the procedure and its choice require careful consideration.

When the behavior to be eliminated is an extraordinarily compelling one that all but demands attention (reinforcement) from those present, or when time-out is difficult to administer because the child is strong, the mother (i.e. a major source of reinforcement) could remove herself, together with a magazine, to the bathroom, locking herself in when the child's temper tantrums erupt and coming out only when all is quiet.

Instructions to parents. The child is warned in advance about those behaviors that are considered inappropriate and the consequences that will follow from them. Time-out may last for as much as five minutes. Three minutes is sufficient for younger children.

In practice, "activity" or "room" time-out should always be preferred before any form of "seclusion" time-out. Techniques such as time-out, which are designed to eliminate inappropriate or undesirable behavior, are unlikely to succeed unless supplemented by the reinforcement of an alternative and more appropriate behavior pattern.

A critical determination of the effectiveness of time-out is the extent to which the child actually enjoys the situation from which he or she is removed. If that situation is positively frightening, anxiety provoking, or boring, it is possible that the time-out procedure might involve removing the child to a less aversive situation and thereby actually increase rather than decrease, the frequency of the inappropriate behavior.

Example of time-out

Gary was six-and-a-half years old at referral and was described as a very unlovable child. He constantly screamed and shouted abuse at his parents and had violent temper tantrums when he would indulge in physical aggression, hitting and punching people and furniture, and screaming at the top of his voice until he got his own way. He was also persistently defiant and disobedient and seemed to enjoy provoking confrontation with his parents. Observation and assessment confirmed that Gary was indeed showing all these behaviors but also revealed that they were being heavily reinforced by attention from his parents and by the fact that the shouting and temper tantrums usually resulted in Gary's getting his own way and were therefore highly functional for him. Not surprisingly, against this background, family relationships were very strained and Gary was so unpopular that on the rare occasions when he did behave appropriately it went unnoticed and unattended to, which meant he was only getting attention for antisocial behavior. To deal with the shouting and temper tantrums his parents removed Gary from the room as soon as he started to shout. This use of "time-out from positive reinforcement" was designed to eliminate the possibility of his receiving reinforcing attention for antisocial behavior and in addition they insisted that he comply with the original request on his return. The parents were able to eliminate these outbursts almost entirely. At the same time great emphasis was placed on rewarding Gary for pro-social behavior with tokens which he could then exchange for privilege (such as staying up later) or a treat (such as a favorite play activity with his parents).

This program was designed to improve the relationship with Gary by providing opportunity for mutually reinforcing activities. By the end of the program Gary was much happier, showing much more pro-social behavior and getting on a good deal better with his parents.

This case illustrates how by changing behavior one can also affect attitudes. Experience at the Center shows that by modifying children's more difficult behavior they become more rewarding to their parents. Mothers who have been at the stage of rejecting and even abusing their difficult children find they can see more positive sides of the child and start to enjoy the experience of being a parent as reflected in the case illustration.

Penalizing Undesirable Behavior

Principle 6: **Response-cost**
The use of *response-cost* procedures involves a penalty being invoked for failure to complete a desired response. This may involve the forfeiture of rewards currently available—as, for example, when failure to complete homework results in the loss of television privileges.

Instructions to parents. To stop a child from acting in a particular way, arrange for him or her to terminate a mildly unpleasant situation immediately by changing the behavior in the desired direction. For example, every time he or she throws a toy in a dangerous manner the offending toy is locked away.

Example of response-cost

A hyperactive boy, Darren, was extremely disruptive and noisy. He made life miserable for his older brothers and sisters, while they read or watched television, by constantly interrupting them—making loud humming and wailing noises and also banging things. An extension of the range of rewards for therapeutic intervention is enshrined in the Premack principle or "Granny's Rule"—where a preferred behavior is made contingent on correctly performing a non-preferred behavior. This principle worked well with Darren. A bottle of marbles representing his pocket money plus a bonus was placed on the mantelpiece. Each transgression "cost" a marble (a penny). As always, sanctions were balanced by rewards. Punishment alone tells children what not to do, not what they are expected to do. He was required to play quietly for set periods—timed with a kitchen timer and if he did this successfully he was rewarded by tokens. These tokens could then be exchanged for treats—for example, he could loudly blow his sister's trombone for five minutes: something he had always wanted to do and something he found a great incentive.

Encouraging Competing Behavior

Principle 7: **Over-correction**
Instruction to parents. Require the child to correct the consequences of his or her misbehavior. Not only must he or she remedy the situation caused thereby, but also "overcorrect" it to an improved or better-than-normal state. In other words, you enforce the performance of a new behavior in the situation where you want it to become routine.

Get the child to practice behaviors that are physically incompatible with the inappropriate behavior.

An example

Gavin, who stole and broke another youngster's penknife, was required to save up enough money not only to replace the knife, but also to buy a small gift betokening regret. He was praised at the completion of the act of restitution. When he deliberately punctured another child's bicycle tire he not only had to repair the tire but also to oil and polish the entire vehicle.

This involves positively reinforcing a particular class of behavior that is inconsistent with, or which cannot be performed at the same time as, the undesired act. In other words, to stop a child from acting in a particular way, deliberately reinforce a competing action.

Summary and Comment

Behavior therapy (modification), unlike psychoanalysis, is increasingly being used not only by clinical psychologists but also by psychiatrists, social workers, nurses, and teachers trained in the approach (see Herbert, 1987a/b; 1994; 2001).

There is a great shortage of professional people with relevant training. This can be mitigated by the fact that clinicians do not have a monopoly of helping skills or such therapeutic qualities as common sense; by providing non-professionals and para-professionals with skills to cope with future problems, behavioral work has moved the focus of therapy toward a preventive model of mental health.

This behavioral approach has been taught to parents. Behavioral Parent Training is among the most painstakingly researched and evaluated approaches and doubtless the most successful (see Kazdin, 1997; Long *et al.*, 1994; Taylor and Biglan, 1998; Webster-Stratton, 1988) in modifying aggressive, disruptive behavior in children. Persons without a considerable amount of psychological knowledge can grasp the concepts, and many persons can be taught at one time as a relatively short training period is needed. The long-term purposes of training are to help parents to become more systematic in their own behavior, so as to be more effective in managing their children.

Parents often prefer a view of problem development that does not assume "sick" behavior based on a medical model (see Chapter 1). In addition, many childhood problems consist of well-defined behaviors that are conducive of behavioral treatment. Various methods were described in the chapter. Guidelines on child behaviour management for parents (Herbert and Wookey, 1998) are described in Appendix I.

CHAPTER 12

Using Life Skills Training

After many years of working with families with a seriously problematic child (or children) we are not surprised when we discover a socially isolated family in which parents seldom go out, and the circle of friends has shrunk. For the mother who often is the primary caregiver, social isolation may result in a loss of social confidence and self-esteem. In some instances the parents were (or felt) unskilled from the beginning; in others a difficult (perhaps developmentally disabled) baby made them feel de-skilled. Overall, skills which assist individuals in the many and varied "life-tasks" which become salient at different stages of life, social and problem-solving competencies are high-priority items.

The self-efficacy theory attempts to explain the interacting and mutual influence of people's self-perceptions and their behavior. You may remember that self-efficacy is a belief in oneself, a conviction that one can produce positive outcomes through effort and persistence. People high in their possession of self-efficacy are convinced of their own effectiveness. Those who are low in self-efficacy believe that their efforts are doomed to failure. Parents with a history of failure in their lives begin to believe that they cannot succeed. Their pessimism leads them to avoid the source of their fear, and avoid further handicaps for them and their children.

For example, there is no opportunity for the child to develop new social skills, let alone practice old ones if the mother doesn't speak to people at the park, take the child to parties or friends' homes. And if unskilled patterns of behavior are allowed to continue uninterrupted, children may never learn how to cope adequately with their social environment; this leads to a sense of isolation, unhappiness, and perhaps "acting out" reactions.

The rationale for social skills assessment and training is to help children and their parents to become more flexible and socially competent, so they have less recourse to self-defeating behaviors and feelings.

In the current enthusiasm for social skills training (SST) as a "package" it is important to remember the need for an ABC analysis and comprehensive assessment in each case of "problematic" behavior (see Chapter 2). "Cookbook" applications of SST without such individualized assessments are likely to fail, mainly because of the multicausal nature of children's problems.

A careful analysis should be made of the types of social situations that upset the child. Parental attitudes (such as over-solicitous concern about the child) can foster timidity and provide a cue for the child to behave in a dysfunctional manner when in the company of others. Parents, thus, become part of the intervention. It may be they themselves who, by excessively authoritarian discipline or excessively demanding attitudes, produce negative self-attitudes in the child. Children may feel unwilling or unable to do what is required of them by their parents, and this may transfer to social situations where they feel they are on display.

If parents themselves lack social skills and graces, they may fail to provide adequate models for their children to identify with or imitate in social situations. Again, parents who are inconsistent in their demands on their children may engender timidity in them because they never know whether what they are doing is right.

The interference model. The interpretation here is that specific skills are, in fact, present but not employed because emotional or cognitive factors interfere with the performance of their skills. The "process" of working out appropriate goals and strategies, of monitoring and setting standards, and then adjusting and controlling one's actions, may be faulty. This could result from severe anxiety, faulty self-attributions, and low self-esteem.

Social Skills Training

This approach involves a structured learning experience for developing skills for interacting with people (see Taylor, *et al.*, 1999). It aims to change specific person-to-person behaviors that influence the quality of relationships, such as:

- assertiveness;
- the ability to listen;
- conversational skills (plus greetings and partings);
- non-verbal skills;
- the ability to be rewarding;
- observational skills (reading social signals, getting information, asking questions); and
- problem-solving skills (the ability to work out solutions to novel and thorny social problems).

Even young people with poor social skills are likely to have several effective components of socially skilled behaviors. These can be built on, improved, and integrated smoothly, by instruction, or by feedback and prompts, during role rehearsal. Role rehearsal allows you to comment on the client's performance. It is a gradual process—building up skills by means of working out the various component tasks making up a particular skill. This "pretend" sort of rehearsal provides an intermediate step in changing behavior and developing new and more effective strategies. The end point is when the client tries out the new skill or role in real life.

Problem Solving

Life is full of crises, problems, and decisions, but many people do not have the appropriate skills to manage them. Much of what we think of as problematic behavior in a client can be viewed as the consequence of ineffective behavior and thinking. The individual is unable to resolve certain dilemmas in his or her life; the unproductive attempts to do so have adverse effects such as anxiety and depression, not to mention the creation of additional problems such as confrontations and interpersonal conflict. For the professional the way to decode the client's sometimes incomprehensible actions is to ask yourself what he or she is trying to "achieve"—seen from their point of view (Kazdin, *et al.*, 1992).

Often, what the client is trying to achieve is the narrowing of the *discrepancy* between his or her *actual* state of affairs and his or her *desired* (or *ideal*) state of affairs. The discrepancy is the problem, and the client's solutions may be making things worse. Problem solving aims to reduce or eliminate this gap with some modification—perhaps a compromise position. Most often as problem solvers we try to improve the actual state of affairs by finding an answer to a difficulty, a solution to a problem.

The process of problem solving involves you in the following activities:

- *defining the problem and its severity* as precisely as possible. This entails:
  - (a) assessing the current (actual) state of affairs; and
  - (b) specifying the desired (ideal) state of affairs (goals) (see Flow Chart 1).
- *assessing the nature and magnitude of the problem.* This entails:
  - (a) listing the "forces" helping the client move toward the desired goals; and
  - (b) listing the "forces" hindering the client from moving toward this goal.

In "force-field analysis," as it is called, the problem is viewed as a balance between forces pushing in opposite directions.

Current State of Affairs
(Sally's/truancy)

(a) Get your client (it may be a family group) to use brainstorming to construct a list of helping (+) and hindering (–) forces.

Helping Forces	*Hindering Forces*
The family's behind her.	Perhaps we put too much pressure on her.

Sally wants to return to school.	She gets panicky when she tries.
The teacher is sympathetic.	Her schoolmates tease her when she appears. There is a bully in her classroom.

(b) Rank the forces in order of their significance in influencing the present situation. Rate the importance of forces according to the relative ease with which they can be resolved. Do not waste time on unrealistic ideas.

- *Formulate alternative strategies.* This entails working out the various means of moving the client (individual or group) from the actual to the desired state of affairs. Creative and divergent (unconventional) thinking, inventiveness, and critical ability are all helpful at this stage. You have to change the helping forces (strengthening them) and the hindering forces (reducing or eliminating them) in order to alter the current state of affairs.

- *Now decide on and implement the strategy.* This entails:
  - (a) selecting the alternatives that seem most likely to succeed;
  - (a) specifying the "know-how," methods, and other resources required to implement the chosen strategy.

- *Evaluate the outcome of applying the strategy.* This entails:
  - (a) defining what a successful outcome means—in terms of explicit criteria;
  - (b) specifying what the effects or consequences of the strategy were.

Group problem solving is generally more fruitful than individual effort, although there is no guarantee of this in particular instances.

In the problem-solving approach "small" is not so much "beautiful" as "manageable." Problems are not manageable when they are conceived in large global terms. (*"Everything* is going wrong"; "He will *never* change"; "There is *no hope*"; "I seem to have the world on my shoulders.")

You break through this rhetoric by trying to establish and obtain the relevant facts—attempting to "unpack" the complicated-looking dilemma. The more your clients can adopt a *mental set* that they *can* cope with a problem, the greater is the likelihood that with your help they will come up with a solution to it.

The feeling of being in control and, conversely, *not* helpless is vital to the successful working through of difficult situations and is invaluable when you are involved in crisis interventions. You "re-label" the problem for the clients, defining what they once thought of as impenetrable as "manageable"—given thought and calm application of a series of interpersonal problem-solving strategies.

The Development of Problem-Solving Skills

Interpersonal problem-solving skills are learned from experiences beginning in the family and wherever the child interacts with others in situations that give rise to interpersonal difficulties. How well the developing child learns these skills is thought to reflect the extent to which the child's caregivers manifest these abilities themselves; also, the degree to which parents communicate in ways that encourage the exercise of such thinking in the child.

The emphasis is very much (but not exclusively) on how the person thinks; the goal in therapy or training is to generate a way of thinking, a way of using beliefs and values in making decisions at such times that problems arise.

George Spivack and his colleagues (Spivack, *et al.*, 1976) have defined a number of differing interpersonal cognitive problem-solving skills. They suggest a series of skills rather than a single ability. The significance of each of these abilities in determining the degree of social adjustment is said to differ as a function of age.

The interpersonal cognitive problem-solving skills include:

- *Problem sensitivity,* which is the ability to be aware of problems that arise out of social interactions and a sensitivity to the kinds of social situations out of which interpersonal difficulties may arise. It also involves the ability to examine relationships with others in the here and now.
- *Alternative solution training.* A close parallel to this is "brainstorming." The key feature is the ability to generate a wide variety of potential solutions to the problem. Judgment about what is best is suspended, and the skill is to draw from a repertoire of ideas representing differing categories of solutions to a given problem.
- *Brainstorming* is the creative art of generating the greatest number of ideas in the shortest possible time. It is ideally suited to group participation as well as individual application. There are some simple rules you apply to your chosen topic:
  - (a) accept every idea that the topic or issue gives rise to uncritically;
  - (b) aim for quantity of ideas rather than quality;
  - (c) at this stage do not initiate any discussion;
  - (d) list the ideas (e.g., write them on a blackboard or flip chart);
  - (e) set a time limit; and
  - (f) code the ideas when the brainstorming session is over.

For example: (i) underline those that are not clear/understood; (ii) put a cross next to those that are impossible; (iii) put an asterisk against those that look useful and/or are worth exploring further.

Work out with the client the likely consequences of the better courses of action you have put forward. What is the utility of these consequences in resolving the problem as it has been formulated? For example, with regard to the proposed solutions put forward by Mrs Hayes for managing Avril's tantrums:

(a) Punishment doesn't seem to work; in fact, it seems to make her more intractable.

(b) If I ignore her she'll probably follow me around, yelling more loudly. Like me she can be very stubborn.

(c) The idea of trying to reason with Avril sounds good, but I find it so hard to keep cool. And we may not be able to resolve things in the heat of the particular confrontation.

(d) My husband won't thank me for insisting that he back me up; he'll say "It's your problem."

(e) Putting Avril in time-out may work but it could also generate trouble, more sulking, and tantrums.

(f) Trying to find occasions to praise Avril should be a possibility; Avril can be reasonable when she's in a good mood—the trick is to catch her at the right time. She is vain and enjoys praise.

- *Means-ends thinking* reflects the ability to articulate the step-by-step means necessary to carry out the solution to a given interpersonal problem. The skill encompasses the ability to recognize obstacles, the social sequences deriving from these solutions, and a recognition that interpersonal problem solving takes time.
- *Consequential thinking* involves being aware of the consequences of social acts as they affect self and others and includes the ability to generate alternative consequences to potential problem solutions before acting.
- *Causal thinking* reflects the degree of appreciation of social and personal motivation and involves the realization that how one felt and acted may have been influenced by and, in turn, may have influenced how others felt and acted.

Any decision to change is likely to involve both benefits and "costs"; benefits for the client, for significant others, and for his or her network. There could also be costs to the client, to others and to his or her social setting. You might construct a list—with your client's help—of the likely benefits and costs of a particular planned change, in terms of these six categories.

Summary and Comment

Many, perhaps a majority of, clients who come for help to social workers and related disciplines, are deficient in life skills—most notably social and problem-solving skills. Fortunately there is a growing literature—theoretical and practical—for improving these skills. It is important not to think of them as a panacea for all social problems. It is also vital not to use them in cookbook fashion without a full and rigorous assessment.

PART IV

Empowerment of Families and Evaluation of Practice

The final two chapters bring us to our natural stopping point which is answering the questions each of us raises in our professional lives. First, did our interventions in the lives of children and families help instead of harm; and did the help experienced have a lasting effect? Second, are the practices and programs we deliver effective in attaining the problem solution hoped for; and were we efficient in their delivery?

Chapter 13 explains the importance of our intervention having lasting benefits for our clients in their daily lives as they continue to interact and cope in their families and communities. Long-term intervention and lengthy follow-up are giving way to demands for cost containment through briefer services as called for by managed care practices. The opportunity for ongoing support from community-based services is an extension of intervention beyond the agency. Healthy participation in social settings extends benefits of treatment into daily living. Focusing on client strengths is important to this extension. Having the capacity to be self-empowered and utilize their strengths, clients do take charge of their situations.

In addition to termination and whatever limited follow-up we provide, linking children and families with support networks is an important addition to our practice. Current mentoring practices are increasing as more and more evidence points to the benefit of mentoring in various life transitions. Examples of mentoring programs with youth are included in this chapter.

Chapter 14 calls for greater attention to ongoing evaluation of practices and programs as means to evaluating both processes and outcomes of our work. A comprehensive list of common purposes of evaluation is provided, not the least of which is the issue of responding to demands for greater professional accountability. Attention is brought to program evaluation and practice evaluation as important in identifying the costs and benefits of both our interventions and the many programs and agencies in the human services arena.

Finally, attention is given to ethical practices of evaluation. We are reminded that ethical, legal, and professional standards inform ethical practice and apply to service delivery, evaluation, and research methodology used in evaluating programs and practices.

Current literature is referenced to enable the reader to pursue the complex issues of research methodology and practice and program evaluation. The enormous challenge of mastering knowledge and techniques necessary for competent practice and its evaluation has implications for all of us.

CHAPTER 13

Beyond the Agency Door: Empowering and Mentoring Families

It is indeed a rare occasion when a client stops by a social work agency to report what a great day it is! Instead, clients seek help with problems, report progress with problems, or hope that the helping process will either keep problems away or will find solutions that work. From such problem presentation, social work intervention can become that of solving problems instead of defining client strengths. As clients have sought help with problems, in the past the helping field has operated mostly from a medical model perspective of identifying and diagnosing problems and then implementing a treatment plan. Helping professions have moved away from exclusive focus on problem configuration. Social workers are particularly aware of personal, social and political systems in the environment where families live and work. The current practice of focusing on client strengths is a shift from the traditional approaches of deficits and disease that have characterized much of social work practice (Cowger, 1997).

In this texts example of Avril Hayes, the family experienced great stress, a loss of self-confidence, feelings of failure and guilt, and a sense of powerlessness to change their personal and social situations. Avril's misbehavior, aggression, demands, and regressive behaviors escalated beyond her parents' control. Reinforced by the situation, Avril only increased her aggressive and demanding behaviors. Through the helping process, Avril's parents were able to verbalize their need for her misbehaviors to stop and to identify new and appropriate behaviors. They learned to support desired behaviors and ignore or punish dysfunctional behaviors. In the problem-solving journey with her family and counselor, Avril learned to respond to her parents' rewards and punishments and to replace misbehaviors with new and positive behaviors.

255

When the family unit gained new ways of interacting together, it experienced control over their interactions in their personal and social environments.

For the Hayes family, the interventive process involved:

(1) identifying problem behaviors and problem parenting;
(2) identifying rewarding and unrewarding interactions;
(3 selecting behaviors desired;
(4) introducing practicing rewards and punishments;
(5) practicing parenting skills;
(6) extending interpersonal relationships beyond the family;
(7) being self-directed as a family unit; and
(8) gaining personal and social competence in their social environment.

Assessment and intervention undertaken by their worker focused on identifying their problem and possible interventions or solutions. This plan for self-direction or "empowerment" of Avril and her parents enabled them to interact successfully together and with others.

As you work with your clients, one measure of your effectiveness is the success your clients have in daily living beyond the intervention. The very capacity to control and direct their lives is empowering and will likely become part of their personal and social worlds after professionals are no longer involved.

Identifying and Utilizing Client Strengths

Even though professions recognize the importance of working with strengths and resources of client systems, assessment often begins with problem identification or diagnosis of pathology. This practice has long been the basis of medical and of social work practices (Cowger, 1999) which have given way to greater reliance on empowerment, problem solving and briefer treatment.

In preceding chapters of this book, utilizing clients' strengths and resources is presented as a crucial part of intervention with them. In Chapter 6 and consistent with working with the strengths and potentials that families and children bring to the intervention situation, we discuss responsiveness in parents and children and promote utilizing their strengths to facilitate development of prosocial behavior. Chapter 8 calls for an inventory of client strengths and involvement of client(s) in their own treatment goals. Throughout the book we identify strengths and weaknesses that clients and client systems bring to the task of problem solving and suggest ways in which the worker can engage those with whom they work in order to build on their own strengths.

Strengths Perspective

Saleebey (1997, 1999b) promotes a strengths perspective for working with clients. Working to discover, build, enhance, and support client strengths so that they can reach their goals and realize their hopes is consistent with the strengths perspective of social work. Recognizing the strong capacities of people to access and to utilize personal and community support systems to grow personally and socially validates qualities of personal resilience and strength. As practitioners in search of identifying and utilizing client strengths and resources, we should approach our clients as "cups half full" and not as "cups half empty." Assessing strengths to cope with great stresses, as well as smaller and more ordinary problems does not ignore the pain, sense of powerlessness, nor inability to take charge of daily living. Practicing assessment from a strengths perspective in no way discounts the pain and suffering experienced by families such as Avril's, nor underestimates the need for care of those experiencing life crises. Instead, the strengths perspective recognizes that clients and their families seek help so that they may live independently and be self-directed to the greatest extent possible.

Viewed as an approach or perspective rather than a theory, strengths assessment is a way of viewing solutions and building capacities of people to grow and change. According to Saleebey (1997), "Practicing from a strengths orientation means this—everything you do as a social worker will be predicated, in some way, on helping to discover and embellish, explore and exploit clients' strengths and resources in the service of assisting them to achieve their goals, realize their dreams, and shed the irons of their own inhibitions and misgivings" (p. 3). Assessing strengths of individuals and multiple client systems and then communicating these strengths and resources to clients provides an opportunity for the client (or client system) to collaborate in the intervention process. Building on strengths of clientele has the potential to allow clients to gain a greater sense of progress, and to become stronger partners and consumers in the helping relationship (Cowger, 1999).

Strengths vary among individuals and are influenced by societal and cultural factors as well. Common human strengths important in assessing coping and growth include (McQuaide and Ehrenreich, 1997):

- cognitive skills involving verbal, logic, memory, intelligence;
- coping mechanisms such as defenses, flexibility;
- dispositional factors including self-esteem and temperament;
- interpersonal skills such as maintaining relationships and solving problems; and
- external factors including resources and society.

Unlike identifying problems, assessing strengths is more straightforward. Nevertheless, conducting assessment from a strengths perspective requires strong observation, listening and interpersonal skills on the part of the workers. The intent in assessment is to gain an understanding of the client—the person and their perspective of pain, trauma, resilience, solution, hopes, dreams, and experiences. Saleebey (1999b) shares strengths assessment possibilities as follows:

- Look around you. Looking involves observing activities, interests, talents, and creativity of the client or client system.
- Listen to clients' stories. Personal accounts, narratives, histories of places and events in time provide rich accounts of life experiences, interests, dreams, and ambitions.
- Ask survival questions. In other words, ask questions

about past coping experiences and survival behaviors that have been helpful.

- Ask support questions. Learn about support systems including family, organizations, special sources, meaningful associations, and other helpful things.
- Ask exception questions. Identify the things that are important, interesting, different, or special in relationships and other experiences.
- Ask possibility questions. What are their goals, hopes, and dreams? Learn what help the client expects or the quality of life they hope for.
- Ask esteem questions. How does the client see him/herself and what is the view of others?

In the client–worker partnership for growth and change, the client becomes the expert about her/his life. For example, who knows better than a welfare mother with three children of how to feed, clothe, shelter, and educate children while managing transportation and health care with a grossly inadequate income? She is also best able to identify how she manages and what alternatives to inefficiencies in service systems there are for her. She can explain her hopes for her children and her means for achieving them. Or, in the Hayes family case example, Avril's parents could best explain the distress experienced in the family and the positive and negative results of their disciplinary efforts.

Identifying and working with strengths of clients and client systems can guide you in your work in interpersonal and social interactions with children and families. Consistent with Saleebey (1999b), some guiding principles of the strengths perspective are:

- Every client, i.e. individual, family, group, and/or community, has strengths—intellectual, physical, financial, or support systems.
- Personal suffering (including abuse, loss, illness, and victimization) can become a source of strength, a motivator or a challenge.
- Upper limits of client capabilities and potential achieve-

ment are unknown and to be discovered sometimes in situations where great adversity is overcome.

- Helping is a collaborative effort, one in which the client may well have the greatest wisdom and resources.
- Great resources abound at all levels of individual and societal systems and can be harnessed for problem solving.

Client strengths and resources are the greatest resources for you as a helper to rely on. For instance, previous research has identified eight cross-cultural curative factors, i.e. healing factors that are common across cultures and found in a variety of situations with a variety of clients (Torrey, 1986; Harper and Lantz, 1996). Two of these cross-cultural curative factors are hope and control. Hope is identified in a variety of situations including one as terrible as a concentration camp during World War II. Sense of mastery or control is linked to increased social functioning and feelings of empowerment. The strengths perspective encompasses individual, social, community strengths, and community resources that provide the greatest opportunity from which clients can experience empowerment over adversity and suffering.

Interestingly, client strengths suggest a "wholeness," a complete configuration of the person involving personal and social domains. For example, in the situation of Avril and her parents, separating the parents from their child and from her social systems was not reasonable. Together, the family members brought not only their struggles and hopes but also their strengths and resources.

Avril and her Parents—Personal and Social Domains

Development in both personal and social domains of the Hayes family, discussed in Chapter 8, reflects the progress experienced by Mrs Hayes as her depression lifted and she gained confidence in her parenting role. Both she and Avril enjoyed social contacts with other families and reported hoping to continue involvement with others outside the family. The case of the Hayes family is one example of increased life-skills development. It builds upon strengths and capacities that enable them to gain new understanding of improved communication, discipline, rewards, and feelings of love and care for each other. Long-term follow-up in this case found that the Hayes family had been able to sustain progress in personal and social domains of their lives a year after treatment ended.

The example of the Hayes family demonstrates the process and outcomes of strengths assessment and treatment where dysfunctional behaviors in the family were directly related to interactions and communications. Avril's parents identified their own sense of personal failure and loss of self-esteem, which they experienced in their struggle to establish appropriate parent–child responses and behaviors. These negative feelings affected the family members in many areas of their lives and reduced their ability to feel rewarded in interactions with friends, work, community activities, and social events. They had avoided taking Avril to social events because of their inability to manage her distracting and embarrassing demands. In these situations, family members often experience stress and frustration that cannot be contained within family boundaries but spill over into other areas of their lives.

This example of inter-connectedness in the Hayes family supports the conclusions of Cowger's work in the strengths perspective literature. The Hayes case example demonstrates that children and families grow and change in both social and personal domains of their lives in response to a renewed sense of power that comes from exercising self-direction. Separating, or discounting, social or personal domains of clients' lives is not consistent with the strengths perspective, because these domains are interdependent and interactive. Growth and energy in one domain positively impacts the other (Cowger, 1997).

The range of problems and stresses that cause families to seek help from professionals is much broader. Domestic violence, marital dysfunctions, childhood disorders, adolescent adjustment, school failure, teen pregnancy, and medical crises are but a few of the problems that families have. Many seek help with failure in their lives and with problems that are beyond the context of dysfunctional interpersonal relationships. These problems may reflect failure to have adequate resources for food, housing, clothing, education, and other necessities for living in today's society. Other problems relate to serious illnesses, medical crises, job failures, and unemployment. In Chapter 8, the mobilization of resources is discussed as an important intervention. Many kinds of support are necessary as social workers, counselors, and other helping professionals join clients in their journey to find solutions to problems and to gain satisfaction in their daily lives.

Helping Beyond the Agency Door

Intervening in the lives of clients is hard work! Individual helping, family therapy, group work, and problem solving all require specialized knowledge and skill to assess, treat, evaluate, and productively join clients in their voyage to problem solution. How often is it that social workers, counselors, psychologists, or health care professionals ask soul-searching questions: Did I help enough?, Is my client going to be able to maintain progress?, How realistic is long-term follow-up?

Many professionals would like to think that intervention toward problem resolution has strong and lasting effects that enhance resiliency of clients on their trajectory toward healthier and happier lives in a successful and self-directed manner. However, "practice wisdom," along with outcome studies and follow-up measures of long-term benefits from service, tell us that those who receive supportive or follow-up services after a period of intense care are more likely to sustain their progress or to prevent more serious or additional dysfunction (Mallon, 1998; Bloom, *et al.*, 1996; Jankowski, *et al.*, 1996). At this juncture in our discussion, it is important to reflect upon the long-term benefits or the quality of life realized from our work. Community services and briefer or short-term services are increasingly important in work with children and families.

Sustaining Benefits: Practice Examples.

Support systems and programs abound beyond the agency. People take charge of their lives and develop strength to become happier and more productive.

In your work with children and families you can find evidence of the importance of supportive networks and services in the lives of children and families. There are a variety of examples in which social networks provide families with the necessary support. For example, youth in out-of-home care have a high likelihood of leaving care for independent living, having missed the opportunity to learn life skills in a family environment. A study of 46 youths discharged from out-of-home care to independent living from Green Chimneys Children's Services in New York City reports the significance of follow-up for the youth (Mallon, 1998). Important supports identified by the youth included family, relatives, friends, teachers, employers, agencies, and churches. Sixty-seven percent reported maintaining contact with staff members of the agency after discharge. Mallon (1998) reports that linking youth with each other and with adult mentors are important measures in providing support for successful independence of these youth.

Another example that illustrates the importance of social support networks is evidenced among adoptive families who participated in post-legal adoption treatment groups. These client families were adoptive families who were served by the Post-Legal Adoption Services Project of Lucas County Children Services in Ohio, a project funded by the Department of Health and Human Services (Harper and Loadman, 1992a). These adoptive children and parents, mostly families with children in early adolescence, were threatened with failed adoptions and were experiencing major stress and conflict in their families. Among families who are on the edge of returning their children to the custody of the public agency, about 10 percent of families who adopt children in the United States eventually experience failed adoptions and do return their adoptees to the agency (Barth and Berry, 1988). Throughout an eight-week period, parents and children from 40 adoptive families participated in post-legal adoptive family treatment groups of eight to 10 members each. There they learned about and explored avenues for coping with problems unique to adoptive families. Parents and children gained skills in communication, explored expectations, gained self-esteem, and met other adoptive families through the group experience. Much empowered by their treatment experience and connected to a new network of adoptive families, these families set about developing community-based support groups for themselves and other adoptive families. Through this continuing social support network they hoped to gain confidence and help other families prevent adoption dissolution. For some, these support groups would complement the individual counseling they planned for themselves and their adoptive child. It is noteworthy that only one of the families served by the program terminated adoption at the end of one year following the post-legal adoption treatment group intervention (Harper and Loadman, 1992b). Other families remained intact and some led support groups for adoptive families in their own communities.

The case example of Avril Hayes follows her only through the intervention period. Nevertheless, she and her family would benefit greatly from ongoing involvement in support networks in their neighborhood and community. Such network linkage would provide the family the opportunity to build upon their personal and family strengths and to build upon the progress they made. Such a group could help the family sustain new management techniques for Avril's behavioral problems and anticipate changing behaviors as she progresses to new ages and stages in her development.

In many ways, the opportunity for ongoing support from community-based services is an extension of intervention beyond the agency. More affordable and consistent with expectations for client independence, participation in natural and social support networks empowers members and allows children and families to utilize much less clinic-based treatment. Such independence and participation in social settings extend benefits of treatment well beyond the agency door and into the daily lives of families.

Mentors: Extending Helping and Building on Strengths

Definition and Roots of Mentoring

Mentoring has not been a common practice of helpers in human services. The practice of mentoring is relatively new for professions like social work and counseling, but it has been a long-standing practice in fields such as business and education. The practice of setting examples, providing senior role models for junior managers and junior partners, has long been a practice in business, law, banking, organizational management, and corporate settings. Those in such partnerships are often protected, promoted, and in turn will mentor their partners and successors. For many, this internal promotion or "favor owed" could be called in. Serving as a path to power in corporate America, mentoring has a history of being a traditional male practice in which one who is older, more experienced, and powerful can create a path for successful growth and promotion of another.

It is noted that early models of corporate power and control have given way to practices of partnering, supporting, and enabling so newcomers to professions and organizations can learn organizational practices (Bell, 1996). Mentoring involves a relationship and requires eventual separatism in which the mentee is free to go on, to exercise individual power and direction, and to surpass the mentor (Jeruchim and Shapiro, 1992).

Mentoring is not a modern phenomenon but one of civilizations past. As told in *The Odyssey*, Telemachus, son of Odysseus, needed to learn wisdom and sensitivity. Telemachus was assigned a teacher named Mentor who was old, experienced, ethical, wise, trusted, and compassionate. Mentor was more than a teacher of facts as he guided Telemachus in preparation to rule the kingdom. Through modeling and thoughtful guidance, Mentor carried out his mission in preparing his protégé for roles involving power and leadership. Anderson and Shannon (1995) conclude from their analyses of Mentor and Telemachus that mentoring is defined as an intentional and insightful effort to nurture, protect, support, and serve as a role model.

A more contemporary example of mentoring is that found in teacher education programs. In much the same way as business and management, the field of education has long had mentors. Teacher education literature is rich with accounts of mentoring, particularly in areas of internships for student teachers. A major role for supervising teachers is to mentor student teachers in classroom teaching and to serve as experts to guide the student teacher in classroom teaching and student/teacher relationships (Campbell and Horbury, 1994; Aspinwall, *et al.*, 1994). The educational model of mentor–mentee is collaborative as the teacher and student work together to bring the student teacher onboard as a teacher and to bring new learning activities to K-12 classroom environments. Upon completion of the supervised teaching assignment, the mentoring relationship ends. Little contact continues between mentor and mentee with the exception of occasional letters of reference. Learning opportunities occur for both student and mentor in these teacher–student relationships; yet, once the purpose of the relationship is accomplished, contact generally terminates. Interestingly, this is not atypical of relationships in clinical settings where meaningful worker/client relationships end with the termination of treatment.

More recently, professional women have become involved in mentoring. Feminist literature gives voice to the need for mentoring and credits mentoring as an important ingredient in many feminine successes and achievements. Moving beyond severe oppression or discrimination in the workplace, women and racial minorities have openly and actively developed networks and mentors for purposes such as employment, promotion, achievement, success, and equal access. Different mentors may be helpful at different ages and stages according to Jeruchim and Shapiro (1992). Women enter careers at various times in their lives, often having reared children and sometimes entering the workforce as single parents. A middle-aged woman with such experiences would have mentoring needs very different from a 20-year-old entering her first job. Perhaps more so than men, women relate to and benefit from mentors of either gender. Women and minorities continue to need mentoring in order to enter the internal working relationships of organizations that are often male dominated and relatively closed. Many professional women and their mentors continue to chip away at the glass ceiling. At a different level, women who are clients experience similar exclusion from access to better jobs, resources, acceptance, and respect. Although different in content and context, mentoring is a process that is useful and appropriate for women in many situations, both in public and private roles, including the range from professional careers to parenting.

Human Services Mentors

Mentoring is not a service typically delivered by social service agencies. However, the practice of mentoring is spreading in public and nonprofit human service organizations. Paraprofessionals, volunteers, and community workers fit easily into roles and jobs of mentors,

Fitting well into the community and closer to "natural helpers," community-based mentors are new to the human services helping arena (Harper-Dorton, 1999b). In addition to familiar helping professionals like social workers, counselors, and psychologists, mentors are becoming a useful extension of other helping professions. Extension of support within familiar home and community contexts is an important follow-up for many clients, including those who benefit from more intensive interventions such as that described in the case of the Hayes family. Other types of client situations in need of some level of follow-up include those involving potential dangers of family violence, child abuse, school failure, teen pregnancy, and elderly or disabled clients. Many children and families are now benefiting from mentors, either natural mentors in their social networks or mentors made available through various community-based service programs.

In human services, as in other arenas, mentoring includes modeling, feedback, and new levels of performance. As a result, mentoring is a means of empowerment—not of "empowering" another but of providing experience and feedback that help overcome past performances or previous feelings of helplessness. In this context, mentoring is a bridge to empowerment processes that become established through collaboration between mentors and mentees.

An example of the empowerment process is described by Webster-Stratton and Herbert (1994) in their application of the collaborative approach. The perceptions of parents with seriously disruptive children have important implications for treatment because learned helplessness and low self-efficacy beliefs can be reversed by experiences of success. The promotion of effective parenting skills undoubtedly starts a reversal process. Parents soon expect that they will eventually be able to control outcomes—notably their children's behavior. Webster-Stratton and Herbert (1994) present their categorization of operations defining therapeutic processes in collaboration with clients. These operations or strategies are classified in terms of knowledge, skills and values, and are detailed in Appendix 4.

Empowering and collaborative work with families requires the therapist to actively work with the parents. Collaborative activities include:

(1) soliciting their ideas and feelings;
(2 understanding their cultural context;
(3) involving them in the joint process of setting goals;
(4) sharing their experience;
(5) discussing and debating ideas; and
(6) solving problems.

The social work role is that of therapeutic partner, to understand the parents' perspectives, to clarify issues, and to summarize important ideas and themes. There is culturally sensitive teaching and coaching. Webster-Stratton and Herbert (1994) suggest that the collaborative process for developing solutions is more likely to increase parents' sense of confidence, self-sufficiency and perceived self-efficacy than are traditional therapy models.

Movements to find role models and mentors reflect the importance of mentoring in the life process (Jeruchim and Shapiro, 1992). Mentoring practices are on the rise in professions like social work, counseling, psychology, and allied health sciences professions.

Practice Examples of Mentoring

Among students. Numerous accounts of successful mentoring programs can be found. One example had the purpose of helping relocated students adjust to living and studying in a new cultural environment. Mowry (1994), a social work educator who served as a mentor to relocated Hmong students, identified some benefits of mentoring. He incorporated his mentoring experience in curricular development to help promote understanding of cross-cultural knowledge, beliefs, and practices.

Teenage mothers. Mentoring is a common practice in working with teenage mothers who have goals ranging from gaining mothering and parenting skills to gaining self-esteem and completing high school. One study of 20 teen mothers with mentors assigned to them credited their mentors with influencing them to continue their education, evaluate options, and build self-esteem by remaining in school, or holding part-time jobs. Nearly half of the group maintained contact with their mentors after completing high school (Zippay, 1995).

Out-of-home youth. Serving youth who are in out-of-home care is a long-term, costly, and challenging arena. There are multiple examples of programs designed to mentor these youth, including the widely familiar Big Brothers and Big Sisters Programs. Among populations of youth in foster care and independent living arrangements, mentoring is an important service. Numerous programs serving these youth exist and can be placed in common categories. These mentoring models serve an important transitional function in the lives of adolescents, some of whom likely experienced multiple foster care arrangements. Although believed to be important preventive programs, little evaluation is available (Mech, *et al.*, 1995). According to Mech, *et al.* (1995), among programs designed to mentor youth, five model programs are:

- Transitional Life Skills: matching adults with adolescents to develop life skills and independent living;
- Cultural Empowerment: same race/ethnicity mentors and gay/lesbian mentors;
- Corporate/Business Mentors: mentoring targets job preparedness and placement;
- Mentors for Young Parents: mentors assist young mothers and serve a preventive function;
- Mentor Homes: adult mentor guides four to six youths and serves as a group-home parent or manager.

Welfare-to-work families. One example stems from recent welfare reform. As a result of current welfare reform, many families are in search of retraining and employment. These client families affected by welfare reform and related welfare-to-work requirements are a population often served by multiple providers. One of the early models of mentoring training developed especially to meet the needs of families participating in welfare-to-work programming is the Family Mentoring Program, operated by West Virginia Community Action Agencies. This program provides a curriculum to train paraprofessionals to serve as mentors to families affected by welfare-to-work requirements. Curricular areas include self-awareness, basic needs awareness, basic interviewing, and problem solving premised on respect, change, and action for independent living and teaching techniques (Randall and Newfield, 1997). Basic interpersonal relationship information, communications training, and daily living skills development including job search and interviewing training are included as well. Once trained, family mentors work with families and children in their homes and communities and support them in their efforts to assess employable skills, search for employment, and reduce barriers to employment such as child care and transportation gaps.

Boundary Concerns In Mentoring Practice

Evaluation from various phases of the ongoing Family Mentoring Program has been completed (Harper-Dorton, 1998, 1999a). One of the interesting findings from rich narratives provided by mentors is that mentors have special boundary concerns:

(1) Being in mentees' homes as often as three days and sometimes five days a week demands clear distinction around the boundaries of mentors. Mentors are not family, friends, nor social workers. Instead roles of teacher, advisor, manager, supporter, and counselor all are included in the mentoring process.

(2) Maintaining professional distance while helping mentee families experience celebrations, empowerment, and support that come with successes like graduation, employment, weddings, etc., requires special effort.

(3) Collaborating and partnering in mentoring require negotiation and mediation abilities so that goals can be established, evaluated and renegotiated if necessary. Such goal development processes must be collaborative and fit well with the value system of the mentee.

Mentoring is a bridging activity—and, depending upon the goals established by mentor/mentee collaboration, can be a bridge of any sort. Mentoring can be a bridge to employment, better parenting, greater self-esteem, leadership, job promotion, etc. Mentored in an assistant principal role, Kirsten Hibert (2000) describes her mentoring experience as being about leadership, power, social justice, compassion, and "honest talk" about self and others. She targets valuing real feelings and real people in the mentor/mentee relationship.

Empowerment: The Glue That Can Hold!

Few citations in the literature clearly voice the responsibility that we have to empower children and families and to study the phenomena of their moving beyond the "disempowerment" that clienthood sometimes brings. Wiley and Rappaport (2000) link research and developmental psychology to build a bridge for advocacy. In your work with families and children, you, too, can advocate for empowering families and children in both personal and political arenas of their lives. Empowerment fits well with social work values and practices and is useful in advocating for those who are oppressed and marginalized (Robbins, *et al.*, 1998).

Having families and children in charge of their lives and taking control of their worlds are common practice goals. Having power over one's life, both in personal and political spheres, is a lifelong adventure full of rewards and greater personal satisfaction (Solomon, 1976). Self-empowerment applies to all people and is defined differently by each person as he or she finds meaning and places value on real life experiences. As workers, we cannot "empower"—we are not omnipotent. However, it is our challenge to help identify and explore processes that enable those whom we work with to find positive meaning in their personal and social environments.

Definition

What is this term "empowerment" that is so important to your clients? Rose (2000) captures its importance for human qualities:

> *Central to this practice (empowerment) was understanding the notion as a relational expression, not a technique or instrument. In empowering relationships, meaning was restored to each person; earned trust was built into explicit acknowledgment of the purpose of the practice; interactions were explored for their links to social structures and their interest; and clients' lives were envisioned simultaneously as unique in terms of meaning, but collective or population-based in terms of patterns of domination and system barriers to validity. (p. 412)*

Another definition hints at the social and political forces of the concept of empowerment. Based on Hodges, *et al.*'s (1998) summation of social work research (Conger and Kanungo, 1988; Deming, 1984; Dunst, *et al.*, 1988), empowerment is a process that enhances self-image and self-efficacy, involves clients in the change process, facilitates access to needed resources and problem solutions, and enables assertive and proactive behaviors. Empowering clients is a long-standing social work practice and comes from a strengths perspective wherein individual, social, and political power, or potentials for such power, is built upon. Empowerment processes continue to include working to increase abilities to identify and utilize personal, social, or political strength in pursuing happiness, self-esteem, and physical and emotional health.

Client empowerment has roots in the charity and settlement house movements of the late 1800s. Poor, immigrant, and illiterate populations were provided aid, taught necessary language skills, and placed in jobs. Throughout the last 50 years, the social work profession has advocated for social changes such as those represented by civil rights and women's movements. During this period, social change involved client participation and political action (Simon, 1998; Kopp, 1989). The history and evolution of empowerment reflects the social and political challenges of social work as a growing profession. From a theoretical perspective, empowerment entailed sup-

porting capacities of oppressed and disenfranchised populations and clients based on identifiable strengths, whether
political or personal (Saleebey, 1999a).

Dimensions of Practice for Empowerment: Personal to Political

Building on personal and political strengths of clients and client
groups is useful in gaining access and bringing about change.
Four dimensions of practice for empowerment are identified by
Parsons, *et al.* (1998). These dimensions call for client–professional partnering in the intervention process:

- Dimension One targets the individual in need of help, the
  need for both a resource and interpersonal help. At this
  level, the worker and client identify and assess perceptions that contribute to feelings of powerlessness.
- Dimension Two calls for educating and building skills to
  form networks and solve problems related to coping and
  inadequate life skills. Together the worker and client identify meaningful information useful in the particular life
  circumstance in the problem configuration.
- Dimension Three identifies gaps and strains in the environment that impact personal problems. For example,
  together the worker and client identify deficits and gaps
  such as lack of jobs or absence of support systems, or the
  lack of information and actions needed to access opportunities or resources. Assistance with job preparation,
  interviewing, placement, and skills in negotiating the
  work setting may occur.
- Dimension Four opens avenues for involvement in social
  and political issues of interest to others, including group
  action for change.

Identifying strengths and supporting client capacities for
growth and change are essential to the empowerment process.
Empowerment in clinical practice is an internal process which
is fueled by identification of strengths, encouraged through
support from others, and fostered by growing self-esteem
through experiencing success in coping with daily living.

Worker–client partnerships shape the process for empowerment. The process serves as a bridge across the chasm of powerlessness. It is important to note that this same process serves to bridge helplessness or powerlessness such as that caused by a personal sense of failure or low self-esteem. Empowerment is about "wellness", a way of looking beyond personal and social problems (Wiley and Rappaport, 2000). Personal empowerment fits with problem solving and the strengths perspective and is an emerging practice theory important to your work as you help clients.

Practice Limitations of Empowerment

Empowerment practice is not a panacea for all troubles that families and other clients seek help with as there are limitations to this approach, not unlike most other approaches or things in our world. In empowerment practice, limitations stream from multiple sources of the helping system—the client or consumer, the service systems involved such as organizations and institutions, and the practitioner or provider (Robbins, *et al.*, 1998; Ackerson and Harrison, 2000). From the client perspective, realizing potential empowerment may be constrained by factors like individual capacities and abilities in physical and intellectual domains as well as in personal and family support systems. From the perspective of institutional settings, the rules of the institutions must be respected even though many limit individual freedoms and choices. Very real personal and legal limitations to empowerment exist for those living in settings such as correctional, psychiatric, or in various sheltered living situations. Depending on the setting, freedoms are bounded by everyday practices that define where and with whom an individual lives, what freedoms there are to leave the institution, and what behaviors will help one survive within the institution or sheltered setting.

In the situation of children, the legal rights of parents and children are bounded by custody responsibilities and by the right of the courts to assume custody if parents are maltreating, neglectful, or absent. Additionally, children are not free to act on their own before reaching legal age. Interestingly, child welfare is the area of practice where social workers and providers make more decisions on behalf of their clients than in any other arena. Children about to enter foster care are not free to select their own foster care family or to choose to remain with their biological family outside the rules of local courts and child welfare.

From the perspective of practitioners, empowerment is often viewed as macro practice—advocacy, social action, social change—and not as micro practice with individuals. Robbins, *et al.* (1998) call for "holistic, systemic, and comprehensive vision of oppression" (p. 107) as they work in direct practice with clients to empower themselves. Empowerment is both personal and political and may be reflected in increased coping abilities just as well as in larger system change.

Summary and Comment

Given the scope of problems that children and families seek help with, the importance of extending helping processes beyond the clinic door has never been more important.

Briefer treatment and utilization of community-based support services are quickly becoming the model of practice. Currently, managed care and cost containment are realities for health and human services across a range of emotional, psychological, and physical needs of children and families (Corcoran and Vandiver, 1996; Greene, 1992). Present practices and cost-containment efforts of managed care reduce the length of care and number of sessions for most types of service, including outpatient and inpatient treatment. Strom-Gottfried (1997) points out that consequences of briefer services and required stronger outcome measures lead to professionals building on client strengths and utilizing social support and natural helping systems in client homes and communities.

Service provision now reflects briefer treatment, cost containment, and increased use of combined, "wrap-around," and triage services involving multidisciplinary teams and a variety of community-based services (Corcoran and Vandiver, 1996; Strom-Gottfried, 1997). Primary providers carry out fewer follow-up services, particularly as managed care changes practices in services to children and families. For helping professionals, meeting demands for cost containment requires brief treatment and reliance on community-based networks and teams found in various helping systems. We must make creative and innovative efforts to develop services for clients who desire or need ongoing support such as that available from paraprofessionals, role models, and mentors in their homes and communities. In your work with children and families, utilizing strengths and empowerment perspectives can help extend support and services into clients' homes and communities. Working with existing networks of various community-based paraprofessionals and natural helpers can facilitate various mentoring activities with your families.

As social workers, counselors, psychologists, and health care professionals we see our clients return to their homes and communities, even after only one visit for assistance or after treatment such as that in the case of the Hayes family. People in search of assistance or treatment represent a plethora of strengths, needs, relationships, families, groups, and communities. The process of identifying strengths and increasing daily living skills builds personal and social capacities necessary for successful participation in increasingly complex demands experienced at all levels of living, particularly in view of the sophisticated information and technology systems spanning global communities and economies that impact personal and social domains of all our lives. It is at this juncture of assessment and decision making that referrals and linkages we make to support networks can extend our intervention further into the homes and communities of those we serve.

CHAPTER 14

Evaluating Practice Processes and Outcomes

Evaluation: An Integral Component of Practice Processes and Outcomes

As we approach this last chapter of *Working with Children, Adolescents, and their Families,* we come to the final phase of intervention—evaluation. Evaluation of our treatment and service intervention is a natural juncture, a point of assessment and closure of our intervention with our client(s). Evaluation produces a measurement, an assessment of intervention for considering the value or quality of practice outcomes, both from the perspective of the worker and from its impact for the client(s). Evaluation of practice educates and informs practitioners and clients of both processes and outcomes of interventions or practice encounters. Intervening in the lives of clients and client systems calls for entering into a process that has both fluidity and vision for desired outcomes as their lives change daily and hoped-for realities become realities. In addition to solid practice knowledge and skills, gaining understanding of the importance of processes as well as outcomes is central to building knowledge and capacities for practice.

Why Evaluate Practice?

Intuitively, our own internal processes inform us a bit about benefits that we expect our clients to gain as a result of our intervention. Regardless of the service we expect to provide, some benefit is intended to be achieved whether the services include counseling, behavioral intervention such as that provided to the Hayes family, or resource provision such as that that comes from referrals for food, housing, health care, or other supports. However positive our intuitive summation of our work and services is, internally consistent and valid measurements of practice outcomes do not just occur! Our intuitive assessment of our practice cannot be systematically communicated to others or used as justification for continued service or program support for future funding and development.

Historically, the question of "Why evaluate practice?" has broad implications for human services, particularly for clinical practices. Early failures to conduct evaluation resulted in accusations of a lack of accountability for much of the social services arena in the 1960s and 1970s. Social workers, counselors, psychologists, and other helping professionals were accused of not systematically conducting or communicating practice outcomes. Questions about treatment effectiveness, costs of treatment, numbers of clients served, and implications for funding and service needs were not answered. Evaluative reports of costs and benefits of services and programs were often just not available. This "accountability gap" or "outcomes gap" resulted in heavy scrutiny of funding for new and existing programs and contributed to calls for cost-benefit analyses of services delivered by human and social service agencies, particularly in health and human services and community mental health organizations.

Political, social, and economic forces demand outcome information and cost containment of social service programs and delivery of services (Rossi and Freeman, 1993). Social and political changes of the 1970s and 1980s produced new standards for consumer awareness and participation. These changes raised awareness for equal access to services for broader populations, including those represented in the civil rights, gay rights, women's, and other movements. Particularly in the United States, these shifts contributed to the growth of private practice, out-sourcing and privatization of many social services. The centralized model of large public service organizations gave way to service delivery by private and nonprofit agencies.

Central to understanding historical evolution of human services delivery, evaluation of the effectiveness and efficiency of social services has been a key to understanding the many points of interest that support human services funding and organization. Practice evaluation is an integral component of the human services—linked to treatment modalities, treatment outcomes, funding, and continuing delivery of services. Some of the questions answered by evaluating practice include:

Clients' questions:	Is my situation better? Did I get help?
Worker's questions:	Was intervention appropriate, ethical, and professional?
Agency's questions:	Are services effective, efficient, timely, needed?
Funders' questions:	Was intervention cost-effective and beneficial?
Politicians' questions:	Do these kind of services need to be continued?

Overall, it is important to gain an estimate of the effectiveness and efficiency of our interventions in direct practice as well as an evaluation of agency programs that guide the delivery of services. The scope of this book does not include comprehensive presentation of strategies for evaluation or research methodology. However, a review of selected literature suggests much common ground in the practice of evaluation of services and service delivery systems (Long, *et al.*, 1994; Rossi and Freeman, 1993; Royse, 1995; Tripodi, 1987; Reamer, 1998; Posavac and Carey, 1985; Sheafor, *et al.*, 1994; Locke, *et al.*, 1998; Gershenson, 1995; Corcoran and Gingerich, 1994; Rossi, 1997). Figure 10 provides a list of many of these common purposes of evaluation, some of which you are quite familiar with.

Careful and consistent attention to measuring and evaluating service delivery practices and programs is occurring in response to managed care and cost containment practices in health and human services in the current era (Corcoran and Vandiver, 1996). Current pressures of managed care and related cost containment call for goal-oriented treatment plans and appropriate intervention that can be evaluated for effectiveness and efficiency in a timely and systematic manner. The challenge of meeting demands of funders for strong performance results has the potential to impact practice so that briefer treatment and cost containment can be accomplished. Funders are demanding results that can be substantiated and that are justified in terms of time and cost involved (Fuscaldo, *et al.*, 1998). On the other hand,

Figure 10   Common purposes of practice evaluation

- Provide feedback to inform nature and scope of agency services, programs, and practices.
- Clarify nature and purpose of intervention(s).
- Identify population served versus population targeted for service.
- Determine service efficiency for problem → interventive effort → outcomes.
- Determine effectiveness, i.e. effectiveness of outcome in relation to the problem.
- Identify ethical practice in view of assessment, intervention, evaluation and client rights.
- Plan program development in response to effective and efficient service delivery.
- Meet expectations for agency/professional accreditation.
- Inform staffing needs.
- Determine value of help received, i.e. impact of outcomes.
- Compare agency performance over time.
- Inform practice for future continuation or change.
- Justify funding for programs operated and services delivered.
- Increase credibility through valid and reliable performance information.
- Establish professional accountability through performance measurement.
- Enhance professional knowledge base.
- Establish evaluation as an ongoing function of practice.

clients expect and need help to restore or improve the quality of their lives—some situations require costly and lengthy treatment.

Constraints in Evaluating Programs and Practices

Despite the many questions and need for information, there are constraints that hamper conducting rigorous and ongoing evaluation of our work. These constraints are found in the context of managing agencies in both public, nonprofit, and private settings. Some of these constraints include:

- Adequate funding to support the time and effort of expert personnel in designing and implementing ongoing evaluation is often not available. In the event that available funding does not support systematic and ongoing evaluation, evaluation may be piecemeal and inconclusive or it may not be done.

- Evaluative or research expertise among agency personnel is crucial. Information, knowledge, and technical skills are essential in conducting practice and program evaluation. Training existing personnel, employing evaluators, and utilizing external consultants are useful corrective actions often undertaken by organizations to increase skills in research and capacities for evaluation.

- Evaluative or research expertise is necessary in order to value the effort and results. Once outcome measurements are established, data are collected and analyzed, and findings reported, valuing findings and translating them into improved services need to occur. Findings that support more services and continuing practices are easy to value. Nonetheless, findings that call for change or termination of certain aspects of practices or services are difficult to value much less to implement. Organizational support and commitment are necessary in order to allow evaluation to inform agency policies and practices in the planning process.

- Continuing attention to identified goals and outcomes to be measured is necessary for changing practices and policies. These demands not only place great expectations on program development and change, but require administrators, practitioners, and evaluators to continually upgrade knowledge and skills.

- Political concerns are to be recognized as they impact practitioners, administrators, public interests, clients, and evaluators. Rossi and Freeman (1993) identify the challenge of clarifying the perspective from which evaluation is undertaken, particularly by those who have particular interests in outcome information. Evaluation has far-reaching professional and political implications, some of which may be powerful enough to affect the direction of social policies developed and human services delivered.

Evaluating Practice

Evaluation as Part of Intervention

Assessment produces a range of information—client strengths to be assessed, problems to be identified and solved, solutions to be achieved, and changes or outcomes to be reached. As we assess strengths and needs, planning for intervention begins. Just as planning for intervention begins, so does planning for evaluation of intervention outcomes.

Practice evaluation is an integral component of intervention from the beginning—not an afterthought nor appendage to intervention! Assessment produces a range of information—client strengths to be assessed, problems to be identified and solved, solutions to be achieved, and changes or outcomes to be reached. Evaluation of these outcomes is an ongoing process throughout intervention and provides opportunities for feedback and renegotiation along the way. Questions like "Did intervention make a difference?" are asked by social workers and other helping professionals and by the clients themselves.

Figure 11 presents a model integrating evaluation with practice. Each phase informs the succeeding phase as information gained in Assessment informs Planning for Intervention that will utilize strengths and provide problem solutions identified. Planning intervention leads to developing a treatment plan which is communicated to the client and agreed upon in the Contracting phase where the client and worker agree on the problem or concern to be addressed, the method of treatment, periodic measures of progress evaluation, and points for renegotiation and/or termination. Intervention involves the application of the agreed upon treatment. Finally, outcome information enters into the Termination phase and this evaluative information completes the feedback loop as it goes back to the Assessment phase. There the information serves to validate that indeed the problem and strengths assessments were addressed by the intervention and that the outcome, in a successful case, was relevant.

Clients, not unlike practitioners, want treatment interventions to produce progress toward solving problems and

Figure 11. Evaluation: An integral part of practice

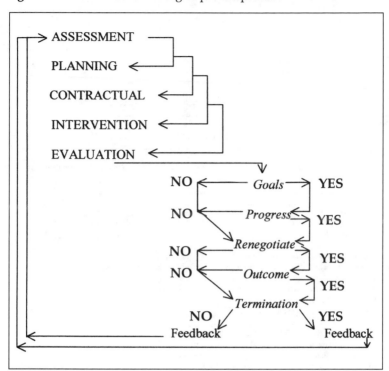

building on strengths as identified in the treatment plan and treatment contract. As part of the plan to intervene and evaluate, the contract for treatment needs to not only identify desired treatment outcomes, but also, ways in which responses to intervention will be evaluated to determine treatment effectiveness and progress toward desired outcomes. The nature of professional contracting requires practitioners to value treatment outcomes that are consistent with treatment plan goals and expectations.

Contracting with clients for services is an open process that involves communicating the results of assessment and planning to the client. Plans for intervention and methods and intervals of evaluating progress toward goals are included in

Figure 12. Sample contract form for services.

Agency Name: _____ Date: ___ / ___ / _____

Client Name: _____ Phone: ____ - ____ - _____

Address Line 1: _____

Address Line 2: _____

City: _____ State: _____ Zip: _____

Statement of Intent for Service:

_____

_____

Service Goals:

Goal A: _____

Action Plan _____

Number of Contacts/Weeks (___ / ___) Progress Review Periods (___ / ___) (___ / ___) (___ / ___) (___ / ___) (Renegotiation may be necessary and alternative goals may need to be identified).

Goal A Evaluation Method: _____ Date Completed: (___ / ___ / ___)

Goal B: _____

Action Plan _____

Number of Contacts/Weeks (___ / ___) Progress Review Periods (___ / ___) (___ / ___) (___ / ___) (___ / ___) (Renegotiation may be necessary and alternative goals may need to be identified).

Goal B Evaluation Method: _____ Date Completed: (___ / ___ / ___)

Tasks:

Evaluation of completion of tasks will occur every ____ weeks.

Renegotiation can occur. Renegotiation is recorded with additional goals and tasks.

Evaluation of progress toward accomplishing goals will be accomplished every ____weeks. We agree that we will put into practice the above goals and action plan. It is agreed that the above tasks will be implemented as part of intervention.

Costs or fees are set by the agency at the rate of $_____ per _____. Fees are to be paid by: Insurance ___ Client ___ Other: _____

Records kept will include: (1) Record of Contacts; (2) Records of Fiscal Actions; (3) Records of Case Progress. Access to records will be handled within the policies of the agency and are restricted to agency personnel including researchers; legal authorities as provided for by law; and for particular uses requested for information purposes by insurance or by the client for referral purposes. Further, agency practices of ethical conduct and professional service apply to services rendered.

Worker signature: _____ Client signature: _____

---

contract agreements as well. A sample contract form for services is reported in figure 12. This particular sample can be adapted to fit many different client and agency situations. Most agencies have similar contract formats that accomplish the purpose of clarifying services to be delivered and outcomes to be achieved. Figure 12 reflects the incorporation of evaluation as an important component of the contract for service.

Evaluating our practice is necessary for gaining an understanding of the effect that our direct intervention has on individuals, families, groups, and communities. Many practitioners take great pride in their competence and appraisal of their work. Self-introspection and self-assessment are important in our streams of thought and self-images as practitioners. This self-assessment and reflection are both painful and joyful in the journey of our professional careers and accomplishments. Regardless of the pain or reward associated with self-assessment of professional practice, it does not replace internally consistent and methodologically sound evaluation of professional practices and direct services delivery. Locke, *et al.* (1998) identify reasons which call for evaluation of practices and processes along the route to problem solution. They call for multiple measures and progress markers during the process of intervention.

First, identifying and evaluating changes throughout the process of intervention are important. Evaluating progress and milestones in the process of reaching intended problem solutions helps to determine accomplishments as well as barriers in the process of treatment. For example, in the process of learning about parenting and behavioral management, Mrs Hayes became aware of her feelings of anger and failure as a parent and was able to change her self-doubts in her mothering role. She was able to gain new confidence and satisfaction as a parent when Avril's behavior began to change. For the Hayes family, the months of the treatment process involved progress markers such as learning to give greater rewards for Avril's positive behaviors. The Hayes family learned to evaluate eventual and lasting reduction of seriously distracting and aggressive behaviors. Evaluating changes in clients' behaviors and lives calls for repeated measures to understand and identify markers of progress. Establishing baseline measures of the problem at the outset of intervention and collecting multiple measures throughout the intervention process informs both practitioner and client(s) of progress and changes that occur (Bloom, *et al.*, 1999).

A second reason for identifying and monitoring even small steps toward accomplishing desirable changes is to inform the practitioner and clients of the change that is occurring. Identifying markers of change which are expected and anticipated to occur in the process toward problem solution is supportive and empowering. Identifying instances of unexpected or troubling changes is equally important and helpful for all involved. Information and knowledge gained in the process of intervention may call for redirecting intervention and involving the client. Renegotiation of both the intervention contract and desired outcomes may occur. Gaining new understanding of changes helps build capacities for future problem solving.

A third reason for evaluating practice is that practitioners gain new understanding of the impact of their intervention. Ongoing practice evaluation provides information about "how well we are doing" as practitioners.

Finally, practice evaluation provides a means of measuring progress in the context of client situations and not just from stark outcomes called for by theoretical perspectives (Parsons, 1998). Linking practice evaluation to identifying client progress and capacities for growth brings a strengths perspective to the interface of practice and evaluation. Involving clients in the design, process, and evaluation of their experience in the practice encounter is empowering. To the extent possible, increasing client participation throughout the process of intervention and its outcome gives voice to clients in their voyage toward problem solution.

In summary, evaluating the process of intervening in the lives of clients and client systems begins with encountering clients in the midst of their need for help and following the process of intervention toward problem solution. Initially assessing the problem to be addressed, engaging clients in the plan for intervention, and identifying desired results produces a process of learning and transition toward successful problem resolution and termination of intervention. This process is depicted in Figure 11 and included in the sample contract in Figure 12. Evaluating these processes and products of intervention are important components in measuring effective and efficient service delivery in direct practice (Berger, 1996; Locke, *et al.*, 1998).

Is Empirical Clinical Practice for You?

As you read this chapter or carry out work with your clients, you may take some comfort in knowing that the accountability concern has received considerable attention and some resolution. The early demand for data, for grouped information, and analyses of client demographics and population characteristics has abated somewhat. Single-subject design, originally seen as mostly behavioral, provides for focus on a single case over time with collection of multiple markers. Single-subject design requires the problem definition be clear, calls for establishing baseline measures of behaviors, and then collects repeated measures of those behaviors. The extent of progress whether it be increased functioning or reduction of problem behaviors is thus evaluated over time (Slonim-Nevo and Anson 1998; Bloom, *et al.*, 1999).

As professionals respond to demands for accountability or effectiveness and cost containment or efficiency, clinical service providers are better prepared than ever to evaluate the outcomes of clinical interventions. According to various sources (Thyer, 1996; Slonim-Nevo and Anson, 1998; Witkin, 1996), evaluation of clinical practice has progressed with the results that you as clinician and evaluator have greater access to a variety of tools to help accomplish evaluation of your practice. Some of these tools include:

- Assessment instruments and inventories that can be administered quickly with strong reliability and validity. (See inventories such as those referenced by Corcoran and Fischer (1999), Wetzler (1989), Schutte and Maloaff (1995), and many others as well.)
- Qualitative methodology has progressed in acceptance and has computerization available for analyses.
- Single-subject research has gained broader acceptance and can produce individual ratings for scrutiny by managed care providers.
- Empirical research has identified "best practices" for many psychosocial practices. Psychosocial and pharmacological interventions are available to help with serious psychiatric problems
- Specialized referral resources provide testing, training, rehabilitation.
- Single-subject design is linked to greater client awareness.
- Evidence reports that many clients are empowered in their treatment in response to feedback from evaluating their own progress and outcomes.

Limitations of Single-Subject Design

Some of the pressure against empirical clinical practice, or practice-based research, criticized empirical practice as being too behavioral and too technically driven. In addition there was overemphasis on causal relationships, inflexible boundaries, and lack of human responsiveness to human concerns (Tyson, 1995; Witkin, 1996). From their exploration of literature, Bloom, *et al.* (1999) report the concern that if carried too far, the goals of evaluation can conflict with the goals of intervention and can divert attention away from practice concerns to those of evaluation. On the other hand, positive involvement of both therapist and client can occur in response to identifying goals and evaluating progress toward those goals. Single-subject research provides little information concerning gender, race, oppression or client advocacy that are common throughout practice in human services (Bloom, *et al.*, 1999).

Noting limitations of single-subject research informs you as evaluator. Nevertheless, the utility and ease of application of single-subject design outweigh the limitations, particularly in the work of an informed practitioner.

Professional Responsibility for the

Practice of Evaluation

It is not within the scope of this chapter to provide a comprehensive overview of the extensive methodologies and techniques available for evaluating human services programs and practices. As mentioned previously, practice evaluation is as varied and unique as is the scope of human services programs and practices. A variety of techniques commonly used in evaluating practice are cited and briefly critiqued by Locke, *et al.* (1998). Among selected techniques are those such as Goal Attainment Scaling, single-subject design, measurement scales for client system outcomes, case study analysis, reflective questioning, journaling, and client system satisfaction surveys. Numerous instruments and scales are available for measuring particular behaviors and functioning (Corcoran and Fischer, 1999; Wetzler, 1989; Schutte and Maloaff, 1995). Royse (1995) discusses ways to find, evaluate, and select scales and measures from existing resources. He provides comprehensive reviews of selected scales particularly designed to measure community living skills, empowerment, prosocial tendencies of children, attitudes toward long-term care, maternal characteristics, helping behaviors, role strains, and job satisfaction.

Numerous reports of practice evaluation can be found throughout professional journals. One example of practice evaluation of treatment of depressed women reports a single-subject design that incorporates standardized instruments in evaluating treatment outcomes of intervention with nine clients. The Beck Depression Inventory was administered weekly. The results were recorded and charted as measures of severity of depression. Pre- and post-test measures of the women's adjustment were gathered by administering the Social Adjustment Scale. Both instruments were administered at the end of a six-month period after treatment ended. This evaluation model measures the impact of cognitive, behavioral, and interpersonal psychotherapies utilized and provides multiple measures of depression throughout the process of intervention. Post-test measures provide data for outcomes achieved and sustained for each of the women and provide overall indicators of the success of the intervention. Professional accountability for practice and evaluation of practice is met in this interesting report of intervention (Jensen, 1994). In this situation, methodology that was not influenced by practice theory was selected by the evaluator and applied to evaluate the effectiveness of practice.

There are few shortcuts to conducting valid and reliable evaluation of professional practice. Summaries of research and evaluation methods, such as those cited, educate and inform practitioners who are faced with evaluating their practice performances. It is the responsibility of the practitioner to become familiar with research methodology in both quantitative and qualitative approaches to evaluative design. Furthermore, professional practices demand that ethical practices be respected in evaluating programs and practice delivery.

Ethical Practice Imperatives (see Sutton, 1999)

"Being ethical is a matter of choosing morally 'right' actions, being a professional who works within professional standards is being a competent practitioner who (on current definitions) uses scientifically verified generalizations to guide practice" (Chambers, *et al.*, 1992). Ethical, legal, and professional standards inform ethical practice and apply to service delivery, evaluation, and research methodology used in evaluating programs and practices.

Competent evaluation of programs and direct practice with clients is a practice in its own right and calls for integrating practice and research knowledge and skills into everyday work. Just as professional ethics apply to program delivery and direct practice with clients, so do they apply to program and practice evaluation. At a minimum, ethically sound evaluation of programs and practices calls for informed consent, willing participation, and explanation of rights.

Clients are not to be harmed in the process of evaluation or in other situations including control and experimental treatment groups. Determining practice effectiveness and efficiency, building knowledge, and planning programs and services delivery based on evaluation of practice are not to be accomplished at any personal, social, or other cost to clients involved. The concern of withholding or delaying services for some in order to determine the impact of services on others raises questions of potential harm in instances where treatment or service is delayed or not provided. Debates about the benefits and harms encountered in such practice are numerous and include concerns of whether receiving delayed services will be harmful and even whether the service or treatment in question is known to be helpful (Williams, *et al.*, 1998).

Best practices and professional standards are to be followed to the best of our ability. Ethical practice is essential in delivering services and intervening in the lives of others. Ethical issues and concerns arise despite our good intentions and sometimes require us as professionals to seek guidance from supervisors and legal experts. Sound and informed practices require that we extend our knowledge base. Informing clients, protecting confidentiality, and avoiding potential harm, are important to conducting practice and evaluation of practice ethically and professionally. Bloom, *et al.* (1999) call for client participation in identifying problem situations, treatment goals, data gathering, and outcomes. Similarly, evaluation of intervention requires client knowledge and participation and should not proceed or be conducted if there is any risk of harm to clients or to the detriment of their progress or recovery. In order to be valid and useful, evaluation of practice processes and outcomes must be independent of practice theory and objective in measuring behaviors, changes, and intended or actual results.

Evaluating Programs

Why Evaluate Programs?

Practice and program evaluation are both necessary to inform good practice and changing programs, particularly in view of changing technology and program management and reimbursement mechanisms. Managed care, third-party reimbursements, and a variety of private and non-profit systems are changing service delivery. It is imperative that both practice and program evaluation be conducted and information exchanged.

"Evaluation research is the systematic application of social research procedures for assessing the conceptualization, design, implementation, and utility of social intervention programs" (Rossi and Freeman, 1993: 5). According to Sheafor, *et al.* (1994), the purpose of program evaluation is to assess the effectiveness and efficiency of a total program intended for serving a large number of people or perhaps even a whole community. Program evaluation involves applied research rather than research for the purpose of theory development or hypothesis testing. In this context, applied research involves research design especially tailored to the program being evaluated. Reamer (1998) identifies four major issues that impact program evaluation design.

First, the "who" and "why" of evaluating a particular program must be taken into consideration. Programs may be funded contingent on satisfactory program evaluation plans, with funders being interested as much or more in appropriate use of funds than in the quality of services so long as the program was implemented as agreed upon. Other situations of program evaluation may be more quality oriented and may call for projections about the program's potential long-range impact on populations served, including national trend comparisons. In other situations, program evaluation may be for organizational purposes ranging from simple accounting of instances of services rendered to various quantitative and qualitative studies which are designed to measure quality of services delivered. Given the breadth of human services delivered, there are nearly as many program evaluation designs as there are programs.

For example, the increasing use of mentoring programs is resulting in new and sometimes quite extensive evaluation designs conducted at the community service level. One such evaluative design measures the impact of mentoring youth who lack close adult attention in a Big Brothers/Big Sisters program (Grossman and Tierney, 1998). This evaluative model, based on a control group and a study group, reports a number of positive behavioral changes for youth who were paired with an adult mentor. This 18-month, comprehensive study included extensive data collection from 1,107 youth (97.3 percent) using baseline data, follow-up questionnaires, and interviews with 959, or 84.3 percent of youths who were served. This effort evaluated quality of services, long-term outcomes, and costs and benefits of the program and had implications for program change and continuation.

Second, clear definitions of the scope and purpose of the evaluation itself are needed so that program evaluation goals can be identified and, therefore, achieved. Just as programs have goals, so does program evaluation. Questions to be answered in identifying these goals include clarifying what the evaluation will be used for. For instance, justifying costs and benefits of program continuation or informing internal activities are reasons to conduct program evaluation. Reamer (1998) emphasizes the importance of identifying goals for program evaluation and notes the potential impact of evaluation on staffing and workload patterns within agencies as well as various segments of community and agency constituencies. Additionally, clarity about the goals of program evaluation are important in navigating the political and funding currents surrounding programs and human services agencies. Clear program evaluation goals inform evaluators of their role and authority. Regardless of whether evaluators are internal or external to the agency, their project of evaluation takes on a structure and direction. Evaluation demands time, energy, knowledge, and attention not only for goal achievement but also for good practices in research and evaluation.

Third, clarifying the intended use of information from program evaluation is important in developing the plan for evaluation (Reamer, 1998). Whether the purpose of evaluation is for the agency's internal use or more for external purposes will determine what information is needed. Sometimes the information needed for internal assessment of service quality and agency expertise may not be the kind of information best shared broadly. Practicality, ethical practice, and objective measurement of performance outcomes enter into practices for evaluating direct practices and programs. From the outset of both program planning and evaluative design, it is important to consider the use of evaluation information and the potential audiences who will receive the information.

Finally, the competence and capacity of evaluators to apply research methodology and data analyses in program evaluation are crucial to the success of evaluation. Evaluators may be internal or external to the organization. Those internal to the organization must have clarity about the purpose, implications, and expected use of their effort. Internal evaluators can be cost effective and can accomplish sound and useful program evaluation. Evaluation that is internally valued and incorporated as part of practice and program development can be an important learning experience for agency personnel. It is noted that funding organizations often require funded programs to have external evaluators. External evaluators are sometimes thought to bring greater objectivity to evaluation and may bring expertise not available internally. A common practice is to bring together both internal and external evaluators and to maximize the strengths of both in a team effort. Again, whatever the approach an agency takes, careful planning must occur at the outset so that goals for evaluation are articulated and become a natural extension of program implementation and service delivery.

Summary and Comment

Evaluating processes and outcomes of programs and practices designed to meet personal and social needs both individually and collectively for families and children is an area of practice with far-reaching implications. "Did my client improve because of my work?" is a question we ask of ourselves. We must answer this question systematically, empirically, and consistently.

The common purposes of evaluation, although sometimes difficult to achieve, are professionally sound and respond to the ever-present demand for knowledge and greater understanding of the effectiveness and efficiency of our many programs and practices. Constraints of funding gaps, available expertise and knowledge, vested interests, and changing practices are hurdles to be overcome and not barriers to continuing our pursuit of evaluating our work with and on behalf of those whom we serve.

Professional standards and conduct call for ethical practices, including their evaluation. The challenges for professionals in both practice and practice evaluation are monumental in the face of changing practices and increased demands for services. Today's increasingly complex and technological world indeed places heavy demands on service systems. It is incumbent that professionals grow and develop in practice delivery and in knowledge and skills for evaluation as we, too, are part of the fluidity of the changing human condition.

Epilogue

Living and working, as we do, in a multi-ethnic society, it is of critical importance that people in the helping professions should be sensitive not only to the norms, sensibilities and sensitivities of clients from different cultures but also the stressful life experiences they endure due to prejudice and discrimination. Racism, for example, extends far too often into service delivery. And it is not only in matters of race, nationality and creed where prejudice has its corrosive influence; it affects women and female children in many subtle and unsubtle ways. In many senses of the word they are "disabled" in our society and demeaned in the way that those of our clients to whom we attach the label "disabled" are patronized and robbed of their self-fulfillment.

We are conscious at the end of this book of a paradox for the reader, whether he or she is a student or experienced practitioner. These pages contain so much about families, parents, children and their problems... and, yet, so little. The subject is so vast that we have only scratched the surface. This is not simply a matter of the limited space available in one volume; it is intrinsic to the topic. We have so much to learn, so much research to initiate. Fortunately, there is no reason for an attitude of pessimism or helplessness. We know enough to be of service to those whose family life is floundering, whose children are in distress, and who, consequently, are calling for help.

We hope you will find the information we provide to be useful to you in your professional practice. Recognizing that our brief chapters are not comprehensive, it now becomes your task to explore practices and theories as they relate to your professional practice.

The potential to expand our knowledge and practices is more promising than ever. As you extend your work in evaluating processes and outcomes of practices and programs there are increasing opportunities to disseminate your research and practice wisdom to contribute to existing knowledge bases. It is this opportunity that we encourage you to take very seriously, as well as the opportunity to share your expertise with those who are just entering helping professions. It will be through all of our involvement and contributions to knowledge and best practices that we will be able to help shape future services and construct a desired program and practice reality that will serve people in the changing world around us.

Parent Training

Behavioral Parent Training programs have been extensively studied. Properly designed studies showing the effectiveness of this approach are more numerous than those supporting any other approach for treating children and families (for reviews see Taylor and Biglan, 1998; Webster-Stratton and Herbert 1994). Programs address themselves to the fact that parents of children with behavior problems tend to flounder because they issue so many commands, provide attention following deviant behavior, are unlikely to perceive deviant behavior as deviant, get frequently embroiled in extended coercive hostile interchanges, give vague commands, and are generally ineffectual in bringing their children's deviant behavior to a halt. They also tend to suffer the kinds of socio-economic disadvantage which have an undermining influence on parenting and family life. At a systemic level, Patterson (1982) has demonstrated an ingrained and pervasive family pattern of escalating coercive interpersonal interactions. Parent training programs therefore emphasize methods designed to reduce confrontations and antagonistic interactions among the family members, to increase the effectiveness of positive interactions and moderate the intensity of parental punishment. Parents are encouraged and guided to increase their positive interactions with the children through the use of play and other activities. They are encouraged to reinforce their children's appropriate behavior with praise, encouragement and other rewards. They are assisted in reducing unnecessary commands, increasing the clarity of the limits they do set, and increasing the consistency with which they follow through on their limits. To do this they are guided in the implementation of brief, mild, non-violent actions such as judicious ignoring, time-out, loss of privileges and logical consequences. They are provided with the means of understanding and analyzing problematic behavior, and ways of negotiating and problem solving their way out of previously corrosive, confrontational situations. They are also encouraged to monitor their children effectively, and to engage in effective communication. Parents' experience of being parented, and of being children themselves in the past, are related to their attitudes and attributions in their ideologies of child-rearing (see Goodnow and Collins, 1990). You may find it useful to train parents in behavioral methods and child management in a group setting.

THE CHILD-WISE PARENTING SKILLS APPROACH

A Collaborative Cognitive-Behavioral Approach

This is a group counseling and applied social learning course for parents with challenging children (three to eight years of age). The course, devised at the Child Development Centre, Plymouth, UK, by Martin Herbert and Jenny Wookey (1998), is described in broad outline below. The course begins with a home visit to introduce ourselves, explain the nature of the program, make a working contract, arrange for some baseline measures, observe the child's interactions with his/her family, discuss practical arrangements, and leave a handout describing what lies ahead. Each session lasts two hours with a 20-minute refreshment and socializing break. (See the manual for details of planning and implementation of the course.)

SESSION 1

INDUCTION

INTRODUCTIONS/WELCOMING
- Personal introductions
- Purpose of groups and ground rules (aims and expectations) discussed
- Ground rules agreed
- Parents show photographs of their children with a brief description (name, age, siblings, etc.)

SHARING PROBLEMS ("I'm not the only one")

- Parents describe their difficulties with their children (written up on a flip chart)
- Video and/or brief case illustration of a challenging child discussed and debated

DESCRIBING AND TACKLING BEHAVIOR

- Defining behavioral/emotional problems
- How to avoid "fuzzies" in observing and describing behavior (flip chart examples followed by discussion)
- How to tease out "ABC of behavior" sequences (e.g. for temper tantrums)

PARENTS' NEEDS

- Parents identify their ideas on parents' needs (flip chart)
- Why needy parents find it difficult to attend to needy children
- Discussion and debate

PRE-TRAINING (BASELINE) QUESTIONNAIRES

- These are filled in along with the weekly evaluation form

HOMEWORK TASKS

Record (track) a chosen behavior (pro-social and problematic) on provided proforma.

SESSION 2

CHILDREN'S NEEDS

PRELIMINARIES

- Refreshments—Welcome—Forms collected

PRECIS

- Highlighting main points from last session

- Discussion of homework—participants' record keeping (to be a regular feature each session)

CHILDREN'S NEEDS

- What are they? Brainstorming—Participants' ideas written up on the flip chart
- Compare parents' needs (from last week) with children's needs and discuss results
- Look at links between the generations

A CHILD'S PERSPECTIVE

- Seeing the world from a child's point of view (Suitable video or role play)
- The child as "learner" and "problem solver" (cartoon/quotations)
- Developmental tasks (handouts/developmental milestones charts given out)
- Discussion and debate of implications for child and parents of their interacting at their respective stages of development

PARENTAL ATTENTION

- Positive attention and its importance
- Finding and creating "special/quality" time
- Negative attention (reinforcing unwanted behavior)
- "Better bad publicity than none" principle in children's behavior
- Differential attention
- Play as special/quality time
- Discussion

SUMMARIZING AND HIGHLIGHTING

HOMEWORK

Find at least 15 minutes daily for "special" time with your child
- Record interesting reactions—yours and her/his (record forms provided)

EVALUATION

- Forms filled in and collected

SESSION 3

PLAY AS "SPECIAL" QUALITY TIME

PRELIMINARIES

- Welcome
- Resumé
- Collect homework

HOMEWORK FEEDBACK

- Individual and group discussion
- Prompts (How did you spend your special time with your child?; Were there any difficulties?; Did you enjoy the time?; Did s/he? If not, why not?)

PARENTS' EXPERIENCE OF PLAY

- Memories of childhood play (flip chart)
- Brainstorm functions and meaning of play

EXPOSITION ON PLAY (VIDEO)

- Role-play (illustrate intrusive joining in; helpful play)
- Demonstrate codes for different kinds of play
- Role-play playing with your child to her/his advantage

HOMEWORK TASK

(a) Play with your child for about 30 minutes each day
(b) Keep a record of what happens

EVALUATION

SESSION 4

EFFECTIVE PRAISE

PRELIMINARIES
- Welcome
- Resumé
- Collect homework

HOMEWORK FEEDBACK
- Individual and group feedback
- Discussion
  Prompts: (a) How many participants found time to play as suggested? (b) What factors affected the quantity/quality of the play periods (e.g. fatigue, lack of time, telephone calls, child's attitude, your feelings about this task). Discuss ways of handling these issues. (c) What effect did the play sessions have on the parent–child relationship? (d) Play can also involve joining parent in, say, baking, cleaning the car. These can be quality-time activities.

IT'S AS SIMPLE AS ABC
- Exposition/Video vignette/Role play to illustrate the ABC of behavior and beliefs (attributions)
- The good behavior rule
- Parents' examples of ABC sequences at home (child's behavior/their beliefs about it; their behavior/the child's likely beliefs and attributions)
- How to encourage desired behavior

HOW AND WHAT TO PRAISE
- Brainstorm these questions (using flip chart)
- Being specific (labeling praise)
- Discussion and debate

SUGGESTIVE PRAISE
- Examples of ways to praise and when
- Schedules of reinforcement
- Praise as reinforcement

HOMEWORK TASKS

(a) Praise your child for behaviors you like to see
(b) Keep a record of some instances (How did you feel? How did s/he react?)

BRIEF RECAP

EVALUATION FORMS
- Filled in and collected

SESSION 5

TANGIBLE AND SOCIAL REWARDS

PRELIMINARIES
- Welcome
- Resumé
- Collect homework

HOMEWORK FEEDBACK
- Individual and group feedback
- Discussion (Prompts: How often and in what situations did parents praise their children? What ways did they do this?)

REWARDS AND INCENTIVES
- Rewards, incentives and privileges
- Parents' experiences in childhood of receiving social and tangible rewards

- Ways of rewarding desired behavior
- Discussion and role play

SYMBOLIC REWARDS

- Rationale
- Illustration of imaginative reward/sticker charts
- Brainstorm of ideas for making charts

HOMEWORK TASK

(a) Design a behavior (reward) chart with your child
(b) Try it out

EVALUATION AND HANDOUTS

SESSION 6

"IT'S AS SIMPLE AS ABC"
(where B stands for beliefs and behavior)

PRELIMINARIES

- Welcome
- Resumé
- Collect homework

HOMEWORK FEEDBACK

- View charts parents have made
- What were the child's responses?
- In what situations were they used?

BELIEFS, THOUGHTS AND FEELINGS

- Explore links between thoughts, feelings and behavior
- Brief exposition on the "stories" people tell themselves, about themselves and their children

- How they impact on behavior and relationships
- Group members describe thoughts and feelings they have linked to their parenting activities and methods
- Notion of "learned helplessness" is explored
- The influence of culture and myth on the so-called "perfect" parent
- Acknowledgment that parenting is a hard and complex job
- How helpful or undermining is the advice/attitudes of friends, relatives and neighbors?

THE ABC OF BEHAVIOR

- The recursive ABC sequence is explained and explored— also role-played
- Its role in learning pro-social and antisocial behavior
- Importance of antecedent/setting events (triggers to actions)

"PAY-OFFS"

- The function of consequences (payoffs)

HOMEWORK TASKS

- Parents apply the ABC model at home with proforma provided

EVALUATION AND HANDOUTS

SESSION 7

DISCIPLINE

PRELIMINARIES

- Welcome
- Resumé
- Collect homework

HOMEWORK FEEDBACK

- Individual and group feedback
- Discuss any difficulties participants had with last week's task
- Examine records

DISCIPLINE

- What is discipline? (Unnecessary equation with punishment only, rather than positive guidance)
- Positive parenting
- Why is discipline important? How is it implemented?

RULES, ROLES AND LIMITS

- Why rules?
- Who rules?
- Setting limits
- Where should they be drawn?
- Firm vs soft limits
- Giving reasons for rules
- Negotiating rules

GIVING INSTRUCTIONS AND MAKING REQUESTS

- What is the difference?
- How to give them
- Parents look back to their childhood to their experience of rules, roles and limits, which is to say what their parents called "discipline"

PHYSICAL PUNISHMENT

- Advantages and disadvantages (brainstorm/flip chart)
- Does smacking actually work on your child?
- The trouble with smacking
- Risks—short and long term
- The issue of authority in the family
- Differences of opinion on discipline and other child-rearing issues within the family

HOMEWORK TASKS

(a) Record instances where you were tempted to smack your child, but used an alternative method
(b) Record how you felt before, during and after the episode
(c) How did your child react?
(d) Draw out the ABC of the incident to tell the group next week

EVALUATION AND HANDOUTS

SESSIONS 8 TO 11

The remaining three course sessions (Number 11 is a "booster" session) contain the following themes:

NUMBER 8

- Planned (judicious) ignoring
- Time-out
- Ethical imperatives (e.g. issues of personal choice for children)

NUMBER 9

- Taking away rewards and privileges
- Problem-solving particular stressful situations (e.g. supermarkets, visiting)

NUMBER 10

- Caring for yourself (stress management)
- Parents' charter/Children's rights—keeping a balance
- Relaxation exercises
- Getting help (sources of help for financial/housing/personal difficulties
- Endings: Arrangements for further contacts/Farewell party

NUMBER 11

BOOSTER SESSION/S: REUNION AND TROUBLE-SHOOTING

* Reminders
* Feedback
* Reassurance re behavioral drift (slippage)
* Social (farewell party)

These methods are fully described in a validated program: CHILD-WISE PARENTING SKILLS MANUAL by Martin Herbert and Jenny Wookey (1998). (Exeter: Impact Publications 1998, PO Box No. 342, Exeter EX6 7ZD)

Treatment Options in Cases of Child Abuse and Neglect
(see Iwaniec, *et al.*, 1988).

Likely target problems (of the excess/deficit/inappropriate categories) that occur in relation to:

- Characteristics of the parents (e.g. alcohol abuse; deficits in bonding and child-rearing skills, faulty expectations of the child).
- Characteristics of the child (e.g. non-compliant aggressive problems, incontinence, inappropriately inflexible response to different situations).
- Unique interaction of the child and his/her parents (e.g. coercive/aversive communications; mutual avoidance; inappropriate, inconsistent (perhaps non-contingent) reinforcement/ punishment).
- Significant others in the family (interference, subversion of maternal authority by grandparents; sexual/physical abuse by relative/lodger, etc.).
- Environmental factors (poverty, overcrowding, social isolation).

Social workers are likely to be faced with any of the following *specific problems* when child abuse cases are referred to them.

Specific Areas of Intervention

1. *Deficits*

- Skill deficits (poor problem-solving skills; ineffective communication skills; ineffective reinforcement skills).
- Social isolation.

- Poor care-giving/socializing skills.
- Withholding attention (ignoring) until there's a crisis (i.e. very annoying activities).
- Failure to track minor incidents before they blow up in major confrontations (e.g. fighting).
- Failure to acknowledge/notice/reward pro-social behavior.
- Few family recreational activities together.
- Low self-esteem/low perception of self-efficacy.
- Less positive emotional expression.

2. *Excessive/surplus problems*

- Use of aversive (negative, coercive, punitive) means of influencing/changing others (criticism/physical assaults).
- Parental yelling, shouting, nagging, threats, complaints.
- Punishment of pro-social behavior.
- High parental stress/distress (marital discord/inadequate income, poor housing, lack of emotional/social support).
- Alcohol/drug use.
- Acting out, antisocial, conduct problems.

3. *Inappropriate beliefs/attitudes/knowledge/behavior*

- Faulty attributions (cause-and-effect inferences).
- Reinforcement of inappropriate/deviant actions.
- Unpredictable/inconsistent.
- Mutual avoidance.
- Faulty expectations due to absence of basic knowledge about child development.
- Inflexible in response to child-disciplinary situations.

Potential Treatment Strategies

1. Systemic Level *(Family)*

- Written contracts.
- Negotiation training.

- Conflict resolving (settling differences).
- Contingency contracting (exchange theory).
- Communication enhancement.
- Clarification of roles and rules.
- Enhancement of social contacts.
- Improvement of physical environment, resources (e.g. child minding/day care).

2. Dyadic Level *(Interactions/relationship)*

- Enhancing positive interactions.
- Operant programs (increasing positive reinforcement— "catching the child out in good behavior").
- Decreasing threats, criticism, negative injunctions.
- Play.
- Increasing consistency.
- Negotiating fair/few/clear rules.
- Marital work.

3. Individual Level *Parents*:

- Training in more effective child-rearing practices.
- Developmental counseling to improve knowledge/decrease family expectations/attributions.
- Cognitive restructuring.
- Decreasing inappropriate anxiety/anger reactions:
  (i) relaxation;
  (ii) self-talk;
  (iii) self-control training.
- Improving skills:
  (i) social skills;
  (ii) problem-solving skills.
- Addiction/substance abuse.
- Self-esteem, self-efficacy enhancement (performance accomplishments).
- Depression/learned helplessness.

Children:
- Training/therapy as in Chapter 11

Separation and Divorce: Helping Parents and Children Cope with the Aftermath

A Collaborative Training and Counseling Course
by Joy Edelstein and Martin Herbert

Course Outline

Session 1: Orientation

In this session, the participants are introduced to each other and to the program facilitator. The approach adopted by the group leader(s) stresses that divorce is a major life event which is transitional in nature; that it *is* possible to mediate and/or train people to cope more effectively with the transitions in their lives, and because children are the parents of tomorrow, that it is of the utmost importance to alleviate divorce-related emotional and other problems that disturb them.

Session 2: Reassurance for the children

This session focuses on ways parents can reassure their children. It details the reactions children have to divorce, the defence mechanisms, such as denial, "acting-out" behavior, and aggression they employ to stave off the hurt and resentment they feel, as they work through the trauma of divorce. Methods for managing the working-through or acting-out behaviors that children frequently display are discussed and debated at this session.

Session 3: Reassurance for the divorced person

This session focuses on providing reassurance for the participants themselves. It includes a description of common (immediate) reactions to the break-up and emphasizes that such reactions are normal; it also recognizes the possible need in some cases to "mourn" a lost marriage. There are suggestions on how to cope with the loneliness that follows a divorce and on ways of handling self-doubt. This session stresses the importance of combating the resentment and bitterness that stem from a broken marriage and outlines constructive ways that participants can help themselves face the future on their own.

Session 4: (a) Looking after yourself
(b) Confronting some thorny issues

The ideas of supportive self-talk and the expression of feelings are introduced, and the concept of "appropriateness" is explained. Skills for managing emotions are described, as are criteria for adequate self-care. Group members participate in a relaxation exercise. The thorny issues of custody, maintenance and access are confronted and ways of dealing with frustrating access problems are discussed and debated.

Session 5: (a) Letting go of the past
(b) Hints for managing difficult childhood behaviors

Pointers are given for explaining divorce to children. The essential step of letting go of the past once the grief of a broken marriage has been worked through is underlined as a fundamental element of emotional recovery. The irrational beliefs and attributions that people harbor are examined and techniques for venting anger constructively discussed. Parents are helped to pinpoint, observe and record unwanted childhood behaviors in terms of the problems-solving ABC of behavior method (Herbert, 1987a).

Session 6: (a) "Know yourself"
(b) More hints for managing difficult childhood behaviors

The important self-knowledge questions, "Would I have chosen for this to have happened?" and "Do I know what I want from this new situation?" are posed and debated. The first question leaves the individual with three possible options, namely, accept and put up with the situation; refuse to accept the situation; or, accept the situation and try to benefit from it. The effects of these options are carefully examined and the usefulness of the question, "What is the worst that can happen?" explored.

The second question, "Do I know what I want from this new situation?" is used to introduce the technique of *values clarification* as a means of crystallizing needs and values, and the differing consequences of proactive and reactive behavior are discussed. Stress control techniques are described and practised.

Session 7: "Loose ends" and farewells final session

In the first half of the session, more hints for managing difficult childhood behaviors are given, and also on managing the consequences outlined (see Webster-Stratton and Herbert, 1994). In addition, effective ways of using rewards and penalties, and encouraging good attending behavior, are discussed. In the second half there is an opportunity to ask questions and raise issues for debate. Participants are invited to comment on aspects of the course that were helpful and/or unhelpful. Farewells are said, and arrangements made for keeping in contact if needed, and for "refresher/booster" sessions.

The course was validated by Joy Edelstein in an unpublished PhD at Leicester University. The manual for the course is published by Edelstein and Herbert (2000). (Exeter: Impact Publications, 2000, PO Box No. 342, Exeter EX6 7Z9)

APPENDIX 4

Sources of Increased Self-Empowerment

	CONTENT	PROCESS
KNOWLEDGE	Child development Behaviour management Individual and temperamental differences	
	Developmental norms and tasks Behavioral (learning) principles Child Management (disciplinary strategies)	Discussion Books/pamphlets to read Modeling (videotape, live role-play, role reversal)
	Relationships (feelings) Self-awareness (self-talk, schema, attributions) Interactions (awareness of contingencies, communications) Resources (support, sources of assistance) Appropriate expectations Parent involvement with children	Metaphors/analogies Homework tasks Networking Developmental counseling Videotape viewing and discussion Self-observation/recording at home Discussing records of parents' own data Teaching, persuading
SKILLS	Communication Problem solving (including problem analysis) Self-restraint/anger management Self-talk (depressive thoughts)	Self-reinforcement Group and therapist reinforcement

Tactical thinking (use of techniques/methods)	Attend-ignore	Self-observations of interactions at home
Building social relationships	Play-praise-encourage	Behavior rehearsal
Enhancing children's academic skills	Contracts	Participant modeling
	Consistent consequences	Homework tasks and practice
	Sanction effectively (Time Out, loss of privileges, natural consequences)	Video modeling and feedback
	Monitoring	
	Social/relationship skills	Self-disclosure
	Problem solving skills	Therapist use of humor/optimism
	Fostering good learning habits	Relaxation training
	Self-assertion/confidence	Stress management
	Empathy for a child's perspective	Self-instruction
	Ways to give and get support	Visual clues at home
VALUES	Treatment/life goals	Discussion/debate
Strategic thinking (working out goals, philosophy of child rearing, beliefs)	Objectives (targeted child behaviors)	Sharing
	Ideologies	Listening
	Rules	Respecting/accepting
	Roles	Negotiating
	Relationships	Demystifying
	Emotional barriers	Explaining/interpreting
	Attributions	Reframing
	Prejudices	Resolving conflict
	Past history	Clarifying
		Supporting
		Adapting

(Webster-Stratton..., J Herb..., 1994, 452-62)

316

Bibliography

Achenbach, T. M. (1974) *Developmental psychopathology*. NY: Ronald Press.

Ackerson, B. J. and Harrison, D. W. (2000) Practitioners' perceptions of empowerment, *Families in Society* 81, 238–44.

Ackerman, N. (1958) *The Psychodyamics of family life*. NY: Basic Books.

Ainsworth, M. D. S., The development of infant mother attachment. In B. M. Caldwell and H.N. Ricciuti (eds) *Review of child development research, vol. 3. Child development and social policy*. Chicago: University of Chicago Press..

Amato, P. R. and Keith, B. (1991) Parental divorce and the well-being of children: A meta-analysis, *Psychological Bulletin* 110, 26–46.

Anderson, E. M. and Shannon, A. L. (1995) Toward a conceptualization of mentoring, in T. Kerry and A. S. Mayes (eds) *Issues in mentoring*. NY: The Open University.

Anderson, R. E. and Carter, I. (1990) *Human behavior in the social environment: A social systems approach* (4th edn). NY: Aldine de Gruyter.

Arlow, J. A. (1995) Psychoanalysis, in R. J. Corsini and D. Wedding (eds) *Current psychotherapies* (5th edn). Itasca, IL: F. E. Peacock Publishers, Inc.

Aspinwall, K., Garrett, V., and Owen-Jackson, G. (1994) "In at the beginning: A pilot partnership," in I. Reid, H. Constable, and R. Griffiths (eds) *Teacher education reform*. London: Paul Chapman Publishing Ltd.

Axline, V. M. (1947) *Play therapy: the inner dynamics of childhood*. Boston, MA: Houghton Mifflin.

Babiker, G. and Herbert, M. (1998) Critical issues in the assessment of child sexual abuse, *Clinical Child and Family Psychology Review* 1, 231–52.

Bandura, A. (1976) *Social learning theory*. Englewood Cliffs, NJ: Prentice-Hall.

Bannister, D. and Fransella, F. (1980) *Inquiring man*. Harmondsworth: Penguin Books.

Barth, R. P. and Berry, M. (1988) *Adoption and disruption: Rates, risks, and responses*. NY: Aldine de Gruyter.

Bateson, G., Jackson, D. D., Haley, J. and Weakland, J. (1956) Toward a theory of schizophrenia, *Behavioral Science* 1, 251–64.

Baumrind, D. (1971) Current patterns of adult authority, *Developmental Psychology Monographs* 4 (1. Pt.2).

Beavers, W. R., Hampson, R. B. (1990) *Successful families: Assessment and intervention.* NY: Norton.

Becker, W. C. (1964) Consequences of different kinds of parental discipline, in M. L. Hoffman and L. H. Hoffman (eds) *Review of child development research.* NY: Russell Sage Foundation.

Becvar, D. S. and Becvar, R. J. (1996) *Family therapy: A systemic integration.* Boston, MA: Allyn and Bacon.

Beech, R. (1985) *Staying together.* Chichester: John Wiley.

Bell, C. R. (1996) *Managers as mentors: Building partnerships for learning.* San Francisco: Berrett-Koehler Publishers.

Berg, I. K. (1994) *Family based services: A solution-focused approach.* NY: W. W. Norton and Company, Inc.

Berger, M. (1996) *Outcomes and effectiveness in clinical psychology practice.* Division of Clinical Psychology Occasional Paper, No. 1. Leicester: British Psychological Society.

Bertalanffy, L. Van. (1968) *Organismic psychology and systems theory.* Worcester, MA: Clarke University Press.

Bettleheim, B. (1987) *A good enough parent.* NY: Knopf: Random House.

Blanz, B., Schmidt, M. H. and Esser, G. (1991) Family adversities and child psychiatric disorder, *Journal of Child Psychology and Psychiatry* 32, 393–450.

Bloom, M., Fischer, J., and Orme, J. G. (1999) *Evaluating practice: Guidelines for the accountable professional* (3rd edn). Needham, MA: Allyn and Bacon.

Bogolub, E. B. (1995) *Helping families through divorce: An eclectic approach.* NY: Springer Publishing Company, Inc.

Bonnie, R. J. and Lynch, B. S. (1997) Teenagers underestimate the risk of addiction, in P. A. Winters (ed.) *Teen addiction.* San Diego, CA: Greenhaven Press, Inc.

Bowen, M. (1978) *Family therapy in clinical practice.* NY: Jason Aronson.

Bowlby, J. (1982) *Attachment and loss* (2nd edn). NY: Basic Books.

Bowlby, J. (1988) *A secure base.* New York: Basic Books.

Browne, K. and Herbert, M. (1997) *Preventing Family Violence.* Chichester: Wiley.

Browne, K. and Saqi, S. (1987) Parent–child interaction in abusing families: possible causes and consequences, in P. Maher (ed.) *Child abuse: An educational perspective.* Oxford: Blackwell.

Bruner, J. S. (1975) *Beyond the information given.* London: Allen and Unwin.

Budney, A. J. and Higgins, S. T. (1998) *A community reinforcement plus vouchers approach: Treating cocaine addiction* (NIH Publication No. 98–4309). Rockville, MD: NIH.

Campbell, B. and Horbury, A. (1994) Mentoring articled science teachers, in I. Reid, H. Constable, and R. Griffiths (eds) *Teacher education reform*. London: Paul Chapman Publishing Ltd.

Carter, E. A. and McGoldrick, M. (1989) *The family life cycle* (2nd edn). Boston, MA: Allyn and Bacon.

Chambers, D. E., Wedel, K. R., and Rodwell, M. K. (1992) *Evaluating social programs*. Boston, MA: Allyn and Bacon.

Children's Defense Fund (1996) *The state of America's children yearbook, 1996*. Washington, DC: Children's Defense Fund.

Cicchetti, D., Toth, S., and Bush, M. (1983) Developmental psychopathology and incompetence in childhood: suggestions for intervention, in B. B. Lahey and A. E. Kazdin (eds) *Advances in clinical child psychology* (Vol. 11). NY: Plenum Press.

Conger, J. V. and Kanungo, R. N. (1988) The empowerment process: Integrating theory and practice, *Academy of Management Review* 13, 471–82.

Corcoran, K. and Fischer, J. (1999) *Measures for clinical practice: A sourcebook*. (Vol. 1. Couples, families and children) (3rd edn). NY: Free Press.

Corcoran, K. and Gingerich, W. J. (1994) Practice evaluation in the context of managed care: Case-recording methods for quality assurance reviews, *Research on Social Work Practice* 4, 326–7.

Corcoran, K. and Vandiver, V. (1996) *Manoeuvring the maze of managed care*. NY: Free Press.

Cowger, C. (1997) Assessing client strengths: Assessment for client empowerment, in D. Saleeby (ed.) *The strengths perspective in social work practice*. NY: Longman.

Crain, W. C. (1985) *Theories of development: Concepts and applications*. Englewood Cliffs, NJ: Prentice-Hall.

Cunningham, C. and Davis, H. (1985) *Working with parents: Frameworks for collaboration*. Milton Keynes, London: Open University Press.

Dadds, H. R. (1995) *Families, children and the development of dysfunction*. Thousand Oaks; CA: Sage.

Dare, C. (1985) Family therapy, in M. Rutter and L. Hersov. (eds) *Child and adolescent psychiatry* (2nd edn). Oxford: Blackwell.

Davis, H. (1993) *Counselling parents of children with chronic illness or disability*. Leicester: BPS Books (The British Psychological Society).

de Shazer, S. (1985) *Keys to solution in brief therapy*. NY: Newton.

de Wilde, E. J., Kienhorst, I. C., Diekstra, R. F., and Wolters, W. H. (1992) The relationship between suicidal behavior and life events in childhood and adolescence. *American Journal of Psychiatry*, 149, 45–51.

Deming, B. (1984) Empowerment: A vehicle to peace, in M. S. White and D. Van Soest (eds) *Empowerment of people for peace* (p. 8). Minneapolis, MN: Women Against Military Madness.

Diagnostic and statistical manual of mental disorders (1994) (4th edn) Washington, DC: American Psychiatric Association.

Duncan, D. E. and Petosa, R. (1994) Social and community factors associated with drug use and abuse among adolescents, in T. P. Gullotta, G. R. Adams, and R. Montemayor (eds) *Substance misuse in adolescence*. Thousand Oaks, CA: Sage Publications.

Dunst, C., Trivette, C., and Deal, A. (1988) *Enabling and empowering families*. Cambridge, MA: Brookline.

Edelstein, J. and Herbert, M. (2000) *Separation and divorce: A collaborative training and counselling course*. Exeter: Impact Publications. (PO Box 342 Exeter EX6 7ZD).

Egan, G. (1986) *The skilled helper*. Monterey, CA: Brooks/Cole.

Eliot, G. (1929) *Silas Marner*. NY: The Macmillan Company.

Epstein, J. F. and Gfroerer, J. C. (1998) *Estimating substance abuse treatment need from a national household study. Analyses of substance abuse and treatment need issues* (DHHS Publication No. [SMA] 98–3227). Rockville, MD: SAMHSA, Office of Applied Studies.

Epstein, N. B., Baldwin, I. M., and Bishop, D. S. (1983) The Mr. Moster Family Assessment Device, *Journal of Marital and Family Therapy 9*, 171–80.

Erikson, E. (1965) *Childhood and society* (Rev. edn). NY: W. W. Norton.

Faller, K. C. (1988) *Child sexual abuse: An interdisciplinary manual for diagnosis, case management, and treatment*. NY: Columbia University Press.

Faller, K. C., Bowden, M. L., Jones, C. O., and Hildenbrandt, H. M. (1981) Types of child abuse and neglect, in K. C. Faller (ed.) *Social work with abused and neglected children*. NY: Free Press.

Falloon, I. R. H., Boyd, J.L., and McGill, C. W. (1984) *Family care of schizophrenia*. London: Guildford.

Farrington, D.P. (1995) The development of offending and antisocial behaviour from childhood: Key findings from the Cambridge Study in Delinquent Development, *Journal of Child Psychology and Psychiatry 36*, 929–64.

Ferris, P. (1998) *Dr Freud: A life*. London: Pimlico/Random House.

Finkelhor, D. (1979) *Sexually victimized children*. NY: Free Press.

Frank, Jerome D. (1973) *Persuasion and healing: A comparative study of psychotherapy* (Rev. edn). Baltimore, MD: Johns Hopkins University Press.

Fraser, M. W. (1997) The ecology of childhood: A multisystems perspective, in M. W. Fraser (ed.) *Risk and resilience in childhood.* Washington, DC: NASW Press.

Freud, A. (1954) *The psycho-analytic treatment of children.* London: Imago Publishing Company.

Freud, S. (1974) *Introductory lectures on psychoanalysis.* Harmondsworth: Penguin Books.

Furstenberg, F. and Cherlin, A. (1991) *Divided families: What happens to children when parents part.* Cambridge, MA: Harvard University Press.

Fuscaldo, D., Kaye, J. W., and Philliber, S. (1998) Evaluation of a program for parenting, *Families in Society: The Journal of Contemporary Human Services* 79, 53–61.

Gambrill, E. (1977) *Behaviour modification.* NY: Jossey-Bass.

Garbarino, J. and Benn, J. L. (1992) The ecology of childbearing and child rearing, in J. Garbarino (ed.) *Children and families in the social environment* (2nd edn). NY: Aldine de Gruyter.

Garvin, C. D. (1997) *Contemporary group work* (3rd edn). Needham Heights, MA: Allyn and Bacon.

Gelles, R. J. and Cornell, C. P. (1997) *Intimate violence in families* (3rd edn). Thousand Oaks, CA: Sage Publications.

Germain, C. B. (1991) *Human behavior in the social environment: An ecological view.* NY: Columbia University Press.

Germain, C. B. and Gitterman, A. (1987) Ecological perspective, in A. Minahan *et al.* (eds) *Encyclopaedia of social work* (18th edn) (pp. 488–99). Silver Spring, MD: NASW Press.

Gershenson, C. (1995) Social policy and evaluation: An evolving symbiosis, in P. J. Pecora, M. W. Fraser, K. E. Nelson, J. McCroskey, and W. Meezan (eds) *Evaluating family-based services.* NY: Aldine De Gruyter.

Gil, E. (1991) *The healing power of play.* NY: The Guilford Press.

Ginott, H. (1969) *Between parent and child: New solutions to old problems.* NY: Avon Books.

Goldenberg, I. and Goldenberg, H. (1991) *Family therapy: An overview.*,Monterey, CA: Brooks-Cole Publishing.

Goldstein, S. (ed.) (1995) *Understanding and managing children's classroom Behavior.* NY: John Wiley & Sons.

Goodnow, J. J. and Collins, A. W. (1990) *Development according to parents: The nature, sources and consequences of parents' ideas.* Hillsdale, NJ: Erlbaum.

Greatbatch, D. and Dingwall, R. (Aug. 1999) The marginalization of domestic violence in divorce mediation, *International Journal of Law, Policy and the Family* 13 (2): 174–90.

Greene, R. W. and Doyle, A. E. (1999) Toward a transactional conceptualization of oppositional defiant disorder: Implications for assessment and treatment, *Clinical Child and Family Review* 2, 129–48.

Greene, R. R. (1992) Case management: An agenda for social work practice, in B. S. Vourlekis and R. R. Greene (eds) *Social work case management*. NY: Aldine De Gruyter.

Greenspan, S. I. and Greenspan, N. T. (1991) *The clinical interview of the child*. Washington, DC: American Psychiatric Press, Inc.

Grossman, J. B. and Tierney, J. P. (1998) Does mentoring work? An impact study of the Big Brothers Big Sisters Program, *Evaluation Research*, 22, 403–26.

Gutierrez, R. J. Parsons, and Cox, E. O. (eds) (1998). *Empowerment in social work practice: A sourcebook*. Pacific Grove, CA: Brooks/Cole.

Haley, J. (1987) *Problem solving therapy* (2nd edn). San Francisco: Jossey-Bass.

Hall, G. Stanley. (1904) *Adolescence: Its psychology and its relationship to physiology, anthropology, sociology, sex, crime, religion and education.* Vols. I and II. New York: Appleton.

Harper, K. V. and Lantz, J. (1996) *Cross-Cultural practice: Social work with diverse populations.* Chicago, IL: Lyceum Books, Inc.

Harper, K. V. and Loadman, W. E. (1992a) *Prevention of adoption disruption/dissolution: Special needs of special children.* Report of funded project, Post Legalization Adoption Services. Toledo, OH: Lucas County Children's Services.

Harper, K. V. and Loadman, W. E. (1992b) Adoption disruption/dissolution: A predictive model, in *Discovering the new world of research and statistics: A federal-state partnership*, proceedings of the 32nd National Workshop of the National Association for Welfare Research and Statistics. Columbus, Ohio, August 1–5, 1992, Vol. II, 107–31.

Harper, K. V. and Shillito, L. S. (1991) Group work with bulimic adolescent females in suburbia. In A. Malekoff (ed.) *Group work with suburbia's children: Difference, acceptance and belonging.* NY: The Haworth Press.

Harper-Dorton, K. V. (1999a) *Family mentoring: Family mentoring with rural families.* Continuing education event, Division of Social Work, West Virginia University, Flatwoods WV, October 28, 1999.

Harper-Dorton, K. V. (1999b) *Family mentoring with rural families affected by welfare reform: Interventions and outcomes.* Paper presentation, 24th National Institute on Social Work and Human Services in Rural Areas, Salisbury, MD, July, 1999.

Helton, L. R. and Jackson, M. (1997) *Social work practice with families*. Boston, MA: Allyn and Bacon.

Herbert, M. (1974) *Emotional problems of development*. London: Academic Press.

Herbert, M. (1987a) *Behavioral treatment of children with problems: A Practice Manual* (2nd edn). London: Academic Press.

Herbert, M. (1987b) *Conduct disorders of childhood and adolescence* (2nd edn). Chichester: Wiley

Herbert, M. (1987c) *Living with teenagers*. Oxford: Basil Blackwell.

Herbert, M., (1993) *Working with children and the Children Act*. Leicester: BPS Books (The British Psychological Society).

Herbert, M. (1994) Behavioral methods, in M. Rutter, E. Taylor, and L. Hersov (eds) *Child and adolescent psychiatry* (3rd edn). Oxford: Blackwell.

Herbert, M. (1996a) *Post-traumatic stress disorder in children*. Leicester: BPS Books (The British Psychological Society).

Herbert, M. (1996b) *Supporting bereaved and dying children*. Leicester: BPS Books (The British Psychological Society).

Herbert, M. (1996c) *Coping with children's feeding problems and bedtime battles*. Leicester, BPS Books (The British Psychological Society).

Herbert, M. (1996d) *Toilet training, bedwetting and soiling*. Leicester: BPS Books (The British Psychological Society).

Herbert, M. (1998a) *Clinical child psychology: Social learning, development and behavior* (2nd edn). Chichester: Wiley.

Herbert, M. (1998b) Family treatment, in T. H. Ollendick and M. Hersen (eds) *Handbook of child psychopathology* (3rd edn). NY: Plenum Press.

Herbert, M. (1998c) Clinical formulation, in M. Hersen. (ed.) *Comprehensive clinical psychology*. NY: Plenum Press.

Herbert, M. (1998d) Cognitive-behavior therapy of adolescents with conduct disorder, in P. Graham (ed.) *Therapy for children and families*. Cambridge: Cambridge University Press.

Herbert, M., Sluckin, W. and Sluckin, A. (1983) Mother-to-infant bonding, *Journal of Child Psychology and Psychiatry* 23, 205–21.

Herbert, M. and Wookey, J. (1998) *Childwise parenting skills manual*. Exeter, Impact Publications, PO Box 342, Exeter EX6 7ZD.

Herbert, M. (2000) Assessment of sexually abused children, *Behaviour Change* 17, 15–27.

Herbert, M. (2001) Behavioural therapies, in M. Rutter and E. Taylor (eds) *Child and adolescent pschiatry* (4th edn). Oxford: Blackwell.

Hibert, K. M. (2000) *Mentoring leadership*. Phi Delta Kappan, 16–18, September.

Hodges, V. G., Burwell, Y., and Ortega, D. (1998) Empowering families, in R. Guiterrez, J. Pousons and E. O. Cox (eds) *Empowerment in social work: a sourcebook.* Pacific Grove, CA: Brooks/Cole Publishing Company.

Hopson, B. and Scally, M. (1980) *Lifeskills teaching: Education for self-empowerment.* NY: McGraw-Hill.

Horne, A. M. (1991) Social learning family therapy, in A. Horne and J. Passmore (eds) *Family counselling and therapy.* Itasca, IL: F. E. Peacock Publishers.

Horne, A. M. and Sayger, T. V. (1990) *Treatment of conduct and oppositional defiant disorders of children.* NY: Pergamon Press.

Hudson, A. (1987) Personal communication. First Author.

Hudson, B. and McDonald, G. (1986) *Behavioral social work: An introduction.* Basingstoke: Macmillan.

Hutter, A. (1938) Endegen ein Fuctionelle Psychosen bei Kindern in den Pubertatsjahren, *A. Kinderpsychiat* 7, 97–102.

Iwaniec, D., Herbert, M. and Sluckin, A. (1988) Helping emotionally abused child who fail to thrive, in K. Brown, C. Davies, and P. Stratton (eds) *Early prediction and prevention of child abuse.* Chichester: John Wiley & Sons, Ltd.

Jackson, D. (1957) The question of family homostasis, *Psychiatry Quarterly Supplement* 31, 79–80.

Jankowski, S., Videka-Sherman, L., and Laquidara-Dickinson, K. (1996) Social support networks of confidants to people with AIDS, *Social Work* 41, 206–13.

Janzen, C. and Harris, O. (1997) *Family treatment in social work.* Itasca, IL: F. E. Peacock Publishers, Inc.

Jehu, D. (1992) Adult survivors of sexual abuse, in R.T. Ammerman and M. Hersen (ed.) *Assessment of family violence: A clinical and legal source book.* NY: John Wiley & Sons, Ltd.

Jensen, C. (1994) Psychosocial treatment of depression in women: Nine single-subject evaluations, *Research on Social Work Practice* 4, 267–82.

Jeruchim, J. and Shapiro, P. (1992) *Women, mentors, and success.* NY: Fawcett Columbine.

Johnson, D. and Johnson, F. P. (1987) *Joining together: Group therapy and group skills* (3rd edn). Englewood Cliffs, NJ: Prentice-Hall.

Jones, D. and McGraw, J. M. (1987) Reliable and fictitious accounts of sexual abuse of children, *Journal of Interpersonal Violence* 2, 27–45.

Jones, D. and McQuiston, M. (1988) *Interviewing the sexually abused child.* Gaskell Psychiatry Series: The Royal College of Psychiatrists, London.

Jordan, C. and Franklin, C. (1995) *Clinical assessment for social workers: Quantitative and qualitative methods.* Chicago: Lyceum.

Kagan, J. (1984) *The nature of the child.* NY: Basic Books, Inc.

Kazdin, A. E. (1978) *History of behaviour modification.* Baltimore, MD: University Park Press.

Kazdin, A. (1995) *Conduct disorders in childhood and adolescence* (2nd edn). Thousand Oaks: Sage Publications.

Kazdin, A. (1997) Conduct disorder across the life-span, in S. S. Luthar, J. A. Burack, D. Cicchetti, and J. Weisz (eds) *Developmental psychopathology: Perspectives on adjustment, risk, and disorder* (pp. 248–72). NY: Cambridge University Press.

Kazdin, A. E. (1997) A model of developing effective treatments: progression and interplay of theory, research and practice, *Journal of Clinical Child Psychology* 26, 114–29.

Kazdin, A. E. (1998) Psychosocial treatments for conduct disorder in children, in P. Nathan and J. Gorman (eds) *A guide to treatments that work.* NY: Oxford University Press.

Kazdin, A. E. (1990) Childhood depression, *Journal of Child Psychology and Psychiatry* 31 121–60.

Kazdin, A. E., Siegel, T. C., and Bass, D. (1992) Cognitive problem-solving skills training and parent management training in the treatment of antisocial behavior in children, *Journal of Consulting and Clinical Psychology* 60, 733–47.

Kelly, G. A. (1955) *The psychology of personal constructs.* NY: Norton.

Kendall, P. C. and Gosch, E. A. (1994) Cognitive-behavioral interventions, in *International handbook of phobic and anxiety disorders in children and adolescents.* NY: Plenum Press.

Kennedy, E. (1981) *Crisis counselling.* Dublin: Gill and Macmillan.

Kernberg, P. A. and Chazan, S. E. (1991) *Children with conduct disorders: A psychotherapy manual.* NY: Basic Books

Kids Count Data Book (1997) *Kids count data book: State profiles of child well-being.* Baltimore, MD: The Annie E. Casey Foundation.

Kilpatrick, A. C. and Holland, T. P. (1995) *Working with families.* Boston, MA: Allyn and Bacon.

King, N. J., Hamilton, D. I. and Ollendick, T. H. (1998) *Children's phobias: A behavioral perspective.* Chichester: John Wiley & Sons, Ltd.

King, N. J., Tonge, B. J., Mullen, P., Myerson, N., Heyne, D. and Ollendick, T. H. (1999) Cognitive-behavioral treatment of sexually abused children: A review of research, *Behavioural and Cognitive Psychotherapy* 27, 295–309.

Knell, S. M. (1998) Cognitive-behavioral play therapy, *Journal of Child Psychology and Psychiatry* 27, 28–33.

Kopp, J. (1989) Self-observation: An empowerment strategy in assessment, *Social Casework* 70, 276–84.

Kubler-Ross, E. (1969) *On death and dying.* NY: Macmillan.

Lask, B. (1980) Evaluation: Why and how?, *Journal of Family Therapy* 2 (2), 119–210.

Lask, B. (1987) Family therapy, *British Medical Journal* 294, 203–4.

Lee, S. G. and Herbert, M. (eds) (1970) *Freud and psychology.* Harmondsworth: Penguin Books.

Locke, B., Garrison, R., and Winship, J. (1998) *Generalist social work practice: Context, story and partnerships.* Pacific Grove, CA: Brooks/Cole Publishing Company.

Long, D., Wood, R. G., and Kopp, H. (October, 1994) *The educational effects of LEAP and enhanced services in Cleveland.* Cleveland, OH: Manpower Demonstration Research Corporation.

Longres, J. F. (1995) *Human behaviour in the social environment* (2nd edn). Itasca, IL: F. E. Peacock Publishers, Inc.

Lorenz, K. (1973) *Motivation of human and animal behaviour: An ethological view.* NY: Van Nostrand Reinhold Co.

Madanes, C. (1981) *Strategic family therapy.* San Francisco: Jossey-Bass.

Madanes, C. (1984) *Behind the one-way mirror: Advances in the practice of strategic therapy.* San Francisco: Jossey-Bass.

Madanes, C. (1990) *Sex, love and violence: Strategies for transformation.* NY: W. W. Norton.

Mallon, G. (1998) After care, then where? Outcomes of an independent living program, *Child Welfare* 76, 61–78.

Mason, M. A., Skolnick, A., and Sugarman, S. D. (1998) *All our families.* NY: Oxford University Press.

Mattaini, M. (1998) Generalist practice: People and programs, in M. A. Mattaini, C. T. Lowery, and C. H. Meyer (eds) *The foundations of social work practice: A graduate text.* Washington, DC: National Association of Social Workers.

McDonald, T. P., Allen, R. I., Westerfelt, A., and Piliavin, I. (1996) *Assessing the long-term effects of foster care.* Washington, DC: CWLA Press.

McQuaide, S. and Ehrenreich, J. H. (1997) Assessing client strengths, *Families in Society: The Journal of Contemporary Human Services* 78, 201–12.

Mech, E. V., Pryde, J. A., and Rycraft, J. R. (1995) Mentors for adolescents in foster care, *Child and Adolescent Social Work Journal* 12, 317–28.

Meichenbaum, D. H. (1974) *Cognitive behaviour modification.* NY: Plenum.

Minuchin, S. (1974) *Families and family therapy*. Cambridge, MA: Harvard University Press.

Minuchin, S. and Fishman, C. (1981) *Family therapy techniques*. Cambridge, MA: Harvard University Press.

Mishne, J. M. (1986) *Clinical work with adolescents*. NY: The Free Press.

Moffit, T.E. and Caspi, A. (1998) Implications of violence between intimate partners for child psychologists and psychiatrists, *Journal of Child Psychology and Psychiatry* 39, 137–44.

Moon, B. L. (1990) *Existential art therapy*. Springfield, IL: Charles C. Thomas Publisher.

Mowry, D. D. (1994) Mentoring the Hmong: A practice outlet for teaching faculty and a possible community development tool, *Journal of Community Practice* 1, 107–12.

Newman, B. and Newman, P. (1991) *Development through life*. Pacific Grove, CA: Brooks/Cole Publishing Company

Nichols, M. P. and Schwartz, R. C. (1991) *Family therapy: Concepts and methods*. Boston, MA: Allyn and Bacon.

O'Hagan, K. (1993) *Emotional and psychological abuse of children*. Toronto: University of Toronto Press.

O'Hanlon, W. H. (1993) Possibility therapy: From iatrongenic injury to iatrogenic healing, in S. Gilligan and R. Price (eds) *Therapeutic conversations*. NY: W. W. Norton.

O'Hanlon, W. H. and Weiner-Davis, M. (1989) *In search of solutions: A new direction in psychotherapy*. NY: W. W. Norton.

Ollendick, T. H. (1998) Panic disorder in children and adolescents: New developments, new directions, *Journal of Child Psychology and Psychiatry* 27, 234–45.

Ollendick, T. H. and Cerny, J. A. (1981) *Clinical behaviour therapy with children*. NY: Plenum.

Ollendick, T. H. and King, N. J. (1997) Empirically supported comprehensive treatments for children with phobic and anxiety disorders, *Journal of Clinical Child Psychology* 27, 156–67.

Olson, D. H. (1986) Circumplex Model VII: Validation studies and Faces III, *Family Process* 26, 337–51.

Open University Course Organisers (1982) *Parents and teenagers*. London: Harper and Row.

Palazzoli, M., Boscoli, L., Cecchin, G., and Piata, G. (1978) *Paradox and counterparadox*. Northvale, NJ: Aronson.

Parke, R. D. (1981) *Fathering*. London: Fontana/Open Books.

Parkes, C. M. (1972) *Bereavement: Studies of grief in adult life*. NY: International Universities Press.

Parsons, R. J. (1998) Evaluation of empowerment practice, in L. M. Gutierrez, R. J. Parsons and E. O. Cox (eds) *Empowerment in social work practice: A sourcebook*. Pacific Grove, CA: Brooks/Cole Publishing Company.

Parsons, R. J., Gutierrez, L. M., and Cox, E. O. (1998) A model for empowerment practice, in L. M. Gutierrez, R. J. Parsons, and E. O. Cox (eds) *Empowerment in social work practice: A sourcebook*. Pacific Grove, CA: Brooks/Cole Publishing Company.

Patterson, G. (1982) *Coercive family process*. Eugene, OR: Castalia.

Pavlov, I. (1927) *Conditioned reflexes* (trans. G. V. Anrey). Oxford: Oxford University Press: Humphrey Milford.

Payne, M. (1991) *Modern social work theory: A critical introduction*. Chicago, IL: Lyceum Books, Inc.

Petr, C. G. (1998) *Social work with children and their families*. NY: Oxford University Press.

Piercy, E.P., Sprenkle, D. and Wetchler, J. L. (1986) *Family therapy sourcebook*. NY: Guilford Press.

Pistole, M. C. (1999) Caregiving in attachment relationships: A perspective for counselors, *Journal of Counseling and Development*, Fall, 77(4), 437–47.

Posavac, E. J. and Carey, R. G. (1985) *Program evaluation: Methods and case studies*. Englewood Cliffs, NJ: Prentice-Hall.

Power, M. J. (1991) Cognitive science and behavioral psychotherapy: Where behavior was there shall cognition be, *Behavioral Psychotherapy* 19, 20–41.

Randall, E. and Newfield, N. (1997) *West Virginia visions: Mentoring manual*. Morgantown, WV: School of Social Work, West Virginia University.

Rappaport, R. N., Fogarty, M. P., and Rapoport, R. (eds) (1982) *Families in Britain*. London: Routledge and Kegan Paul.

Reamer, F. C. (1998) *Social work research and evaluation skills*. NY: Columbia University Press.

Reimers, S. and Treacher, G. (1995) *Introducing user-friendly family therapy*. London: Routledge.

Richards, M. and Dyson, M. (1982) *Separation, divorce and the development of children: A review*. Cambridge: Child Care and Development Group.

Robbins, S. P., Chatterjee, P., and Canda, E. R. (1998) *Contemporary human behavior theory: A critical perspective for social work*. Boston: Allyn and Bacon.

Robins, L. and Rutter, M. (eds) (1990) *Straight and deviant pathways: From childhood to adulthood*. Cambridge: Cambridge University Press.

Rogers, C. R. (1951) *Client-centered therapy*. Boston, MA: Houghton-Mifflin.

Rose, S. M. (2000) Reflections on empowerment-based practice, *Social Work* 45, 403–12.

Rossi, P. H. (1997) Program outcomes: Conceptual and measurement issues, in E. J. Mullen and J. L. Magnabosco (eds) *Outcomes measurement in the human services*. Washington, DC: NASW Press.

Rossi, P. H. and Freeman, H. E. (1993) *Evaluation: A systematic approach*. Newbury Park, CA: Sage Publications.

Royse, D. (1995) *Research methods in social work*. Chicago: Nelson-Hall Publishers.

Rutter, M. (1972) *Maternal deprivation reassessed*. Harmondsworth: Penguin Books.

Rutter, M. and Quinton, D. (!977) Psychiatric disorder – ecological factors and resistance to psychiatric disorder, *British Journal of Psychiatry* 147, 598–611.

Rycroft, C. (1970) Causes and meaning, in S. G. Lee and M. Herbert (eds) *Freud and psychology*. Harmondsworth: Penguin Books.

Saleebey, D. (1997) Introduction: Power in the people, in D. Saleeby (ed.) *The strengths perspective in social work practice*. NY: Longman.

Saleebey, D. (1999a) Community development, group empowerment, and individual resilience, in D. Saleeby (ed.) *The strengths perspective in social work practice* (2nd edn). NY: Longman.

Saleebey, D. (1999b) Introduction: Power in the people, in D. Saleeby (ed.) *The strengths perspective in social work practice* (2nd edn). NY: Longman.

Sanders, M. R. (1996) New directions in behavioral family interventions with children, *Advances in Clinical Child Psychology* 18, 284–330.

Satir, V. (1982) The therapist and family therapy: Process model, in A. M. Horne and M. M. Ohlsen (eds) *Family counseling and therapy*. Itasca, IL: F. E. Peacock Publishers.

Satir, V. (1983) *Conjoint family therapy* (3rd edn). Palo Alto, CA: Science and Behavior Books.

Schaefer, E. S. (1959) A circumplex model for maternal behaviour, *Journal of Abnormal and Social Behaviour* 59, 226–35.

Schaffer, H. R. (1990) *Making decisions about children: psychological questions and answers*. Oxford: Basil Blackwell.

Schaffer, H. R., Seligman, M., and Darling, R. B. (1997) *Ordinary families, special children*. NY: The Guilford Press.

Schneider, K. (1959) *Clinical psychopathology*. NY: Grune and Stratton.

Schutte, N. S. and Maloaff, J. M. (1995) *Sourcebook of adult assessment strategies*. NY: Plenum.

Seligman, M. E. P. (1975) *Helplessness: On depression, development, and death*. San Francisco, CA: Freeman.

Seligman, M. and Darling, R. B. (1997) *Ordinary families, special children*. NY: The Guilford Press.

Sgroi, S. (1982) *Handbook of clinical intervention in child sexual abuse*. Lexington, MA: Lexington Books.

Sheafor, B. W., Horejsi, C. R., and Horejsi, G. A. (1994) *Techniques and guidelines for social work practice* (3rd edn). Boston: Allyn and Bacon.

Sheldon, B. (1980) *The use of contracts in social work*. Birmingham: British Association of Social Workers.

Shulman, L. (1999) *The skills of helping individuals, families, groups, and communities* (4th edn). Itasca, IL: F. E. Peacock Publishers, Inc.

Simon, B. L. (1998) *The empowerment tradition*. NY: Columbia University Press.

Skinner, B. F. (1953) *Science and human behavior*. NY: Free Press.

Skolnick, A. (1998) Solomon's children: The new biologism, psychological parenthood, attachment theory, and the best interests standard, in M. A. Mason, A. Skolnick, and S. D. Sugarman (eds) *All our families*. NY: Oxford University Press.

Slonim-Nevo, V. and Anson, Y. (1998) Evaluating practice: Does it improve treatment outcomes? *Social Work Research* 22, 70–74.

Sluckin, W. and Herbert, M. (eds) (1986) *Parental behaviour*. Chichester: John Wiley & Sons, Ltd.

Sluckin, W., Herbert, M., and Sluckin, A. (1983) *Maternal bonding*. Oxford: Basil Blackwell.

Snyder, H. N., Sickmund, M., and Poe-Yamagat, E. (1996) *Juvenile offenders and victims: 1996 update on violence*. Washington, DC: Office of Juvenile Justice and Delinquency Prevention.

Solomon, B. (1976) *Black empowerment: Social work in oppressed communities*. NY: Columbia University Press.

Speck, R. and Atneave, C. (1974) *Family networks*. NY: Vintage Books.

Spencer, J. R. and Flin, R. H. (1990) *The evidence of children: The law and the psychology*. London: Blackstone Press.

Spivack, G., Platt, J. J., and Shure, M. B. (1976) *The problem-solving approach to adjustment*. San Francisco, CA: Jossey-Bass.

Stevenson, J. (1999) The treatment of the long-term sequelae of child abuse, *Journal of Child Psychology and Psychiatry* 40, 89–112.

Stewart, S. D. (Nov. 1999) Nonresident mothers' and fathers' social contact with children, *Journal of Marriage and the Family* 61 (4): 894–907.

Strom-Gottfried, K. (1997) The implications of managed care for social work education, *Journal of Social Work Education* 33, 7–18.

Substance Abuse and Mental Health Services Administration, Office of Applied Studies (1996) *National household survey on drug abuse: Main findings 1994.* (DHHS Publication No. [SMA] 96–3085.) Rockville, MD: SAMHSA, Office of Applied Studies.

Sturmey, P. (1996) *Functional analysis in clinical psychology.* Chichester: John Wiley & Sons, Ltd.

Sutton, C. (1994) *Social work: Community work and psychology.* Leicester: BPS Books (The British Psychological Society).

Sutton, C. (1996) *State of America's children yearbook.* Washington, DC: Children's Defense Fund.

Sutton, C. (1999) *Helping families with troubled children: A preventive approach.* Chichester: John Wiley & Sons, Ltd.

Sutton, C. (2000) *Child and adolescent behaviour problems.* Leicester: BPS Books.

Sutton, C. and Herbert, M. (1992) *Mental health: A client support reference pack.* Windsor: NFER Educational.

Taylor, T. K. and Biglan, A. (1998) Behavioral family interventions for improving child-rearing: A review of the literature for clinicians and policy makers, *Clinical Child and Family Psychology Review* 1, 41–60.

Thurman, S. (1997) LSD on the playground? Teen drug trends: Users get younger, substances harder, *Christian Science Monitor* 89, 3.

Thyer, B. A. (1996) Forty years of progress toward empirical clinical practice? *Social Work Research* 20, 77–81.

Tomm, K. (1984) One perspective of the Milan systemic approach: Part 1. Overview of development, theory and practice, *Journal of Marital and Family Therapy.* NY: Plenum Press.

Torrey, E. (1986) *Witchdoctors and psychiatrists.* NY: Harper and Row.

Tower, C. C. (1996) *Understanding child abuse and neglect.* Boston, MA: Allyn and Bacon.

Treacher, A. and Carpenter, J. (eds) (1984) *Using family therapy.* Oxford: Basil Blackwell.

Tremblay, R. E., Vitaro, F., Bertrand, L., LeBlanc, M., Beauchesne, H., Boileau, H., and David, L. (1992) Parent and child training to prevent early onset of delinquency: The Montreal longitudinal-experimental study, in J. McCord and R. Tremblay (eds) *Preventing antisocial behavior: Interventions from birth through adolescence* (pp.117–138). NY: Guilford Press.

Tripodi, T. (1987) Program evaluation, in S. M. Rosen, D. Fanshel, and M. E. Lutz (eds) *Encyclopaedia of social work* (19th edn). Silver Spring, MD: National Association of Social Workers.

Tyson, K. (1995) *New foundations for scientific social and behavioural research.* Needham Heights, MA: Allyn and Bacon.

U.S. Bureau of the Census (1993) *Current population reports. Population profile of the United States.* Washington, DC.

Vetere, V. and Gale, A. (1987) *Ecological studies of family life.* Chichester: John Wiley & Sons, Ltd.

Wachtel, P. L. (1997) *Psychoanalysis, behavior therapy and the relational world.* Washington DC: American Psychological Society.

Waddell, C., Lipman, E., and Offord, D. (1999) Conduct disorder: Practice parameters for assessment, treatment, and prevention, *Canadian Journal of Psychiatry.* October, Supplement 2, Vol. 44: 35–41.

Wallerstein, J. and Blakeslee, S. (1989) *Second chances.* NY: Ticknor and Fields.

Webb, N. B. (1991) *Play therapy with children in crisis.* NY: The Guilford Press.

Webster-Stratton, C. (1988) *Parents and children videotape series: Basic and advanced programs.* 1–7. 1411 8th Avenue West, Seattle, WA 98119, USA.

Webster-Stratton, C. and Hammond, M. (1999) Marital conflict management skills, parenting style and early conduct problems: processes and pathways, *Journal of Child Psychology and Psychiatry* 40, 917–27.

Webster-Stratton, C. and Herbert, M. (1994) *Troubled families: Problem children. Working with parents: A collaborative process.* Chichester: John Wiley & Sons, Ltd.

West Virginia Kids Count Fund (1999) *Kids count data book: 1999 County profiles of child well-being.* Morgantown, WV: Survey Research Center, West Virginia University.

Wetzler, S. (ed.) (1989) *Measuring mental illness: Psychometric assessment for clinicians.* Washington, DC: American Psychiatric Press.

White, R. (1991) Examining the threshold criteria, in M. Adcock, R. White, and A. Hollows (eds) *Significant harm: Its management and outcome.* Croydon: Significant Publications.

Wiley, A. and Rappaport, J. (2000) Empowerment, wellness, and the politics of development, in D. Cicchetti, J. Rappaport, I. Sandler, and R. P. Weissberg (eds) *The promotion of wellness in children and adolescents.* Washington, DC: CWLA Press.

Williams, M., Unrau, Y. A., and Grinnell, Jr., R. M. (1998) *Introduction to social work research.* Itasca, IL: F. E. Peacock Publishers, Inc.

Wing, J. K. (ed.) (1978) *Schizophrenia: Towards a new synthesis.* London: Academic Press.

Winnicott, D. (1958) *Collected papers.* London: Tavistock.

Winters, K. (1998) Treatment recognizes link between delinquency and substance abuse, *Corrections Today* 60, 118–23.

Witkin, S. L. (1996) If empirical practice is the answer, then what is the question?, *Social Work Research* 20, 69–75.

Yelloly, M. A. (1980) *Social work theory and psychoanalysis*. London: Van Nostrand Reinhold.

Zastrow, C. and Kirst-Ashman, K. K. (1997) *Understanding human behaviour and the social environment*. Chicago, IL: Nelson-Hall Publishers.

Zippay, A. (1995) Expanding employment skills and social networks among teen mothers: Case study of a mentor program, *Child and Adolescent Social Work Journal* 12, 51–69.

Index